Cloud Native Development with Google Cloud
Building Applications at Speed and Scale

Daniel Vaughan

Beijing · Boston · Farnham · Sebastopol · Tokyo

Cloud Native Development with Google Cloud

by Daniel Vaughan

Copyright © 2024 Daniel Vaughan. All rights reserved.

Published by O'Reilly Media, Inc., 1005 Gravenstein Highway North, Sebastopol, CA 95472.

O'Reilly books may be purchased for educational, business, or sales promotional use. Online editions are also available for most titles (*http://oreilly.com*). For more information, contact our corporate/institutional sales department: 800-998-9938 or *corporate@oreilly.com*.

Acquisitions Editor: Megan Laddusaw
Development Editor: Sara Hunter
Production Editor: Beth Kelly
Copyeditor: nSight, Inc.
Proofreader: Brandon Hashemi

Indexer: Potomac Indexing, LLC
Interior Designer: David Futato
Cover Designer: Karen Montgomery
Illustrator: Kate Dullea

November 2023:   First Edition

Revision History for the First Edition
2023-11-10:   First Release

See *http://oreilly.com/catalog/errata.csp?isbn=9781098145088* for release details.

978-1-098-14508-8

[LSI]

Table of Contents

Part II.   Hands-On Projects

Part III. The Facilities

Part IV.   Going Further

Preface

Many organizations have faced disappointment with cloud migration when expected productivity gains and cost savings weren't realized. Often, the mistake is treating the cloud as just another data center. This book highlights the distinctiveness of a cloud native approach and how it can truly harness the power of the cloud.

Who This Book Is For

This guide is for software developers and architects who are either newcomers to cloud computing or already on their cloud journey and want a deeper understanding of Google Cloud. While Google offers numerous professional certifications for its cloud platform, they can be rather theoretical. This book bridges that gap, offering a holistic view of Google Cloud services and how they come together to create a powerful toolkit for cloud native application development.

Conventions Used in This Book

The following typographical conventions are used in this book:

Italic
: Indicates new terms, URLs, email addresses, filenames, and file extensions.

`Constant width`
: Used for program listings, as well as within paragraphs to refer to program elements such as variable or function names, databases, data types, environment variables, statements, and keywords.

`Constant width bold`
: Shows commands or other text that should be typed literally by the user.

Constant width italic

> Shows text that should be replaced with user-supplied values or by values determined by context.

 This element signifies a tip or suggestion.

 This element signifies a general note.

How This Book Is Organized

This book is organized into four distinct parts, each serving a different purpose.

Part I lays the groundwork by introducing cloud native development, Google Cloud, and the fundamental concepts of cloud native applications.

Part II is a hands-on guide, designed to help you get building with Google Cloud. After preparing your Google Cloud environment, you will work through five projects that form the building blocks of an example application, becoming acquainted with essential Google Cloud services and gaining practical experience.

Part III delves into the "facilities" you can build with Google Cloud to streamline the development and management of your applications. It introduces techniques and tools to enhance your efficiency and make your life easier.

Part IV of the book serves as a gateway for the next phase of your cloud journey. It first gives you ideas of how to scale the example application using the more advanced Google Cloud services and then offers information, tips, and resources to help you explore further and continue your learning.

Using Code Examples

The code that accompanies this book, Skills Mapper, is available in a single project on GitHub at *https://github.com/SkillsMapper/skillsmapper*. At the beginning of each chapter that uses code, the directory within the project will be indicated.

If you have a technical question or a problem using the code examples, please send email to *bookquestions@oreilly.com*.

This book is here to help you get your job done. In general, if example code is offered with this book, you may use it in your programs and documentation. You do not need to contact us for permission unless you're reproducing a significant portion of the code. For example, writing a program that uses several chunks of code from this book does not require permission. Selling or distributing examples from O'Reilly books does require permission. Answering a question by citing this book and quoting example code does not require permission. Incorporating a significant amount of example code from this book into your product's documentation does require permission.

We appreciate, but generally do not require, attribution. An attribution usually includes the title, author, publisher, and ISBN. For example: "*Cloud Native Development with Google Cloud* by Daniel Vaughan (O'Reilly). Copyright 2024 Daniel Vaughan, 978-1-098-14508-8."

If you feel your use of code examples falls outside fair use or the permission given above, feel free to contact us at *permissions@oreilly.com*.

O'Reilly Online Learning

 For more than 40 years, *O'Reilly Media* has provided technology and business training, knowledge, and insight to help companies succeed.

Our unique network of experts and innovators share their knowledge and expertise through books, articles, and our online learning platform. O'Reilly's online learning platform gives you on-demand access to live training courses, in-depth learning paths, interactive coding environments, and a vast collection of text and video from O'Reilly and 200+ other publishers. For more information, visit *https://oreilly.com*.

How to Contact Us

Please address comments and questions concerning this book to the publisher:

O'Reilly Media, Inc.
1005 Gravenstein Highway North
Sebastopol, CA 95472
800-889-8969 (in the United States or Canada)
707-829-7019 (international or local)
707-829-0104 (fax)
support@oreilly.com
https://www.oreilly.com/about/contact.html

We have a web page for this book, where we list errata, examples, and any additional information. You can access this page at *https://oreil.ly/cloud-native-dev-with-GC*.

For news and information about our books and courses, visit *https://oreilly.com*.

Find us on LinkedIn: *https://linkedin.com/company/oreilly-media*

Follow us on Twitter: *https://twitter.com/oreillymedia*

Watch us on YouTube: *https://youtube.com/oreillymedia*

Acknowledgments

This book is lovingly dedicated to my wife, Michelle, who has been as supportive as ever on this journey. My gratitude goes to the wonderful team at O'Reilly for bringing my ideas to fruition. A special note of thanks to the astute technical reviewers Shreya Chakravarty, Pankaj Gajjar, Michael Hopkins, Nodir Siddikov, and Wietse Venema; your insights have been instrumental. To my friends, colleagues, and well-wishers, I am deeply appreciative of your encouragement.

Most of this book was written during early morning and early evening sessions at Starbucks in Saffron Walden, UK, where I was often the first customer to arrive or the last to leave. I'm grateful to the staff for their patience and for keeping me well-caffeinated. On many such occasions, my baby son Alex was my silent partner. While he might not have contributed in words, his companionship was inspirational.

PART I

Cloud Native Google Cloud

In this part, you'll discover the origins of cloud and cloud native applications and understand why Google Cloud is an excellent platform for them.

CHAPTER 1

Why Cloud Native and Not Just Cloud?

In the late 1990s when I started my career, the digital landscape was in the early stages of transformation. Companies were introducing email servers for the first time as employees began to familiarize themselves with PCs sitting on their desks. As the hands-on tech guy, my job was to set up these PCs and install email servers in server rooms, connecting them to the internet through dial-up modems or ISDN lines.

Back then, a computer room was often just an air-conditioned cupboard that housed the company's entire computing infrastructure. I distinctly remember installing a server next to a washing machine–sized DEC VAX (*https://oreil.ly/IaobX*), a computing relic from the 1980s, which continued to run just as it was pictured in my computer science textbooks.

With the dot-com boom of the early 2000s, a robust and uninterrupted internet presence became critical for businesses. Large corporations responded by investing in on-premises data centers, specialized facilities equipped to host IT equipment with multiple redundant internet connections and power supplies.

However, building a dedicated data center wasn't feasible for smaller companies. Instead, they could rent space in shared colocation data centers, or "CoLos." But this posed a significant challenge for emerging internet startups: What happens if you become an overnight success? What if your user base explodes from a thousand to a million users overnight?

Would it be wiser to start with servers that can accommodate a thousand users and risk your website crashing if you can't scale quickly enough? Or should you preemptively invest in the capacity to serve millions of users, in the event of rapid growth? The latter choice would require significant funding, possibly reliant on a venture capitalist with deep pockets. Balancing this risk and potential growth became a pressing question for many businesses during this time.

Emergence of the Cloud Era

The advent of the public cloud marked a significant turning point. Launched in 2006, Amazon Web Services (AWS) began offering on-demand EC2 servers, and by 2008, anyone with a credit card could virtually set up a server in an instant. The ability to seamlessly scale up server capacity as demand increased was a game changer. Startups could begin with modest infrastructure and then expand as they became more profitable, thus minimizing initial investments and reducing the cost of innovation.

In 2008, Google followed suit with the Google App Engine (GAE), pioneering one of the first platforms as a service (PaaS). With GAE, developers could write a web application in PHP or Python and deploy it on Google's public cloud, all without the need to manage server infrastructure. Despite GAE's potential, it presented challenges for developers like me, accustomed to working with traditional applications and relational databases, due to its unfamiliar restrictions.

As the 2010s unfolded and cloud computing surged in popularity, companies with pricey on-premises data centers began eyeing their *digital native* competitors with envy. Companies like Netflix, Airbnb, and Slack. These newer entities, born in the cloud and deploying software on platforms like AWS, Google Cloud, and Microsoft Azure, were rapidly releasing competitive products without bearing the burdensome costs of maintaining a data center. They were also leveraging additional on-demand cloud services, including machine learning and AI, which offered unprecedented capabilities.

Established companies, rooted in traditional data center operations, found the allure of the cloud irresistible for several reasons, as shown in Figure 1-1.

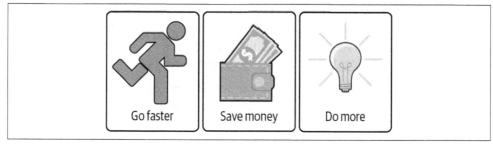

Figure 1-1. Go faster, save money, and do more

These were typically:

Go faster

Enhance developer productivity by leveraging the cloud's on-demand, scalable resources and a wide range of prebuilt services. This allows developers to focus on core application logic instead of infrastructure management.

Save money
> Decrease infrastructure or operational costs by shifting from capital expenditure (CapEx) for hardware and maintenance to operational expenditure (OpEx) for on-demand services, improving cash flow and reducing upfront investments.

Do more
> Access resources and services that are impractical in an on-premises setup, such as vast scalable storage options, powerful data analytics tools, machine learning platforms, and advanced AI services.

The critical misstep these organizations often make is migrating to the cloud without understanding its unique nature, the added complexity, and how it necessitates changes in software development practices. As a result, rather than enhancing efficiency and reducing costs, the cloud can sometimes introduce additional complications and expenses, thus slowing progress and increasing expenditure. Therefore, the frequently promised benefit of "run your mess for less" rarely materializes, underscoring the importance of a well-informed and strategic approach to cloud migration.

Navigating the Cloud Migration

I am a great admirer of Marie Kondo (*https://konmari.com*), the Japanese organizing consultant who brings joy to homes by transforming cluttered spaces into realms of tranquility and efficiency.

Picture a cupboard brimming with two decades of accumulated possessions—a mix of obsolete, broken, and unopened items. Among these are items you've bought in duplicate, unaware of their existence deep within the cluttered confines. Amid the chaos, a few handy objects await discovery. However, trying to excavate them could cause a catastrophic avalanche. Trust me, I possess such a cupboard.

This scenario aptly represents a typical on-premises data center, a labyrinth of applications without discernment of their significance.

In the quest for cloud benefits, companies were urged to execute a "lift and shift" strategy—moving their existing applications to the cloud wholesale. This strategy often feels akin to relocating your cluttered cupboard into a rented garage in another part of town. You still grapple with the same amount of stuff; it's just more inconvenient to access and secure. Not to mention, the garage comes with an additional rental cost.

An alternative to "lift and shift," companies were also recommended to "containerize" their applications before cloud migration. Using the cupboard analogy, this would equate to packing your belongings into plastic crates before moving them to the garage. Containerization simplifies the transportation and management of applications and facilitates future moves between different storage units. Nonetheless, it inherits the downsides of garage storage, along with the added expense of containers. This "move and improve" strategy seems appealing, but the motivation to sort out the clutter often dwindles once it's out of sight.

The Pitfalls of an Unplanned Journey

The ideal scenario involves decluttering the cupboard entirely. Broken items should be repaired or discarded, obsolete belongings removed, and duplicated or unused possessions donated. Following Marie Kondo's mantra, you should retain only the items that "spark joy." Once this selection is complete, you can consider whether to display these cherished items prominently or store them away, neatly and securely.

In the realm of cloud technology, this approach translates into cloud modernization: a comprehensive review and restructuring of applications for optimal cloud performance. This topic, however, lies beyond the scope of this book. As many companies have discovered, cloud modernization can be a lengthy and costly process. Many firms have resorted to the lift and shift or containerization strategies, only to find their applications harder to manage and secure and more expensive to run in the cloud.

Less than optimal experiences with cloud migration have resulted in scepticism and disappointment surrounding the cloud. Companies have been reminded that there is no one-size-fits-all solution or quick fix. Despite this disillusionment, digital native competitors continue to leverage the cloud's advantages, warranting a deeper exploration into what sets these companies apart in their cloud strategy.

More Than Just an Online Data Center

Digital natives understand that the real power of public cloud services lies in their massive, globally distributed, shared, and highly automated data centers. These features enable the provision of pay-per-use billing, virtually limitless scalability, and a self-service consumption model, as shown in Figure 1-2.

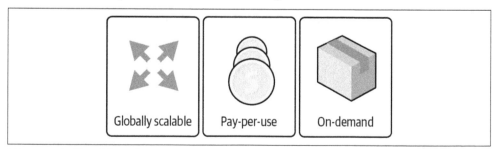

Figure 1-2. Cloud benefits

Nevertheless, public clouds are constructed from commodity hardware connected by networks that have been selected to minimize the total cost of ownership. The hardware is managed by a third-party provider and shared among multiple clients. It's crucial to understand that cloud computing isn't inherently more reliable, cost-effective, or secure than running your own data center:

- Data center hardware is often built for redundancy and task-specific optimization, while in the cloud, hardware is generic, commoditized, and designed with the expectation of occasional failure.

- In a data center, you own the hardware and change is difficult. In contrast, the cloud provides rented hardware on a minute-to-minute basis, allowing for easy change, but at a premium over your hardware.

- A physical data center has an effective *wall* around it, engendering a level of implicit trust in the infrastructure inside. In the cloud, however, a *trust nothing* approach should be adopted.

Transitioning to the cloud isn't simply a matter of transferring your traditional data center operations online. It represents an opportunity to leverage a powerful technology that can fundamentally reshape business operations. However, this requires the correct approach. Simply replicating your on-premises setup in the cloud without adapting your methods can lead to higher costs, heightened security risks, and potentially reduced reliability, as shown in Figure 1-3. This fails to utilize the full potential of the cloud and can be counterproductive.

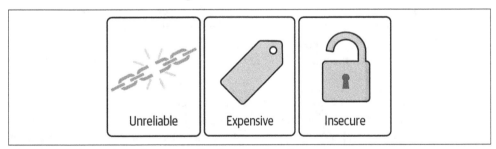

Figure 1-3. The reality of treating cloud as another data center

Instead, acknowledging the unique characteristics and requirements of the cloud and fully embracing these can be truly transformative. Harnessing the elasticity, scalability, and advanced security features of the cloud can lead to levels of operational efficiency, cost-effectiveness, and innovation that surpass what traditional data center environments can offer.

The cloud isn't just an online variant of your current data center. It's a different paradigm that demands a different approach. When navigated adeptly, it can unlock a world of opportunities far surpassing those offered by traditional infrastructure. Embrace the differences, and the cloud's full potential is vast.

Embracing the Cloud as a Distributed System

The essential truth of the cloud is that it functions as a distributed system. This key characteristic renders many assumptions inherent in traditional development obsolete.

These misconceptions, dubbed the fallacies of distributed computing (*https://oreil.ly/ PWnjs*), were first identified by L Peter Deutsch and colleagues at Sun Microsystems:

- The network is reliable.
- Latency is zero.
- Bandwidth is infinite.
- The network is secure.
- Topology doesn't change.
- There is one administrator.
- Transport cost is zero.
- The network is homogeneous.

Each of these points represents a hurdle that must be surmounted when attempting to construct a cloud from scratch. Thankfully, cloud providers have devoted substantial engineering resources over the past two decades to build higher-level abstractions through APIs, effectively addressing these issues. This is precisely why digital natives have an edge—they are attuned to cloud native development, a methodology that leverages this groundwork.

Cloud native development acknowledges the distinct characteristics of the cloud and capitalizes on the high-level abstractions provided by cloud provider APIs. It's a development style in tune with the realities of the cloud, embracing its idiosyncrasies and leveraging them to their full potential.

Distinguishing Cloud Hosted from Cloud Native

Understanding the difference between cloud hosted and cloud native applications is fundamental. To put it simply, the former is about *where*, and the latter is about *how*.

Applications can be cloud hosted, running on infrastructure provided by a public cloud provider, but architectured traditionally, as if they were operating in an on-premises data center. Conversely, applications can be designed in a cloud native manner and still be hosted in an on-premises data center, as shown in Figure 1-4.

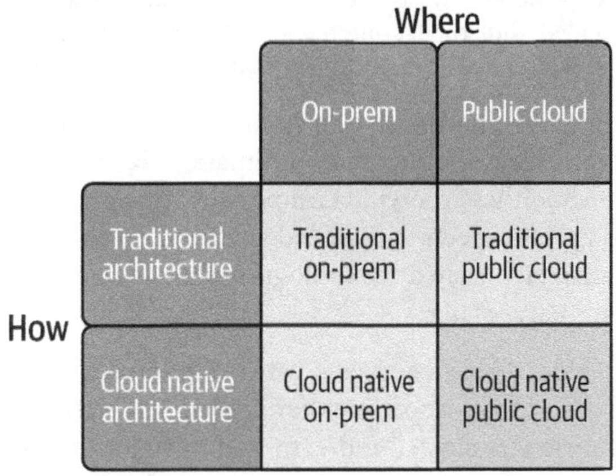

Figure 1-4. Cloud hosted is where, cloud native is how

When I refer to cloud native, I am discussing the development style, application architecture, and abstraction provided by the cloud APIs, rather than the hosting location.

This book primarily explores the construction of cloud native applications using Google Cloud, which embraces both cloud hosted and cloud native principles, the bottom right in Figure 1-4. However, keep in mind that much of the information shared here is also applicable to on-premises private and hybrid clouds, particularly those built around containers and Kubernetes, such as Red Hat OpenShift (*https:// oreil.ly/cQfxg*), VMWare Tanzu (*https://oreil.ly/7xZl4*) and Google Anthos (*https:// oreil.ly/XRSlB*), bottom left in Figure 1-4.

Unraveling the Concept of Cloud Native

The term "cloud native" used to make me cringe, as I felt its significance had been diluted by software vendors leveraging it merely as a stamp of approval to signify their applications are cloud compatible and modern. It reminded me of other buzzwords such as "agile" or "DevOps,'" which have been reshaped over time by companies with something to sell.

Nevertheless, the Cloud Native Computing Foundation (CNCF) (*https://www.cncf.io*), a Linux Foundation project established to bolster the tech industry's efforts toward advancing cloud native technologies, provides a concise definition:

> Cloud native technologies empower organizations to build and run scalable applications in modern, dynamic environments such as public, private, and hybrid clouds. Containers, service meshes, microservices, immutable infrastructure, and declarative APIs exemplify this approach.

These techniques enable loosely coupled systems that are resilient, manageable, and observable. Combined with robust automation, they allow engineers to make high-impact changes frequently and predictably with minimal toil.

In my early advocacy for cloud native technology, I commonly characterized it as encompassing microservices, containers, automation, and orchestration. However, this was a misstep; while these are vital components of a cloud native solution, they are just the technological aspects referenced in the first part of CNCF's definition. Mistaking cloud native as purely a technological shift is one of the key reasons why many cloud native initiatives fail.

Introducing technologies like Kubernetes can be quite disruptive due to the steep learning curve and the added complexity they present to developers. If developers are merely handed a Kubernetes cluster and expected to manage it, problems are bound to arise. A common misconception is that cloud native begins and ends with containers or Kubernetes, but this is far from the truth.

There are also issues related to cost and security. Both these aspects undergo significant changes with the cloud, especially in a cloud native scenario. Developers need to work within appropriate boundaries to prevent costly mistakes or security breaches that could compromise an organization's reputation.

What's more crucial in the CNCF definition is the second part—the techniques. These reflect a development style that capitalizes on the cloud's strengths while recognizing its limitations.

Cloud native is about acknowledging that hardware will fail, networks can be unreliable, and user demand will fluctuate. Moreover, modern applications need to continuously adapt to user requirements and should, therefore, be designed with this flexibility in mind. The concept of cloud native extends to considering the cloud's limitations as much as utilizing its benefits.

Embracing cloud native means a mental shift toward designing applications to make the most of the abstractions exposed by cloud providers' APIs. This implies a transition from thinking in terms of hardware elements such as servers, disks, and networks to higher abstractions like units of compute, storage, and bandwidth.

Importantly, cloud native is geared toward addressing key issues:

- Developing applications that are easy to modify
- Creating applications that are more efficient and reliable than the infrastructure they run on
- Establishing security measures that are based on a zero-trust model

The ultimate goal of cloud native is to achieve short feedback cycles, zero downtime, and robust security.

So, "cloud native" no longer makes me cringe; it encapsulates and communicates a style of development that overcomes the cloud's limitations and unlocks its full potential.

In essence, cloud native acts as a catalyst, making the initial promise of cloud computing achievable: accelerated development, cost savings, and enhanced capabilities.

Embracing Cloud Native Architecture

Cloud native architecture adopts a set of guiding principles designed to exploit the strengths and bypass the limitations of the cloud. In contrast to traditional architecture, which treated changes, failures, and security threats as exceptions, cloud native architecture anticipates them as inevitable norms.

The key concepts in Figure 1-5 underpin cloud native architecture.

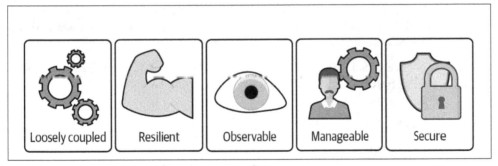

Figure 1-5. Cloud native architecture principles

Let's explore each of these concepts:

Component independence
> An architecture is loosely coupled when its individual system components are designed and changed independently. This arrangement allows different teams to develop separate components without delays caused by interdependencies. When deployed, components can be scaled individually. Should a component fail, the overall system remains functional.

Built-in resilience
> A resilient system operates seamlessly and recovers automatically amidst underlying infrastructure changes or individual component failures. Cloud native systems are inherently designed to accommodate failure. This resilience may be achieved through running multiple instances of a component, automatic recovery of failed components, or a combination of both strategies.

Transparent observability

Given that a cloud native system encompasses multiple components, understanding system behavior and debugging issues can be complex. It is therefore crucial that the system is designed to allow a clear understanding of its state from its external outputs. This observability can be facilitated through comprehensive logging, detailed metrics, effective visualization tools, and proactive alert systems.

Declarative management

In a cloud native environment, the underlying hardware is managed by someone else, with layers of abstraction built on top to simplify operations. Cloud native systems prefer a declarative approach to management, prioritizing the desired outcome (*what*) over the specific steps to achieve it (*how*). This management style allows developers to focus more on addressing business challenges.

Zero-trust security

Given that everything on the public cloud is shared, a default stance of zero trust is essential. Cloud native systems encrypt data both at rest and in transit and rigorously verify every interaction between components.

As I explore these principles in later chapters, I will examine how various tools, technologies, and techniques can facilitate these concepts.

Building a Cloud Native Platform

Cloud providers offer a broad range of tools and technologies. For cloud native architecture to flourish, it is crucial to synergize these tools and apply them using cloud native techniques. This approach will lay the foundation for a platform conducive to efficient cloud native application development.

Laboratory, Factory, Citadel, and Observatory

When conceptualizing a cloud native platform, envision the construction of four key "facilities" on top of the cloud: the laboratory, factory, citadel, and observatory, as shown in Figure 1-6. Each one serves a specific purpose to promote productivity, efficiency, and security:

Laboratory

The laboratory maximizes developer productivity by providing a friction-free environment equipped with the necessary tools and resources for application innovation and development. It should foster a safe environment conducive to experimentation and rapid feedback.

Factory

The factory prioritizes efficiency. It processes the application—originally created in the laboratory—through various stages of assembly and rigorous testing.

The output is a secure, scalable, and low-maintenance application ready for deployment.

Citadel
The citadel is a fortified environment designed to run the application securely and effectively, protecting it from potential attacks.

Observatory
The observatory serves as the oversight hub for all services and applications running in the cloud.

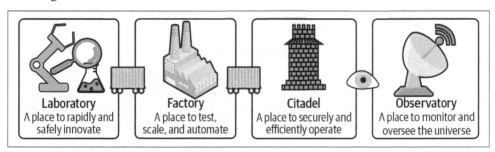

Figure 1-6. Developing effective cloud facilities

Ensuring a smooth transition of applications from the laboratory, through the factory, and into the citadel is critical. The same immutable code should be automatically transported between different facilities.

The Need for More Than Just a Factory

During the 90s, when I was thinking about what to study at university, I found inspiration in an episode of the BBC TV program *Troubleshooter*. The imposing Sir John Harvey-Jones visited the struggling classic car company, Morgan, suggesting they replace their outdated manufacturing methods with a modern factory to enhance production and product consistency. From then on, I was captivated by the idea of improving companies' efficiency.

Yet, a decade later, a follow-up episode revealed that Morgan had defied Sir John's advice entirely, instead capitalizing on their unique craftsmanship as a selling point. Remarkably, the TV program itself ended up promoting their craftsmanship and drawing new customers.

For many enterprises, the prospect of establishing a factory presents an enticing solution to streamline what is often perceived as the chaotic landscape of the cloud. As an engineer, I naturally gravitate toward such systematic order. However, confining and regulating development solely within an automated production line risks sacrificing innovation and craftsmanship, attributes that often set a product apart. A factory-only approach could undermine the creative freedom facilitated by the on-demand public cloud, which is skillfully exploited by digital natives.

To harness the cloud's full potential, it's not enough to have a factory for automating testing and ensuring quality consistency; a laboratory is equally crucial. In this space, developers can craft and rapidly innovate a product in a safe environment, with a wide array of tools at their disposal, before transitioning smoothly to the factory.

Once the factory has produced thoroughly tested and trusted applications, a third facility, the citadel, is necessary where the application can function securely in a production setting.

The Potential for Developers

Throughout my career as a developer, I've experienced both technical and bureaucratic hurdles that have hampered my productivity and, over time, dented my morale. A classic example might be the painstaking wait of weeks for a new virtual machine to be approved or provisioned, or simply awaiting permission grants.

Several years ago, when I began using the public cloud for my personal projects, I was astounded by the difference. It felt akin to running unimpeded rather than wading through muck. As cloud platforms have matured in recent years, this experience has only gotten better.

Marie Kondo, well-known for advocating order, also underscores the importance of joy. For developers, joy is not a mere pipe dream; it can be realized within a friction-free environment that enables developers to work in a state of flow (*https://oreil.ly/n-As5*). With a cloud native platform that puts the developer experience at the forefront, you too can relish this experience.

Equipped with the support of a laboratory, a factory, a citadel, and an observatory, an individual sitting in a coffee shop with merely a laptop and an internet connection has the power to design and deploy an application that can scale to millions of users, just like the most sprawling multinational organization. Adding to the thrill, numerous cloud giants are locked in competition to make this task even easier for you.

As a digital native individual, you're not tethered to a data center or traditional applications. You can commence developing in a cloud native style right away. As you relish the perks of being a digital native, you can either continue on this path or lend your expertise to an organization that seeks to adopt a cloud native development style. Either way, your skills will be highly sought after and valuable.

I recall a conference speaker's words from the late 2000s, as smartphones began to dominate the market. They described mobile phone manufacturers and network operators as engaged in a war, with mobile app developers serving as the ammunition. Today, as organizations strive to exploit the cloud's full potential, cloud native developers have become the new ammunition.

This book consolidates my learnings over the years to help you experience the same joy—a term I use with utmost sincerity—that I have derived as a cloud native developer. It aims to offer you an accessible and low-cost route to experiencing the productivity of cloud native development as an individual, by crafting a developer experience (DX) that truly works for you.

Additionally, it offers enough insight into enterprise concerns to successfully introduce cloud native development into a scaled environment. Achieving the same level of productivity at work as in your personal projects can help you experience this joy at the workplace as well.

Summary

Cloud native represents an architectural approach and development methodology that fully exploits the potential of the cloud. It's characterized by specific techniques, tools, and technologies designed to enhance the strengths and mitigate the weaknesses inherent in cloud computing. Importantly, the scope of cloud native isn't confined to Google Cloud or even the public cloud. It encompasses a broad spectrum of methodologies applicable wherever cloudlike abstractions are present.

To thrive in the cloud native ecosystem, developers need to harness the potential of four distinct yet interdependent facilities: a laboratory for innovative exploration, a factory for streamlined production automation, a citadel for robust defense of live applications, and an observatory for comprehensive system oversight.

The remainder of this book will guide you through these cloud native methodologies, demonstrating how to create and optimize a laboratory, factory, citadel, and observatory using Google Cloud. The aim is to equip you with the knowledge and strategies that maximize your chances of achieving cloud native success. Before you embark on this journey, let's first examine why Google Cloud, among others, offers a particularly conducive environment for cloud native development.

CHAPTER 2

Why Google Cloud Platform?

You can't build a great building on a weak foundation.

—Gordon B. Hinckley

At the time of writing, Google Cloud Platform (GCP) holds the third place in the public cloud market, trailing behind Amazon Web Services (AWS) and Microsoft Azure. With AWS commanding a significant mindshare and Azure capitalizing on Microsoft's expansive corporate presence, one might question the rationale behind opting for Google Cloud. Why not consider other players such as IBM Cloud, Oracle, or Alibaba?

One reason I choose Google Cloud for cloud native development is the integration of services. AWS famously has two-pizza teams (*https://oreil.ly/PG5NG*) that work on each service independently. This produces a wide range of services quickly, often with overlapping capabilities. On the other hand, Google seems to put more emphasis on integration, having fewer services that work well end to end, making it easier to build the laboratory, factory, citadel, and observatory.

Although Google Cloud represents approximately 10% of the cloud market share, it powers 70% of tech unicorns at the time of writing. This disproportionate representation suggests that Google Cloud resonates with digital natives for valid reasons. AWS and Azure may host a multitude of traditional applications, but digital natives, unhindered by legacy infrastructure, favor a cloud native development style, and Google Cloud aligns better with this approach. In essence, Google Cloud is built by cloud native engineers for cloud native engineers, and this resonates with developers.

However, it's important to note that many services discussed in this book also have equivalents in other public clouds. The techniques and considerations, therefore, can be adapted to other platforms. It's a Herculean task to understand every feature and service of a single cloud, such as Google Cloud, let alone grasp multiple services across diverse cloud platforms.

In my experience, focusing on services built on open standards or those that have become de facto standards can be particularly beneficial. These services are universally accessible, both on-premises and across multiple clouds. Learning them once gives you the ability to apply them anywhere. Containers, Kubernetes, Knative, PostgreSQL, and HTTP are a few notable examples where Google Cloud's support for standards shines.

If you are familiar with and favor these abstractions, applications will be more portable, and you will minimize "vendor lock-in." This is where you become reliant on a particular provider's service. Some cloud providers seek to minimize these concerns. Still, if suddenly they decide to double the price, discontinue service, or stop offering a service in a region you need to run your application, you are stuck. This means vendor lock-in should always be at least a consideration. I use the Google Cloud services that are widely available.

Ultimately, the real strength of Google Cloud lies in its robust foundational infrastructure, the hidden backbone built by Google's engineers to run their global services. This strength truly sets Google Cloud apart from its competitors.

Strong Foundations

Google Cloud data centers are purpose-built with proprietary power distribution, cooling, and networking. The compute hardware within them is also custom designed and standardized throughout.

Google uses the term *machine* to refer to a unit of hardware and server for a piece of software that implements a service. As all hardware is standardized, any machine can run any server.

Machines are the smallest building block, with 10 machines assembled into a rack. Racks stand in a row. One or more rows make a cluster. A data center contains multiple clusters. Multiple data centers make a zone, and a region is then made up of three or four zones.

Each machine in a data center is linked together using a high-speed network fabric called Jupiter. Data centers are then connected using B4, a global software-defined network.

Even though Google Cloud is vast, think of it as thousands of standardized machines distributed around the globe, linked together by a fast network.

Powerful Abstractions

What makes Google Cloud stand out is the software Google has built to manage the massive global pool of machines. Although the hardware Google uses is custom-designed, it is nothing special—simply hardware constructed to minimize the total cost of ownership. Given the sheer number of components, failures of machines and disks are frequent. The software introduced next manages hardware failures so that any problems are abstracted away.

Borg

Whether you need to run serverless code for 100ms, need a virtual machine that runs indefinitely, or consume compute through a Google Cloud managed service, Borg will manage the compute. When you make a request, a job is sent to Borg that finds suitable machines to run tasks on. Borg will monitor each task, and if it malfunctions, it will be restarted or moved to a different machine. Borg inspired Kubernetes, so the concepts may be familiar.

However, as a user of Google Cloud, you will know nothing about Borg but will benefit from its abstraction. You request, directly or indirectly, the resources you require in terms of CPU cores and RAM. Borg fulfills everyone's request behind the scenes, making the best utilization of the machines available and seamlessly working around any failures.

Colossus

While machines have local disks, these are only used for temporary storage. For managing permanent storage, Google uses a system named Colossus.

Storage pools consist of spinning discs and flash disks of different capacities. Again, these are selected to minimize their total cost of ownership, so they can and will fail. Colossus sets out to work around any failures and fills the disks as optimally as possible, as any empty space is wasted capacity.

Colossus constantly rebalances where data is stored. Frequently accessed (hot) data is stored on the more expensive fast disks. Less frequently accessed (cold) data is on slower, cheaper disks. As with compute, this means the details of storage are abstracted away. As a user, or more accurately, a service requesting on your behalf, you request the bytes and performance characteristics (or input/output operations per second [IOPS]) required, and Colossus takes care of it.

Spanner

Colossus also forms the foundation of two core database abstractions that support petabytes of data. Bigtable is a petabyte-scale NoSQL database that is eventually consistent across regions. Spanner is a SQL-compatible database that offers strong consistency across regions. Google uses Spanner internally for many systems. For example, Google Photos stores metadata for 4 trillion photos and videos from a billion users in Spanner. Some public references are available in a Spanner blog (*https://oreil.ly/Xxzd6*). These abstractions allow the decisions to be about the type of consistency and level of availability needed rather than the details of how it is achieved.

Andromeda

Like Borg efficiently allocates compute resources, Andromeda manages network bandwidth over Google Cloud's global network. This software-defined network ensures traffic from a service or user is routed most efficiently. Google Cloud is a single extensive network, and everything is software. Features like the global load balance or firewalls are just software configurations via an API rather than a physical device. This powerful feature defines how you want the network to appear with code alone.

An enormous benefit for me is having my development environment on the same Google network as my deployment environments with security between them. Gone are the days of having to transfer data over slow VPN connections.

Combining Abstractions

Taken together, this combination of abstractions is powerful. Being able to request a unit of compute or a unit of storage and knowing that the contract will be met without having to worry about the capacity or reliability of hardware means work is done for you. Similarly, with networks, data replication, and security, being able to declare behavior and being confident that requirements will be met is a liberating way of working. It gets better as Google Cloud combines these building blocks to make higher-level services so a developer can focus on the code, not the infrastructure.

Why Not DIY?

It can be tempting to use the infrastructure as a service (IaaS) of Google Cloud and treat it like a normal data center with virtual machines, disks, and networks, and run vendor's products as you would on-premises. Effectively, this is resorting to the lowest common denominator to remain cloud agnostic. This is particularly popular when deploying databases and Kubernetes platforms like OpenShift, and it will work. You will have to pay for licenses and people to operate the services to go down that road, though. This may be practical for a large organization, but it may be no cheaper than an on-prem data center adding complexity for little benefit.

However, I hope by explaining the abstractions that Google Cloud provides, you will see how you are missing out if you do this. Google's abstractions allow you to work at a higher level and leverage many years of Google engineers' work. Moreover, you would also be missing out on the managed services Google provides on top of the foundations that raise the abstraction even further. Being able to take advantage of the higher levels of abstraction is what cloud native development is all about.

As an individual developer, you don't have the choice of doing it yourself. If you have followed Kelsey Hightower's "Kubernetes the Hard Way" (*https://oreil.ly/pcK7K*), for example, you will have some idea of the effort involved. That is why using Google Cloud can be seen as a powerful toolkit to build what you want without needing an organization behind you. However, suppose you are developing as part of a large organization and adopting the same cloud native approach. In that case, there is no reason for complexity and cost to rise, which is how a traditional organization can keep up with any digital-native competitor.

If you work for an enterprise organization, you may have access to a private cloud platform like Red Hat OpenShift, VMWare Tanzu, or even Google Anthos, Google Cloud's on-premises offering. Like Google Cloud, all these platforms' applications are container based. Although tools and services vary, the principles of cloud native development I describe for Google Cloud in this book will still be applicable. The difference is that these solutions require a significant initial investment. If you are an individual developer, they are unlikely to be available. Google Cloud, however, has a much lower barrier to entry, especially if you take advantage of the free trial. For an individual developer, it is a much more accessible way to learn.

Summary

Google Cloud stands out in cloud native development due to its focus on service integration and support for open standards, minimizing vendor lock-in. It boasts a robust infrastructure, built on custom hardware and high-speed networking. Powerful software abstractions like Borg, Colossus, Spanner, and Andromeda manage compute, storage, databases, and networking, respectively, freeing developers to focus on coding rather than infrastructure. A do-it-yourself approach, treating GCP as a typical data center, limits the benefits of these high-level abstractions and may lead to extra costs. Leveraging GCP's cloud native principles is beneficial for individual developers and large organizations alike.

Google Cloud provides the foundations for building cloud native applications. In Chapter 3, you will look at the characteristics of a cloud native application and the tools, techniques, and technologies that support them.

Cloud Native Applications

So far in this book, the discussion about the motivations and principles behind cloud native technologies addressed the *why* and *what*. Now, let's dive into the *how*. This chapter introduces the techniques, tools, and technologies that make the cloud native approach possible, specifically in the context of Google Cloud.

Autonomous Components Communicating with Messages

Alan Kay, a prominent computer scientist primarily known for pioneering object-oriented programming and the development of the Smalltalk programming language in the 1970s, envisioned computer software as akin to a biological system constituted of interlinked cells. His model fosters a mindset that promotes application modularity and reusability.

The cornerstone of Kay's concept is *messaging*, a mechanism that allows application cells to communicate with each other. Unlike traditional methods that rely on a shared state, messaging ensures interaction through sending and receiving of information. Essentially, Kay advocated for a world of autonomous components, interacting seamlessly through messages.

Interestingly, cloud native applications share striking parallels with Alan Kay's vision, principally the attribute of loosely coupled components. This idea, in itself, is not novel. However, the innovation lies in the amalgamation of contemporary tools, techniques, and technologies that create a robust toolkit for building cloud native applications. Let's explore this in detail, shedding light on how such elements blend to architect modern, efficient, and scalable applications in the cloud.

Harnessing Cloud Potential with the 12-Factor App Principles

Heroku, a cloud platform service established in 2007, quickly became a favorite among developers. It offered an effortless environment for hosting applications, a haven that provided support right from the development phase to secure deployment, albeit within the platform's specific constraints. Many of today's cloud native platforms, including Google Cloud, strive to emulate this developer-friendly experience while minimizing limitations.

In 2012, after extensive engagement with their customers, Adam Wyner and his team at Heroku began to recognize common patterns among applications that performed exceptionally well on their platform. This observation led to the consolidation of these patterns into a cohesive set of guidelines and best practices for developing cloud native applications, known as the 12-factor app principles (*https://12factor.net*).

The 12-factor app principles found extensive application in Cloud Foundry, another platform inspired by Heroku. As cloud platforms continue to evolve, these principles have proven enduring, gaining widespread acceptance as a comprehensive blueprint for designing cloud-ready software.

If you're interviewing for a cloud native developer position, it's likely the concept of 12-factor applications will emerge as a foundational topic. While many candidates might recollect some of the factors' names, similar to recalling catchy acronyms like SOLID or DRY, understanding the underlying concept is far more critical. You should comprehend the problem each factor addresses and how to practically implement them.

Moreover, it's worth noting that the 12-factor app principles were originally devised with a specific platform in mind. Therefore, it's essential to revisit these principles in that original context before applying them to Google Cloud, to ensure their most effective use and relevance.

I. Codebase: One Codebase Tracked in Version Control, Many Deploys

When initially encountering this factor, you might interpret it as advocating for monorepos, which advocate for housing the code for multiple projects within a single version control repository. However, this interpretation isn't accurate.

The principle of *one codebase* dictates that a singular codebase should serve all deployment environments, such as development, staging, and production. This approach negates the practice of having separate repositories configured for each environment or, even worse, maintaining a repository with a production-specific fix that hasn't been integrated back into earlier environments.

The primary goal here is to ensure consistency. By deploying code from the same repository across all environments, you significantly reduce the potential for inconsistencies and, consequently, unexpected bugs. This practice bolsters reliability and predictability across all stages of the application life cycle.

II. Dependencies: Explicitly Declare and Isolate Dependencies

Applications often rely on a multitude of external libraries and frameworks. A common mistake is to assume that a specific version of a library installed on one developer's machine will be equally available on another's, or even in a production environment. This assumption can lead to unexpected errors and the infamous "it works on my machine" defense.

To sidestep this issue, it's critical to explicitly declare all dependencies, inclusive of their precise version numbers. This approach ensures all necessary components are readily available across all development and deployment environments, thus fostering consistency and eliminating potential errors.

Later in this chapter, you will see how containers can greatly facilitate this process, further enhancing the robustness and reliability of your applications.

III. Config: Store Config in the Environment

In the application of the one codebase principle, the challenge emerges of how to manage environment-specific configurations, like database connection details or API keys, which aren't suited for inclusion in the codebase. The answer lies in utilizing the environment itself as the storage medium for these configurations, thereby allowing them to be injected directly into the application. This can be accomplished through environment variables or distinct configuration files.

However, when dealing with sensitive information such as API keys, passwords, or other credentials, storing them directly in the environment can introduce unnecessary security risks. Exposure of environment variables, especially in multitenant environments or open source projects, could lead to unintended access to these secrets.

To mitigate this, a more secure alternative involves the use of secret management services. These specialized services, such as Google Cloud Secret Manager, offer a secure and convenient method to handle sensitive data. They store, manage, and access secrets like API keys, passwords, or certificates in a centralized and secure manner. These secrets are encrypted at rest and in transit and can be accessed programmatically by applications that require them. They also provide auditing and versioning capabilities, which help to monitor and control access to your secrets.

So, while environment-dependent configurations are stored within the environment, sensitive data should be managed using dedicated secret management services. This combination ensures that each environment is correctly configured while maintaining the confidentiality and integrity of your credentials, hence enhancing the overall security posture of your application.

 Storing sensitive information within the codebase poses a significant risk. Cybercriminals employ sophisticated, automated tools that scour code repositories like GitHub, looking for any vulnerabilities such as embedded credentials. Once discovered, these credentials can be exploited in numerous ways. For instance, cloud credentials could allow a hacker unauthorized access to private data. Even worse, they could harness these acquired privileges to spawn an army of cloud-based virtual machines for their purposes, such as Bitcoin mining. In such scenarios, you, the account owner, might end up bearing the brunt of substantial unforeseen expenses.

IV. Backing Services: Treat Backing Services as Attached Resources

A backing service refers to any resource or service upon which an application depends but is not incorporated within the application itself. Common examples include databases and message queues. Treating these backing services as attached resources implies that the application receives the service details through its configuration, thereby eliminating the need for any hardcoded dependencies within the application.

For instance, the application might be supplied with a uniform resource identifier (URI) and credentials to access a particular database. This approach allows for the independent scaling and management of the backing service, offering enhanced flexibility and seamless transitions between different environments. For instance, a database utilized in a development environment could be purposefully scaled down to a size significantly smaller than that in a production environment, aiding in resource management and cost efficiency.

V. Build, Release, Run: Strictly Separate Build and Run Stages

The principle of strictly separating the build and run stages of the software development life cycle aligns with the earlier discussion of the factory and the citadel.

The factory stage is focused on building the application efficiently. The objective here is to minimize the build time and ensure the reliability of the application through rigorous testing before it is released. This phase is fully automated and generates an immutable artifact, which assures reproducibility. Consequently, this makes debugging simpler, as it limits the potential variables that could cause changes.

The citadel stage, on the other hand, is where the application artifact from the factory is run. It's optimized for security, providing only the necessities to securely run the application artifact. If you were to include tools for building the application at this stage, it could create additional avenues for security vulnerabilities.

By separating the build and run stages, you can optimize each for different factors—efficiency and reliability in the build stage, and security in the run stage. This clear division minimizes the risk of security breaches when the application is operating within the citadel.

VI. Processes: Execute the App as One or More Stateless Processes

At the beginning of this chapter, I compared the architecture of cloud native applications to Alan Kay's analogy of cells—individual, loosely coupled components working together. To expand on this, each component is recommended to operate as an independent, stateless process under this principle.

Stateless doesn't mean a process without any state. Rather, it emphasizes that any state a component maintains should be stored externally, such as in a database, rather than being held in the process's memory or local disk storage. This principle becomes especially relevant when a process restarts, as locally stored states could be lost. Notably, in the Heroku platform, persistent storage was not available, making state holding an impossibility, and necessitating this approach. Nonetheless, even in cloud native platforms where persistence is available, this principle remains important and beneficial.

Adherence to statelessness facilitates the scaling of processes, as there is no state to be lost when instances are scaled down or acquired when scaling up. It also mitigates the risk of process failures due to corruption of the internal state, thus enhancing reliability. Importantly, the absence of state allows for flexibility in relocating processes to different hardware or environments in case of failure, enabling the creation of cloud native applications that are more reliable than the infrastructure on which they run.

Although the 12-factor app principles predate microservices, the notion of a cloud native application as multiple stateless processes is foundational to the convergence of microservices and cloud native. It's worth noting that the Heroku platform was built upon small instances called *dynos*, essentially small stateless processes, allowing for no alternative. While loose coupling is a key attribute of cloud native applications, the question of whether each component must be deployed as a separate microservice is a topic I will explore further.

Addressing a common question, the concept of statelessness doesn't necessarily preclude all forms of state. For instance, buffering unsent data for efficiency, such as batching insert statements, might seem like a form of state. However, this represents a temporary or transient state, which is intended to be cleared in the short term. Such transient states can be lost without disrupting the overall functionality or correctness of the application. Therefore, such practices can still be considered in line with state-less principles, provided they don't affect the overall functionality or lead to data loss.

VII. Port Binding: Export Services via Port Binding

The principle of port binding is a fundamental aspect of how services communicate within and outside of an application. It allows a service to become accessible by attaching itself to a specific port number on a host machine. This mechanism ensures that different services can coexist on the same host machine without interfering with each other. For instance, it's quite common for a service with an HTTP endpoint to be exposed on port 8080. As you delve deeper into the intricacies of Google Cloud in subsequent sections, you will discover how much of this port binding management is seamlessly handled by the platform itself.

VIII. Concurrency: Scale Out via the Process Model

Traditional applications often achieve scaling through a vertical approach, which involves bolstering a single process with additional resources like CPU and memory. Given the availability of multiple CPUs, this necessitates concurrent threads to effectively utilize the added resources, consequently increasing the complexity. It's noteworthy that Heroku, originally designed for Ruby applications, adhered to this principle likely because concurrency wasn't a forte of Ruby at that time.

This principle of concurrency advocates the more efficient alternative of horizontal scaling, which involves adding more, smaller instances of the service rather than augmenting the size of existing instances. This approach optimizes the usage of the underlying infrastructure without escalating the complexity. An additional advantage of this strategy is the enhancement of application reliability through multiple instances, thereby reinforcing its place as a key principle in the cloud native paradigm.

IX. Disposability: Maximize Robustness with Fast Startup and Graceful Shutdown

Cloud native applications are designed with the expectation of potential failure of the underlying infrastructure. Consequently, at any given moment, an instance may need to be terminated and restarted. This principle highlights the importance of treating instances as disposable, emphasizing their ability to shut down gracefully—avoiding data loss, for example. It's equally crucial for new instances to be capable of starting up swiftly, thus minimizing periods of unavailability. This focus on disposability not only maximizes the robustness of the system but also prepares it to handle unexpected disruptions or demand fluctuations efficiently.

X. Dev/Prod Parity: Keep Development, Staging, and Production as Similar as Possible

The dev/prod parity principle is another step to solving the "but it runs on my machine problem." The idea behind it is that the development, testing, and production environment should be as similar as possible to avoid unexpected behavior when an application moves to a new environment. This includes having the same operating system, dependencies, services, and configuration wherever possible. As I will discuss later in Chapter 12, containers and infrastructure as code (IaC) do a lot to help with this.

XI. Logs: Treat Logs as Event Streams

In a conventional application operating on a single machine, logs can be written to a local file for subsequent examination. However, in a cloud native system with numerous instances of components distributed across multiple machines, managing an assortment of log files on various machines is hardly practical. Rather than dealing with disparate log files, logs should be treated as event streams that are directed toward a centralized logging solution. This method enables efficient processing, correlation, and searchability of logs, thereby improving the overall visibility of system activities and aiding in debugging. In Chapter 13, I'll delve into how services like Google Cloud offer outstanding features to facilitate these log management practices.

XII. Admin Processes: Run Admin/Management Tasks as One-Off Processes

Admin and management tasks, such as database migrations, data imports, or system updates, are often required in systems and are typically run on a schedule or on demand. This principle advises isolating these types of tasks from the main application execution. By doing so, these tasks can be run independently, reducing potential side effects and simplifying their maintenance.

When making architectural decisions, it's beneficial to refer back to the 12 factors. These principles should be viewed as guidelines rather than stringent rules. However, if you choose to deviate from them, it's important to understand why.

Beyond the 12 Factors

In 2016, Kevin Hoffman revisited the 12-factor app in *Beyond the Twelve-Factor App* (O'Reilly). His book revised and expanded the 12 factors to encompass 15 factors, accounting for advancements and learnings since 2012.

The additional factors—"API first," Telemetry, and Security highlight the growing significance of security and observability in cloud native applications.

API First

The "API first" principle posits that any functionality that your application provides should be exposed through a well-documented and versioned API. This approach benefits both the development of your application and its potential integration with other systems.

From a development perspective, "API first" encourages a clean separation of front end and back end code, making it easier to develop, test, and scale each independently. It also provides a clear contract for what functionality the back end provides and how it should be used, which can help to reduce bugs and improve consistency.

From an integration perspective, an "API first" approach means your application can be more easily combined with other systems. This is increasingly important in modern cloud environments, where complex systems are often composed of multiple smaller services.

Telemetry

Telemetry involves the collection and analysis of data generated by remote systems to gain insights into their operation, usage, and performance. In a cloud native context, telemetry usually involves tracking metrics, logs, and traces from your application and its underlying infrastructure.

Telemetry is crucial for monitoring the health of your system, understanding how it's being used, and diagnosing issues when they arise. It is also an essential part of many modern practices such as observability and site reliability engineering (SRE).

Security

While the original 12-factor app principles include some security considerations, the renewed focus on security reflects its growing importance in the modern software landscape. This principle acknowledges that security is not an afterthought or an optional extra, but a fundamental concern that should be integrated into every stage of application development and operation.

In a cloud native context, this can involve practices like secure coding, automated vulnerability scanning, use of encryption for data at rest and in transit, proper management of secrets and credentials, use of least-privilege access controls, and ensuring regular updates and patches to all software components to protect against known vulnerabilities. This principle emphasizes that security is a shared responsibility across developers, operators, and security teams.

When considering the 12 factors, remember that they were originally devised for the Heroku platform and subsequently adopted by Cloud Foundry, a similar platform. While these principles remain relevant for modern cloud platforms, some are shaped by the constraints of the Heroku platform, which may not be applicable to Google Cloud in certain scenarios.

Defining Components with Microservices

Traditional applications are often referred to as monolithic. In a monolithic application, all of the functionality is deployed as a single unit.

This itself is not a bad thing. Deploying a single unit is easy to manage. The problems come from not having a good separation of concerns. In a cloud native application, it is important to have a good separation of concerns by splitting the system into separate components that can be developed and tested independently. The idea is that if each component only has one reason to change, then changes do not cause side effects to other components. This allows different developers to work on different components at the same time and quickly, as they are not stepping on each other's toes.

Unfortunately, many monolithic applications do not separate concerns sufficiently and they become "big balls of mud" that are difficult to change, killing developers' productivity.

I joke that any book about cloud native can be measured by the time it takes to mention Martin Fowler, who popularized microservices in the early 2010s. My colleague Jeff will be disappointed I only managed to get to the third chapter. I learned about microservices from a talk by James Lewis, the often-forgotten co-coiner of the term. At first, I did not get it, but when I applied it to my work, I saw the value.

I handled an application that allowed users to submit data and produce reports on the data. If a change was needed to the reports, the whole system needed to be deployed, and at that time, no one could submit new data. By breaking apart the monolith into a data submission and a data reporting service, I could deploy changes to reporting without any interruption to submission. Similarly, I could change the submission service without interpreting reporting. This is a simple example, but it led to much happier users and made my life a lot easier as deployment became a lot easier.

Microservices are now a widely adopted approach to building modern, scalable, and resilient cloud native systems. However, because they are deployed and managed independently, there is an overhead of complexity.

When beginning an application, it may not be clear where the boundaries are, and it is not necessary to jump to microservices straight away; the important part is to separate the application into modules that have the potential to be deployed independently. If an application is initially developed as a single modular monolith, this is not a problem. As the application grows and different components need to be deployed or scaled independently, a well-structured monolith can be broken into microservices later.

However, for the rest of the book, I will use microservices synonymously with components as the building blocks of your cloud native applications. To go into much more depth on the subject of microservices, I recommend *Building Microservices* by Sam Newman (O'Reilly).

Determining Component Granularity

How granular should a component be?

Simply put, if aspects of your component—like changes, failures, or scaling—can occur together, it should remain a single unit. However, the moment it requires independent alterations, failure management, or scaling, it's time to consider breaking it down into separate services.

In his manufacturing process improvement book *The Goal* (North River Press), Eliyahu Goldratt observes that "technology can bring benefits if, and only if, it diminishes a limitation."

This is analogous to our cloud native approach, where our aim is to streamline the process of building and operating applications. Hence, the only rationale for dividing a component into smaller entities should be to overcome a limitation:

- When a component doesn't yet need to change, fail, or scale independently, it is fine to keep them as modules in a modular monolith.
- When separate teams come across limitations due to sharing the code, it makes sense to split components out.
- When a piece of functionality is limited on how much it can scale, it makes sense to split it out.

Remember, the more you break a system down into fine-grained components, the more complexity you introduce. While automation and observability can mitigate this complexity to an extent, it's crucial to always be mindful of the reasons for downsizing a component and to consider the trade-offs involved.

Leveraging Domain-Driven Design for Defining Microservice Boundaries

In cloud native system design, one key consideration is the delineation of boundaries between microservices. Each microservice should ideally have a single responsibility, providing it with only one reason to change, thereby promoting a clear separation of concerns.

Domain-driven design (DDD), a technique centered around domain knowledge, plays a vital role in this context. When implemented in a microservices environment, DDD can enhance the system's design and maintainability by establishing a laser focus on the business domain and enforcing a clear demarcation of responsibilities among the various microservices.

Implementing DDD within microservices offers several advantages:

Domain-driven architecture
>   DDD facilitates the identification and modeling of the core business domains within a system. These domains subsequently guide the microservices' design, leading to an architecture that's intuitively aligned with business requirements and exhibits logical consistency.

Bounded contexts
>   A crucial principle of DDD is defining clear boundaries—termed *bounded contexts*—for each microservice. Identified by the specific business capabilities they represent, these boundaries ensure that each microservice has a distinct scope and purpose, simplifying their understanding and maintenance.

Domain language
>   DDD promotes the use of a shared domain language, enhancing communication and collaboration within the development team. In a microservices environment, where different teams might handle different microservices, this is particularly important.

Evolvability
>   DDD supports the concept of continuous evolution and improvement, perfectly aligning with a microservices environment where the system often evolves in tandem with the business and incorporates new features over time. By maintaining focus on the business domain, DDD ensures that any changes align with the system's overall goals and objectives.

Domain-driven design is an expansive subject with a vibrant community and dedicated conferences. Numerous resources are available for learning its concepts and practices. *Domain-Driven Design* by Eric Evans (Addison-Wesley) serves as the definitive reference. However, *Learning Domain-Driven Design* by Vlad Khononov (O'Reilly) serves as an accessible starting point for newcomers.

Intercommunication Between Microservices: APIs and Events

In multicomponent applications, effective communication is key, and it heavily relies on well-defined contracts between components. Microservices predominantly employ two communication approaches: event-driven and API-first.

Event-Driven Architecture

Event-driven architecture is a paradigm where microservices communicate by generating and consuming events. Triggered by system internal or external changes, events serve as contracts in an event-driven structure.

API-First Approach

The API-first design is characterized by APIs serving as contracts that facilitate communication with a service. Essentially, the API is the intermediary between the system components. APIs, particularly HTTP APIs, are the primary means for external systems and developers to access system functionality and data.

HTTP APIs usually employ one of two protocols, REST or gRPC:

REST
> Leverages a text-based format (typically JSON), offering more flexibility than gRPC but potentially leading to increased maintenance challenges.

gRPC
> Utilizes a binary format (Protocol Buffers) and has a more rigid structure than REST. The API is specified in a contract (a *.proto* file) that outlines the request and response messages and permissible operations. Owing to its defined structure, gRPC APIs can be easier to maintain and more efficient due to their binary format.

A gRPC or REST API can be designed for either synchronous or asynchronous communication. The choice is dictated by its design and implementation.

In a synchronous communication model, the client sends a request and waits for a response before proceeding. The client is blocked until a response is received or a time-out occurs. While synchronous communication is straightforward to use, it may be less efficient as the client must wait for a response before continuing.

In contrast, asynchronous communication allows the client to send a request and continue processing while waiting for a response. The client is not blocked while waiting for the response before continuing. Asynchronous communication can be more efficient as it allows the client to continue processing while waiting for a response, but it might introduce complexity due to the asynchronous handling of responses.

Both REST and gRPC can be implemented in either synchronous or asynchronous styles depending on the requirements. However, due to ease of use and familiarity, REST is often chosen when exposing APIs externally, while gRPC might be preferred for internal microservices communication due to its performance and strong contract enforcement.

gRPC: Up and Running by Kasun Indrasiri and Danesh Kuruppu (O'Reilly) offers a comprehensive discussion on gRPC. API design, a vast subject in itself, is covered in many dedicated books.

Harmonizing APIs and Events for Effective Microservice Communication

Both API-first and event-driven architectures come with distinct advantages and challenges. Understanding these, one can ingeniously combine these approaches for a more robust and flexible system design. In a composite model, an event-driven system could utilize APIs to expose its functions and data to external systems. However, the primary emphasis remains on the internal event flow, with APIs serving as the conduit rather than the focal point. As you delve further, you'll explore how a strategically designed API can serve as a powerful gateway into an event-driven system, effortlessly harmonizing these two paradigms for superior microservice communication.

Event Storming: A Collaborative Approach to System Design

One of the instrumental techniques often employed in conjunction with DDD is Event Storming. This collaborative, workshop-style method is particularly effective in shaping event-driven systems.

Event Storming serves as a powerful tool to comprehend, design, and enhance an organization's processes. Its primary objective is to map out the system's event flow and business processes, while also identifying opportunities for improvement.

In an Event Storming session, participants collaboratively chart the system's event flow using sticky notes, each representing a distinct event such as a customer placing an order, a payment being processed, or an item being shipped. These notes are then arranged and rearranged on a board, visually depicting the event sequence and their interrelationships.

Beyond identifying process inefficiencies or bottlenecks, Event Storming can be employed to architect new processes or systems and to refine existing ones. This method synergizes effectively with other approaches such as agile development and lean principles, creating a comprehensive toolset for system improvement.

For those keen to delve deeper into Event Storming, Alberto Brandolini's book, "EventStorming" (*https://oreil.ly/U1eUq*) (Leanpub), provides practical insights. As the technique's creator, Brandolini offers invaluable guidance on how to leverage Event Storming to its full potential.

Achieving Portability with Containers

When I was a child, the town where I lived had a dock where ships would be unloaded of loose cargo using a crane that scooped it up and deposited it into a row of waiting trucks. Shipping containers had not made it to our town.

A few years ago, I saw huge cranes unloading standardized containers from ships and autonomous vehicles moving the containers around the terminal to await collection. It is a whole different level of scale and efficiency.

Shipping containers' strength lies in their durability and standardized size and shape, making them easily manageable with cranes and forklifts, loading them onto trucks and trains for further transportation. Their ability to be stacked and stored efficiently, coupled with their locked and sealed nature, ensures they are secure and tamper-proof. By abstracting the cargo from the infrastructure that transports it, they revolutionize shipping logistics.

Just as shipping containers were standardized by the International Organization for Standardization (ISO) in the 1960s, containers for applications were standardized by the Open Container Initiative (OCI). Although practitioners often talk about Docker containers, this is just one implementation of the OCI container standard.

A container encapsulates everything necessary for the application to run—the application code, libraries, dependencies, and runtime—into a lightweight, standalone, and executable package. This concisely addresses the second factor of the 12-factor application methodology (see "II. Dependencies: Explicitly Declare and Isolate Dependencies" on page 25).

The primary advantages of containers, much like their physical counterparts, lie in their packaging and portability. When run on a host, containers are isolated from others, mitigating the risk of conflicts between coexisting applications and services.

The thing to remember is that containers are both a packaging and an isolation mechanism, and by using them, you get both benefits. Sometimes, for example, in a Python application with many dependencies, there will be a great advantage in packaging it up as a container. Other times, such as packaging to a single Go binary, the packaging will be less useful. However, in both cases, the content will give isolation at runtime.

The containers can also be immutable, and like having a locked and sealed shipping container, the content is immutable. As containers are a standard, there is also a wide range of tools for working with them, from building to checking security.

There are arguments against the need to use containers for cloud native applications around complexity and overhead. However, Google Cloud services are container-centric, so using containers gives a lot of flexibility in where those containers can run.

As you will see, Google Cloud also has tools that take away a lot of the complexity and overhead concerns.

Flexible Running with Container Runtimes

You have a container nicely packaging your microservice; now you need to choose where to run it—a container runtime. Many people automatically associate Kubernetes, the container orchestrator, with cloud native. "Containerized microservices running on Kubernetes" is almost the definition of cloud native for some. However, in this book's definition of cloud native, I prioritize efficiency; and Kubernetes will not always be the most efficient way of running a container on Google Cloud.

To illustrate this, consider a container as a person and the container runtime as a vehicle. If you have a family of four and use a car multiple hours each day, owning a standard five-seater car makes sense. At times, the car may transport all four individuals; other times, only one or two. While the car may not be fully utilized at all times, it is always ready and possesses adequate space. Occasionally, you might even squeeze an additional passenger into the middle seat. This scenario reflects the versatility of Kubernetes.

However, if there are times when you need to accommodate more people—say, when grandparents visit monthly, and you need six seats—you might consider purchasing a seven-seater car, perhaps with two extra seats that fold away when not needed. This mirrors the functionality of Kubernetes with autoscaling, where the capacity can expand to accommodate additional load when required.

On the flip side, consider a different scenario where:

- You are living in a city.
- You undertake short, solo journeys every other day.
- Once a week, you travel for an outing with a group of friends.
- A few times a year, you travel a hundred miles to visit family with your partner.

In such a situation, does owning a car make sense? Probably not.

Now imagine a service like Uber offering an on-demand transportation service where you can order a self-driving car to accommodate anything from one to twenty people. You merely specify the number of passengers, a suitable car arrives within 30 seconds, and you pay per minute of use. Would you still own a car, or would you prefer this "carless" service?

This scenario is akin to running containers using a serverless container runtime. Yes, there may be a cluster of machines (perhaps a Kubernetes cluster) somewhere behind the scenes, but they're so abstracted that you don't need to worry about them.

However, imagine if you changed jobs and had a 60-minute daily commute where punctuality is critical. You might opt to own a two-seater sports car for daily commuting and use the Uber service for larger, less frequent trips. Here, the ownership of the car provides a guaranteed capacity, and on-demand service is the perfect solution for situations where you don't need that assurance.

Likewise, different services exist on Google Cloud for running containers. Although Kubernetes is a powerful abstraction, it has a steep learning curve, and sometimes running a cluster 24/7 will not be efficient. You can use Kubernetes directly on Google Cloud using Google Kubernetes Engine (GKE) but you don't need to. If your services run all the time with occasional spikes, it may make sense to have a Kubernetes cluster. It may make sense to use just the serverless container runtimes. It may make sense to use a combination.

Cloud Foundry, an earlier cloud native platform, introduced a succinct haiku that elegantly encapsulates the essence of cloud native services:

> Here is my source code
> Run it on the cloud for me
> I do not care how
>
> —@onsijoe

Drawing parallels with Cloud Foundry's approach, once you have a service running in a container on Google Cloud, you can adopt a similar philosophy: "Here is my containerized service, ensure it's ready to handle incoming requests." This approach offers immense flexibility. The specifics and trade-offs of various services will be explored in detail in later chapters.

Avoiding Lock-In with Abstractions

Avoiding vendor lock-in with a particular cloud provider is always a consideration when building cloud native applications. Even though this is a book on Google Cloud, it is still worth considering the potential switching costs of moving to another cloud.

There are several strategies to mitigate lock-in:

Infrastructure based
> Aim for the lowest common denominator in infrastructure. This involves building only on IaaS primitives, such as disks, databases, and virtual machines, that are universally available across all clouds. This strategy typically includes self-managing a Kubernetes distribution on the infrastructure to ensure consistency across clouds.

Kubernetes based

Target a managed Kubernetes service as the lowest common denominator. All major cloud providers offer managed Kubernetes services, so it seems logical to use Kubernetes as the common abstraction layer. However, managed Kubernetes services differ across providers, especially regarding versions and maintenance requirements, making this solution less straightforward than it may initially appear.

Open standards based

Embrace open standards and protocols that are supported across various clouds. This approach favors managed services that offer a technology available on other clouds through a higher-level abstraction since these have often become a de facto industry standard. Examples include the PostgreSQL wire protocol, Kubernetes API, Knative, and OCI Containers.

Single-cloud based

Choose the most suitable service on a single cloud, on the assumption that the benefits of using the managed service will outweigh even high switching costs if the probability of needing to switch is low. Technologies like AWS Lambda might fit this category. Even then, implementing patterns that allow developers to abstract away from specific services can make potential transitions more manageable.

As I discussed in Chapter 2, I believe the first two strategies often sacrifice many benefits of cloud native, particularly the ability to use managed services and the integrated experience they provide. By striving for a generic abstraction, you may reduce the switching cost, but it might also lead to losses in speed, efficiency, and potential security. Therefore, the likelihood of needing to switch should be carefully evaluated. I believe this approach only makes sense when an application must be deployed across multiple clouds simultaneously.

If Google Cloud is your chosen platform and the chances of needing to switch to another cloud are minimal, I advocate for the third approach, which is the primary focus of this book. This strategy involves favoring technologies and high-level abstractions available in any cloud, rather than focusing on individual services. While I will discuss many specific Google Cloud services in this book, I'll always attempt to highlight where these services support an open standard or protocol that's also available in other environments.

Responding to Change with Extreme Programming (XP)

Cloud native benefits greatly from the techniques of extreme programming (XP) first put forward by Kent Beck and Cynthia Andres in *Extreme Programming Explained* (Addison-Wesley). These are a set of techniques that aim to build quality into code by emphasizing simplicity, communication, and feedback. It is a type of agile software development, which means that it is optimized to be flexible and responsive to change.

Principles include:

Small releases
> XP emphasizes the importance of delivering small, usable increments of software frequently, rather than waiting until the end of the project to deliver a large, monolithic product. In cloud native, these increments can correspond to micro-services.

Collaborative development
> XP emphasizes the importance of collaboration between developers, customers, and other stakeholders.

Test-driven development
> XP encourages developers to write automated tests for their code before writing the code itself, to ensure that the code is correct and meets the needs of the users.

Refactoring
> XP encourages developers to regularly review and improve their code to keep it simple and maintainable.

XP is a flexible approach that can be adapted to the needs of different projects and organizations. It is designed to be adaptable to change and to encourage frequent communication and feedback between everyone involved in the development process.

Test-driven development in particular is a useful tool for cloud native development, as having the tests in place first means that any changes or refactoring can be made with confidence. *Learning Test-Driven Development* by Saleem Siddiquif (O'Reilly) is a good practical introduction to this subject.

Building Confidence with Testing

For effective cloud native development, going beyond test-driven development to embrace testing in a broader sense is indispensable. Comprehensive testing procedures lay a foundation of confidence, enabling developers to make changes with the assurance that any newly introduced issues would be promptly identified and addressed. Given the intricate nature of cloud native applications, comprised of numerous interconnected components, it is virtually impossible to sustain a desirable pace of development without a robust testing regime.

Here are some critical testing methodologies for cloud native applications:

Unit testing

Focusing on testing isolated functional units within each microservice. It verifies the correctness of individual functions without considering their interactions with other parts of the system.

Integration testing

Concentrates on testing the interaction between microservices, or between a microservice and external services such as databases or messaging systems. It ensures that all components work harmoniously in conjunction.

Contract testing

This involves the verification of the contract between microservices, which could be event-driven or API-based. Contract testing ensures that all services adhere to the agreed-upon interfaces.

Performance testing

This evaluates the application's performance under various load conditions, determining the system's behavior under peak load, identifying bottlenecks, and understanding its scalability potential.

Disaster recovery testing

Critical for validating the application's ability to recover from failures, disruptions, or catastrophes, ensuring that recovery procedures and contingency plans are effective.

Security testing

Ensures the application's resilience against threats such as hacking or data breaches. It verifies the robustness of the system's security measures, aiming to safeguard both the system and user data.

User acceptance testing

This is conducted from the perspective of the end user to ensure the application aligns with user expectations and requirements, affirming that it's ready for deployment.

While testing is a cornerstone of software development regardless of the paradigm, cloud native applications, with their microservices architecture and specific scalability and resilience attributes, demand a nuanced approach. The loose coupling of components, which communicate through APIs or respond to events, calls for an increased emphasis on contract testing to secure the reliability of these interactions. Throughout this book, I will delve into these methodologies and demonstrate how they fortify cloud native development.

Eliminating Toil with Automation

When I first started learning to program at school, my teacher said to me, "if you are doing the same thing manually more than three times, you are probably doing it wrong."" That has stuck with me. Another way of looking at it is that the best developers are lazy developers. They don't want to build a container by hand, manually deploy a new version multiple times a day, or spend ages trawling through logs to debug errors. The most productive developers consider this work "toil" and seek to eliminate it and get back to building applications.

This is where DevOps comes from, a set of practices that combines software development (Dev) and operations (Ops) to speed up the development and increase software quality. As you will see in later chapters, this includes:

Continuous integration
> Automatically building and testing changes in the factory (Chapter 12)

Continuous delivery
> Automatically making the output of the factory ready for deployment to the citadel (Chapter 11)

Monitoring and logging
> Exposing what is happening inside the citadel in the observatory (Chapter 13) to make correcting problems straightforward

Infrastructure as code
> The mechanism for building the infrastructure of the factory and the citadel in a reproducible way

Managed services
> Using services managed by the cloud provider in the citadel in preference to self-management

Ultimately, when working with cloud native apps, there is the approach of "you build it, you run it." As it is the developers that are on the hook if the applications fail at 2 a.m., there is a great incentive to make sure that doesn't happen. If it does, there is the incentive that it be easy to fix so the developer can get back to bed. DevOps is operations performed by a developer who prefers to be writing code *and* getting a good night's sleep.

Google has developed a particular implementation of DevOps called site reliability engineering (SRE) that it uses for running production systems. This is explained in *Site Reliability Engineering* by Betsy Beyer et al. (O'Reilly). You will see how SRE principles permeate into Google Cloud in Chapter 13.

Summary

Successfully developing cloud native applications relies on a comprehensive understanding of various tools, techniques, and technologies. While each of these subjects merits detailed study, here are the primary points to remember:

- Cloud native applications tend to be made from *autonomous components* communicating by *messages*, not by sharing state.
- The 12 factors are useful recommendations, but remember that they were designed for earlier platforms.
- Microservices are one destination but don't have to be the starting point.
- Event-driven and API-driven architecture are both useful approaches.
- Domain-driven design helps identify the boundaries between microservices.
- Event Storming helps map out communication in event-driven systems.
- Containerizing components provide flexibility and portability.
- Kubernetes is just one way of running containers.
- Patterns exist to help address common problems and mitigate the risk of vendor lock-in.
- Extreme programming techniques help sustain fast feedback, especially test-driven development.
- Testing increases quality and provides the confidence needed to keep going fast.
- Automation saves time, provides consistency, and lets developers focus on solving business problems.

One crucial thing to remember is that everything comes with trade-offs. There aren't any definitive rules dictating what a cloud native application should be. Instead, there are proven principles that generally provide good results. Cloud native doesn't impose the use of Kubernetes, microservices, or even containers. Situations may arise where these principles don't apply, and it's these shades of gray that underline the importance of knowing the options available and making informed decisions based on your specific circumstances.

In Part II, you'll begin your exploration of Google Cloud, focusing on how it can be leveraged to build cloud native applications.

Hands-On Projects

In this part, you'll dive headfirst into Google Cloud, building the *Skills Mapper* application through a series of projects.

CHAPTER 4

Preparing Google Cloud

In this chapter, you'll embark on a journey that will fully equip you to work with Google Cloud. This includes account creation to the installation of essential tools designed to aid and enrich your experience in the project chapters that follow. You will also be introduced to the example project, which you will build into five separate projects in the subsequent chapters.

Create a Google Account

The first step toward using Google Cloud is creating an account. This can be accomplished by visiting the sign-up page (*https://oreil.ly/pKvnv*) and selecting the "Start free" button (Figure 4-1) in the upper right corner of the page.

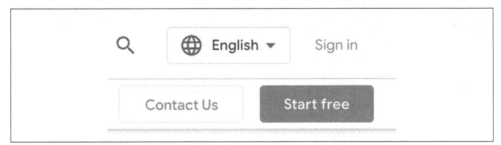

Figure 4-1. Start free button

For those new to Google Cloud, a $300 free credit is available, which can be used over a period of 12 months to explore the platform's services. This amount should cover the exercises in this book, allowing you to experiment without needing to spend money. In Chapter 15, there is information about the Google Innovators Plus program, an education subscription that also offers discounted Google Cloud credit.

Install the gcloud CLI

When signing into Google Cloud through a web browser, you will see the Google Cloud Console. Although the console provides access to nearly all Google Cloud's services, this book focuses primarily on the *gcloud* CLI for its productivity and ease of explaining in writing.

The gcloud CLI is a command-line tool that provides interaction with Google Cloud Platform APIs. It is compatible with Windows, macOS, and Linux. Follow the steps outlined in the Google Cloud documentation (*https://oreil.ly/Qnova*) for installation on your machine.

If, like me, you're using a Mac with Homebrew, you can shortcut the installation process by running:

```
brew install google-cloud-sdk
```

Alternatively, you can use the Google Cloud Shell. This is a browser-based environment that is preinstalled with the gcloud CLI. You can access the Google Cloud Shell from the Google Cloud Console.

When signed in, look at the top right corner of the console and click the icon that looks like a command prompt labeled `Activate Cloud Shell`. This will give you an up-to-date gcloud CLI logged into your account, like the one shown in Figure 4-2.

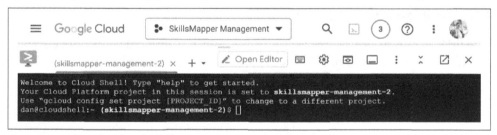

Figure 4-2. Google Cloud Shell

If using Google Cloud Shell, you can skip the next two steps, which are only applicable when using the gcloud CLI from your own machine.

Update Your gcloud Client

Since Google updates gcloud components frequently, if you already have your gcloud client installed, it is often worth updating to the latest versions before starting work. You can do that with this command:

```
gcloud components update
```

If updates are available, you will be prompted for confirmation before installation.

Log In to gcloud

With an up-to-date gcloud client, you can now authenticate with your account using this command:

```
gcloud auth login
```

This will give you a link to open in your browser that will ask you to sign in with your Google account and then automatically authenticate your client. You will then be ready to start working with Google Cloud.

Set Your Default Region and Zone

Resources in Google Cloud are zonal, regional, or multiregional. That is, they apply to a single zone (location), multiple zones within a region, or distributed across multiple regions.

It is useful to specify defaults for your region and zone so that you do not have to specify them every time you create a resource. For example, if you are working in London (like me), you may want to specify the default region as `europe-west2` and the default zone as `europe-west2-a`.

These commands set the default region and zone:

```
gcloud config set compute/region europe-west2
gcloud config set compute/zone europe-west2-a
gcloud config set run/region europe-west2
```

These settings are stored on your local machine; for example, on a Mac, in `~/.config/gcloud/configurations/config_default`, they are set for your machine rather than for an account.

> If you encounter a message like "API [compute.googleapis.com] not enabled on project [your-project-id]," it means that the specific service—in this case, the Google Compute Engine service—is not enabled for your project by default.
>
> Not all services are enabled for new projects to avoid unnecessary usage and cost. When you create a new project, only a subset of services that are commonly used or required by other core services will be enabled automatically. This approach helps keep the project environment clean and reduces potential security risks.

Alternatively, you can use the `gcloud init` command to be guided through the process of setting up the gcloud CLI.

Create a Project

All Google Cloud Platform resources live in a project. A project is a container for resources that allows you to manage access and billing. Each project has a unique ID and a name. The name is unique to your account, but the ID is unique across all Google Cloud Platform accounts.

 You will create several projects in this book. Rather than explaining how to set up a project each time, you will be referred back to this section.

I find it useful to store the PROJECT_ID in an environment variable so that I can easily reference it later on. As you move on to the projects, you will make a lot of use of this pattern:

```
export PROJECT_ID=[PROJECT_ID]
```

To create the new project, enter the following gcloud command:

```
gcloud projects create $PROJECT_ID
```

Then set the gcloud CLI to use the new project as the default:

```
gcloud config set project $PROJECT_ID
```

Similarly, if you have an environment variable named $REGION you could set the default region and zone like this:

```
gcloud config set compute/region $REGION
gcloud config set compute/zone $REGION-a
gcloud config set run/region $REGION
```

At any time, you can check your current project using:

```
gcloud config list project
```

If you ever want to set your current project to an environment variable again you use the output of the gcloud command like this:

```
export PROJECT_ID=$(gcloud config get project)
```

Enable Billing

By default, projects do not have a billing account enabled. This means you cannot create billable resources. Therefore, you need to enable billing by linking your project with an active billing account you have permission to use. With a new Google Cloud account, you should just have one billing account, and it should be active.

First, find `ACCOUNT_ID` for a billing account to use for the project by listing the billing accounts associated with your Google Cloud account. This is three blocks of six characters separated by hyphens:

```
gcloud beta billing accounts list
```

Now assign it to a `BILLING_ACCOUNT_ID` environment variable like you did with `PROJECT_ID`:

```
export BILLING_ACCOUNT_ID=[BILLING_ACCOUNT_ID]
```

You can then assign the billing account to the project using this command:

```
gcloud beta billing projects link $PROJECT_ID --billing-account $BILLING_ACCOUNT_ID
```

Note that here the gcloud command includes `beta`. You will see this occasionally. It just means it is a newer feature of the gcloud CLI. By the time you read this, the command may be fully integrated and `beta` will not be needed.

Checking Billing Is Enabled

You can check that billing is enabled on a project using the following command:

```
gcloud beta billing projects describe $PROJECT_ID --format="value(billingEnabled)"
```

This will return `True` if billing is enabled and `False` if it is not. If you see `True`, your project is now configured with a billing account and ready to use.

A nice feature of Google Cloud is that you can also remove the billing accounts from projects and be confident that you will not be billed. This will shut down the services in your project, so it is better to shut them down yourself first.

However, having worked with AWS, I still find I am billed a few dollars a month for forgotten resources I have not tracked down and removed, so I appreciate this Google Cloud feature.

The command to unlink a billing account from your project is:

```
gcloud beta billing projects unlink $PROJECT_ID
```

Doing More with the gcloud CLI

You will be using the gcloud CLI throughout this book. Although you can do nearly everything through the Google Cloud Console, as you get more familiar, the gcloud CLI you will find your productivity rise.

A good way to do this is to use the gcloud interactive environment by running the following command:

```
gcloud beta interactive
```

This gives you command completion and provides inline documentation, helping you to learn the commands and options available.

Key Google Cloud Concepts

Let's take a moment to review some key concepts that will be used throughout this book.

Environment Files

Throughout the projects, values are stored in environment variables. This is a common pattern in the world of DevOps. It allows you to easily change values without having to change code. It also allows you to keep sensitive values out of your code and version control. Rather than setting the environment variables each time you start a new terminal session, you can store them in a file and then load them into your environment. This is what the *.env* file is for. Each project has a *.env.template* file that you can copy to *.env* and then fill in the values. At the root, there is also an environment file that holds common environment variables.

In each project, execute the `set-env.sh` script to set environment variables for you. This will apply the values in the *.env* file in the current directory together with the shared environment variables in the root *.env* file.

Enabling Services

Upon the initial creation of a project in Google Cloud, a number of services are not active by default. Attempting to utilize these services may result in an error. These services, however, can be easily activated using either the Google Cloud Console or the gcloud CLI. For instance, if you wish to activate the Cloud Run API, you can do so by executing the following command:

```
gcloud services enable run.googleapis.com
```

Whenever you use a service for the first time, you will see the command to enable it.

Identity and Access Management

Every Google Cloud Platform project has an identity and access management (IAM) policy. This policy specifies who has what type of access to which resources. Unlike what may be the case for an on-premises system, almost every resource or service in Google Cloud needs implicit permission to be accessed. This is a powerful and flexible system that allows you to control access to your resources.

In general, a principal (user) has roles that grant them permission to perform actions on resources.

It is important to understand that changes to IAM roles and permissions are eventually consistent and can take several minutes. This means that if you revoke a role or permission, it may still be available for a few minutes. Similarly, if you grant a role or permission, it may not be available for a few minutes.

Service Accounts

Service accounts are a special type of account used by applications acting as the principal to access Google Cloud services and resources. They are not intended for use by humans. They are used by the Google Cloud services themselves. As you start to join up services, you will be using service accounts to allow services to access other services.

While you can use a default service account for this, it is better to create a specific service account for each service. This allows you to control access to resources more granular. To follow this best practice, you will be using a service account for each service created in the projects.

Recommended Tools

Let's review the tools you will be using throughout this book. These are not essential, but they will make your life easier, and they will be referenced in the projects.

Google Cloud Architecture Diagramming Tool

The Google Cloud architecture diagramming tool (*https://oreil.ly/xqBsv*) has been used to create the diagram architecture in this book. It supports all Google Cloud services and is free to use.

Command-Line Utilities

While much of this book assumes that you're using a POSIX-compliant shell, such as those found on Linux or macOS systems, it's not a hard requirement. You can still follow along using Windows PowerShell or the Windows Subsystem for Linux (WSL). Alternatively, the Cloud Shell, which I mentioned earlier, can also be used.

Let's move on to some command-line utilities that you'll find handy:

envsubst
> envsubst is a handy command-line tool that substitutes environment variables in a file. It's part of the gettext package and works across Windows, macOS, and Linux. Refer to the installation instructions (*https://oreil.ly/PAI2j*).

Use envsubst for replacing environment variables in configuration files. This lets you maintain configuration settings for your gcloud environment separately from your code.

jq

jq is a command -line tool for parsing JSON (*https://oreil.ly/obnwx*). Many commands you will use have the option of outputting results in JSON format. Being able to extract information for use elsewhere is handy. jq is available for Windows, macOS, and Linux. Follow the instructions (*https://oreil.ly/lnmRo*) to install.

yq

yq is like jq but for YAML (*https://oreil.ly/kt7mR*) allowing extracting information from commands that output YAML. It is available for Windows, macOS, and Linux. Follow the instructions (*https://oreil.ly/tD21X*) to install.

pack

In some projects, you will be using Cloud Native Buildpacks (*https://build packs.io*) to build container images. The pack CLI is a tool for building container images using buildpacks. It is available for Windows, macOS, and Linux. Follow the instructions (*https://oreil.ly/S-49y*) to install.

cURL

cURL is a command-line tool for sending HTTP requests. You will use this for testing HTTP endpoints from the command line. It is available for Windows, macOS, and Linux and is sometimes installed already. However, follow the instructions (*https://oreil.ly/5RI9p*) to install it on your local machine.

Apache Bench

Apache Bench is a tool for benchmarking web requests. It is a command-line tool that can be used to send a large number of requests to a web server and measure the response time.

If you are using a macOS, Apache Bench is already installed. If you are using Linux, you can install it using your package manager. If you are using Windows, you can install it using Chocolatey.

However, if you are using the Google Cloud Shell, Apache Bench is not installed by default. You can install it using the following command:

```
sudo apt-get install apache2-utils
```

Siege

Siege is a similar tool to Apache Bench, but Siege can provide log files of the test with more details, including the response of each request. Follow the instructions (*https://oreil.ly/hAmW5*) to install it.

Kubernetes

While the main Kubernetes command-line tool kubectl is provided as part of the Google Cloud SDK, there are a number of other tools that you will find useful:

k9s

k9s is a command-line tool for managing Kubernetes clusters. It is available for Windows, macOS, and Linux. Follow the instructions (*https://oreil.ly/VzbUg*) to install. It provides a command-line interface to Kubernetes that is much easier to use than the standard kubectl command, and it also looks cool, as shown in Figure 4-3.

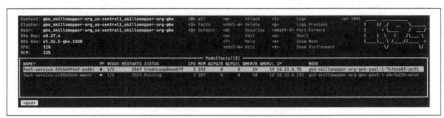

Figure 4-3. k9s

kubectx *and* kubens

kubectx and kubens are a pair of command-line tools for managing Kubernetes clusters and namespaces. They are available on GitHub (*https://oreil.ly/Goz81*).

Terraform

Terraform is a tool for managing infrastructure as code that will be introduced toward the end of the book. It is available for Windows, macOS, and Linux. Follow the instructions (*https://oreil.ly/Y7eLE*) to install. As well as Terraform itself, there are several other tools that you may find useful:

TFLint

TFLint is a tool for linting Terraform code. Follow the instructions (*https://oreil.ly/EPNvw*) to install.

TFSec

TFSec is a tool for checking Terraform code for security issues. Follow the instructions (*https://oreil.ly/G1C6p*) to install.

Infracost

Infracost is a tool for estimating the cost of Terraform code. It is useful for keeping track of potential Google Cloud expenses. Follow the instructions (*https://oreil.ly/fTUYG*) to install.

Introducing the Example Application

To better illustrate how Google Cloud services can be used, this book utilizes an example application named Skills Mapper.

Introducing Skills Mapper

The transition to a cloud native style of development involves more than just adopting new technologies and techniques. It also requires equipping your team with the necessary skills to build and support the applications. Understanding the existing knowledge and experience within your team, as well as the broader organization, can be invaluable in this transition.

While learning, it can be beneficial to identify peers with similar interests or those who are also learning. Knowing any existing experts in a particular topic can be a source of support and mentorship.

This is where our project, Skills Mapper (*https://oreil.ly/kl07P*), comes into play. Skills Mapper is a web application designed to track and map skills—tools, technologies, and techniques—that individuals are interested in, are currently learning, have experience in, or are planning to phase out. It maps these skills to a common ontology, providing an organized view of skill sets.

For individual users, Skills Mapper provides an API that can be utilized to generate a dynamic "living CV." This CV can be displayed on a web page or incorporated into an online resume. For groups of users, Skills Mapper illustrates how their combination of skills compares to their peers, suggests what they should learn next, and provides insights into trending interests.

Within an organization or a community where Skills Mapper is in use, it serves as a tool to locate experts, construct job profiles, and suggest communities of practice. It can also support the planning of training, and study groups, or identify the skills individuals are seeking to acquire.

Throughout this book, the Skills Mapper project will be developed and scaled as a microservices architecture, evolving from a tool for individuals to an application that can efficiently serve thousands of users.

Skills Mapper Architecture

The Skills Mapper application consists of three microservices, each utilizing a different type of storage. The architecture of the application is displayed in Figure 4-4.

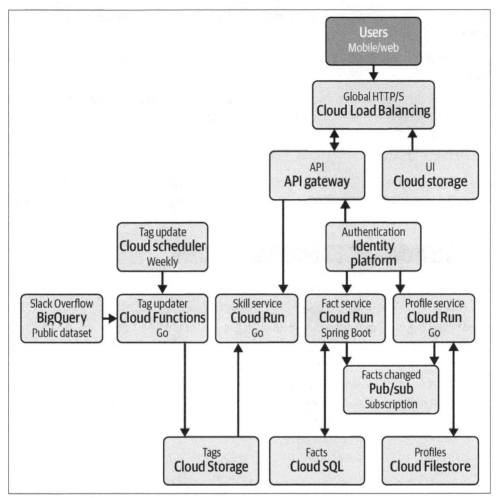

Figure 4-4. Skills Mapper architecture

Each microservice is responsible for a single function, with its capabilities exposed through a REST API:

Skill service (Chapter 6)
This service suggests skills from a list gathered from Stack Overflow.

Fact service (Chapter 7)
This service allows authenticated users to manage their skills.

Profile service (Chapter 8)
This service automatically creates a profile and provides authenticated users with profile information.

A common API exposes the microservices and, in turn, a user interface interacts with the API in Chapter 9.

In the background in Chapter 5, a utility function is used to refresh the list of tags weekly.

To ensure security, everything is placed behind a load balancer with a public IP address associated with a DNS name in Chapter 11.

Services Used

Here is a comprehensive but nonexhaustive list of the services you will be using throughout this book. The chapters in which each service is used are also shown in the table.

Service	Description	Chapters used
BigQuery	Data warehouse	Chapter 5
Cloud Functions	Serverless functions	Chapter 5
Cloud Run	Serverless containers	Chapters 6, 7, and 8
Cloud Storage	Object storage	Chapters 5, 8, and 9
Cloud Build	CI/CD	Chapter 12
Cloud Scheduler	Scheduled tasks	Chapter 5
Cloud Pub/Sub	Messaging service	Chapter 8
Cloud Firestore	NoSQL document database	Chapter 8
Cloud SQL	Relational database	Chapter 7
Cloud Spanner	Distributed relational database	Chapter 14
Identity Platform	Authentication provider	Chapter 7
Global HTTP Load Balancer	Load balancer	Chapter 11
Cloud Armor	Web application firewall	Chapter 11
GKE Autopilot	Managed Kubernetes	Chapter 14

Summary

Now that you've set up a project and installed the necessary tools, you're fully prepared to begin building on Google Cloud Platform. You will start the journey in Chapter 5.

Project 1: Tag Updater
with Cloud Functions

In this initial project, you will write the first part of the Skills Mapper application. You will be introduced to some of the higher-level abstractions in Google Cloud and be shown how you can solve a real-world problem at a minimal cost.

You will learn how to solve the requirement in three ways:

- Manually, using the gcloud CLI alone
- Automated, using a Cloud Function and Cloud Scheduler
- Fully automated, using the Cloud Function and Terraform to deploy

> The code for this chapter is in the `tag-updater` folder of the Git-Hub repository (*https://oreil.ly/os8n4*).

Requirements

Let's dive into the requirements for this project.

User Story

The user story for this piece of functionality can be written as shown in Figure 5-1.

Figure 5-1. Project 1 user story

Elaborated Requirements

This project also has the following specific requirements:

- The list of skills should include technologies, tools, and techniques, and be comprehensive and unambiguous.
- Although new skills emerge frequently, it is not every day so limiting updates to weekly is sufficient.
- The solution should be reliable, require minimal maintenance, and be low cost.
- The resultant list of skills should be easy to consume by future services.

Solution

Maintaining a list of technical skills is a big undertaking. Fortunately, Stack Overflow (*https://oreil.ly/kpLAQ*) is already doing that by maintaining a crowdsourced list of over 63,000 tags, terms which are used to categorize questions. Google Cloud provides all Stack Overflow data, including tags, as a public dataset in BigQuery, the enterprise data warehouse service.

To obtain an up-to-date list of technical skills, you can extract them from the public dataset of BigQuery directly.

With cloud native solutions, we favor simplicity. The simplest way is to store a list of terms in a file. Cloud Storage is the Google Cloud service for storing object data like this. If you store a file in Cloud Storage, it will be easily consumable by other services.

You need a small amount of code to extract Stack Overflow tags from the BigQuery dataset and to store the resultant list of skills as a file in Cloud Storage. Cloud Functions is an effective way of running this type of glue code, as you only pay for the short amount of time the code is running. This is a serverless solution, meaning it is a fully managed service with no servers to maintain.

You need to update the list of skills once a week. Cloud Scheduler is a fully managed service that runs jobs on a schedule. You can use this to schedule the execution of a

Cloud Function. You can use this to create a new list of skills every week and retry if there is a failure.

Architecture Diagram

Figure 5-2 is a diagram of the architecture you will be implementing.

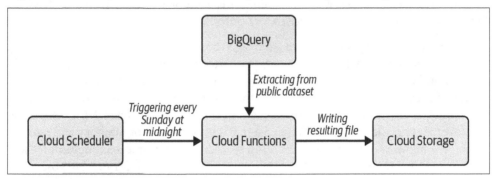

Figure 5-2. Tag updater design

You can draw similar diagrams using the Google Cloud architecture diagramming tool (*https://oreil.ly/ZAtlE*), which is a great tool for drawing cloud architectures.

Summary of Services

Here is a summary of the Google Cloud services you will be using in this solution.

BigQuery

BigQuery is a Google data warehouse solution designed for performing analytics on vast amounts of data. It uses SQL syntax, like a relational database. However, here you will just be using it to query a relatively small set of public data.

Cloud Storage

Cloud Storage is Google Cloud's object store, similar to S3 on AWS. This is designed to store objects, text, and binary files containing unstructured data that does not need to be queried. It is a low-cost way of storing data.

Cloud Functions

Cloud Functions is Google Cloud's highest-level abstraction for running code. To start with, you will use Cloud Functions because it is the simplest and most cost-effective option for running code occasionally. This is Google's serverless offering and the nearest equivalent to AWS Lambda or Azure Functions. It is great for running the sort of glue code we need for this service.

If Cloud Functions was a means of transport, it would be like a taxi; it takes you where you want to go, but your involvement in driving is minimal. You just state the destination and Cloud Functions gets you there. It is ideally suited for short trips, and maintenance of the car is not your concern.

Cloud Functions has two generations. I will concentrate on the 2nd gen, as it is more flexible and has a larger memory limit. This supports code written in Node.js, Python, Go, Java, Ruby, PHP or .NET Core (*https://oreil.ly/_P06t*).

Code is automatically packaged into a managed container that is invoked by an event, but the container itself is hidden from you. Execution is in a slice of virtual CPU (vCPU) and memory, the slice of which you can specify. You can use a maximum of 16GiB of memory and four vCPU cores and execute for a maximum of 60 minutes. For more details, see the quotas documentation (*https://oreil.ly/sheUK*). This is a big improvement on the 1st gen, which had a maximum of 8GiB of memory and a maximum of 9 minutes of execution time. However, the default of a maximum of 60 seconds, one vCPU core, and 256 MB of memory will be sufficient for this purpose.

In fact, Cloud Functions (2nd gen) is effectively a wrapper around two other services, Cloud Run and Cloud Build, which you will use in Chapter 6. Cloud Run is a managed container platform that allows you to run containers that are invocable via HTTP requests or events. Cloud Build is a managed build service that allows you to build containers.

Cloud Scheduler

Cloud Scheduler is a fully managed enterprise-grade job scheduler similar to Cron. In this case, you are going to use it to schedule the execution of the Cloud Function.

Command Line Implementation

Before getting hands-on, make sure you have a gcloud CLI client either on your local machine or in Cloud Shell and create a new project, as described in Chapter 4; store the PROJECT_ID in an environment variable using:

```
export PROJECT_ID=$(gcloud config get project)
```

BigQuery

To start with, you can use the bq command-line tool to try out the query you will use to retrieve the Stack Overflow tag names from the public dataset. This tool is installed as part of the Google Cloud SDK:

```
bq query --max_rows=10 --nouse_legacy_sql --format=csv \
"SELECT tag_name FROM bigquery-public-data.stackoverflow.tags order by tag_name"
```

Use the following flags:

`--max_rows`
> Limits the number of results to 10 instead of the default 100

`--nouse_legacy_sql`
> Uses Google Standard SQL (*https://oreil.ly/3Q01I*) for the query

`--format=csv`
> Formats the result as a CSV file

The results of this command should show the first ten Stack Overflow tag names. You will use a similar query in your service. For now, let's output all the tags to a file named *tags.csv*. There are approximately 63,000 Stack Overflow tags, so setting the maximum rows to 100,000 will retrieve them all.

 It is good practice to always specify the maximum rows with Big-Query, as it is billed by the amount of data queried. One day, you may accidentally write a query that queries trillions of rows and be left with a hefty bill.

Define an environment variable for the FILE_NAME (e.g., *tags.csv*); even when programming at the command line, it is good to follow the cloud native principle of externalizing configuration:

```
export FILE_NAME=[FILE_NAME]
```

Now you can issue the `bq` command to write the tags to the file:

```
bq query --max_rows=100000 \
  --nouse_legacy_sql \
  --format=csv \
  "SELECT tag_name FROM bigquery-public-data.stackoverflow.tags order by tag_name" >$FILE_NAME
```

You can check that it was successful by listing the number of lines in the file:

```
wc -l $FILE_NAME
```

If all goes well, the result should be approximately 63,654 lines, allowing one line for the CSV header.

Cloud Storage

You now need to create a Cloud Storage bucket to store the file you generate from your query. You can do that with the `gsutil` command, which is also included with the gcloud CLI.

First, create a BUCKET_NAME environment variable with the bucket to use. Like a project ID, the bucket name must be globally unique. As your project ID is unique, you can use that as a prefix to the bucket-name (e.g., `skillsmapper-tags`):

```
export BUCKET_NAME="${PROJECT_ID}-[BUCKET_SUFFIX]"
```

Then use the `gsutil` command to create the new bucket:

```
gsutil mb gs://$BUCKET_NAME
```

With the bucket created, you can then copy the file containing the list of tags to the bucket:

```
gsutil cp $FILE_NAME gs://$BUCKET_NAME/$FILE_NAME
```

You can check that the file has been created successfully by again counting the number of lines and making sure that matches the approximately 63,654 lines you had in the file you generated:

```
gsutil cat gs://$BUCKET_NAME/$FILE_NAME | wc -l
```

Running commands like this would be one way of keeping the tags up to date. Alternatively, you could automate it into a bash script and save it as a file named *update-tags.sh*:

```
include::code/update-tags.sh
```

Then run the script providing the bucket name and file name as variables:

```
./update-tags.sh $BUCKET_NAME $FILE_NAME
```

You could then manually run the script periodically or use a cron job on a machine with Google Cloud credentials; however, there is a better cloud native approach where you can implement the task programmatically using a Cloud Function.

Cloud Native Implementation

Here, you will implement the same functionality as the manual implementation but using a Cloud Function scheduled with Cloud Scheduler. This will allow you to automatically update the tags periodically without any manual intervention.

Cloud Functions

As mentioned earlier, Cloud Functions can only be written in certain programming languages. The code accompanying this book includes a Cloud Function written in Go (*https://oreil.ly/W6HJk*). This effectively performs the same task as the gcloud CLI steps but uses the BigQuery and Cloud Storage client libraries for Go.

Don't worry too much about the code if you are not familiar with Go, but there are some key points to note:

```go
func init() {
        // err is pre-declared to avoid shadowing client.
        var err error
        bigQueryClient, err = bigquery.NewClient(ctxBg, projectID)
        if err != nil {
                log.Fatalf("bigquery.NewClient: %v", err)
        }
        storageClient, err = storage.NewClient(ctxBg)
        if err != nil {
```

```
                log.Fatalf("storage.NewClient: %v", err)
        }
        // register http function
        functions.HTTP("tag-updater", updateTags)
}
```

In the init block above, a BigQuery and Cloud Storage client is created. These are initialized once and then reused for each invocation of the function. This is good practice, as it reduces the time needed to respond to requests. At the end of the block, a function named updateTags is registered as the HTTP trigger. This is the entry point for the function and is called when the function is invoked:

```
func updateTags(w http.ResponseWriter, r *http.Request) {
        var err error
        numberOfTagsRetrieved, data, err := retrieveTags()
        if err != nil {
                log.Printf("failed to retrieve tags: %v\n", err)
                http.Error(w, "retrieving tags failed", http.StatusInternalServerError)
        }
        err = writeFile(data)
        if err != nil {
                log.Printf("failed to write file: %v\n", err)
                http.Error(w, "writing file failed", http.StatusInternalServerError)
        }
        message := fmt.Sprintf("%v tags retrieved and written to %s as %s",
                numberOfTagsRetrieved, bucketName, objectName)
        log.Println(message)
        w.WriteHeader(http.StatusOK)
        fmt.Fprint(w, message)
}
```

The updateTags function in the code is handling an HTTP request. In response, it calls a function that retrieves the tags from BigQuery Stack Overflow dataset using the BiqQuery client. It then calls another function that writes the tags to Cloud Storage using the Cloud Storage client in a similar way to the gcloud CLI steps. Note that errors are handled by logging the error and returning an HTTP error response; success is handled by logging the success and returning an HTTP success response. This is important, as it is the HTTP response that is used by Cloud Functions to determine whether the function invocation was successful or not.

Configuration

Just like the bash script version, the configuration for the Cloud Function should be externalized. In this case, you don't have any secrets like passwords, but you do have three arguments to pass as environment variables, shown in Table 5-1.

Table 5-1. Environment variables

Environment variable	Description
PROJECT_ID	The ID of the Google Cloud project
BUCKET_ID	The ID of the Cloud Storage bucket
OBJECT_NAME	Cloud Storage is an object store, so when files are uploaded to it, they are referred to as objects.

You can provide these as a YAML file when you deploy the function. The code accompanying this book (*https://oreil.ly/O56i7*) shows an example of the structure:

```
PROJECT_ID: $PROJECT_ID
BUCKET_NAME: $BUCKET_NAME
OBJECT_NAME: $FILE_NAME
```

As you set environment variables earlier, you can generate an *env.yaml* with this command:

```
envsubst < env.yaml.template > env.yaml
```

The main difference between this function and the bash script is that it writes the retrieved tags to an object in Cloud Storage directly rather than storing them to a file and then uploading the file.

Cloud Functions run in a Google Cloud region. In Chapter 4, you specified a default region for the Google CLI using this command:

```
gcloud config set functions/region [REGION]
```

However, I like to declare an environment variable for the region I want to deploy to (for example, `europe-west2`), so I explicitly know which region I am deploying to:

```
export REGION=[REGION]
```

Then use this to set the default region for Cloud Functions:

```
gcloud config set functions/region $REGION
```

The services Cloud Functions needs are not enabled by default, so you need to enable them for the project. As mentioned earlier, the Cloud Build service is used for building a container. The container is stored in Artifact Registry, Google Cloud's container registry. The container is run using Google's Cloud Run service. This means you need the following services enabled:

- `cloudfunctions.googleapis.com`—Cloud Functions
- `cloudbuild.googleapis.com`—Cloud Build
- `artifactregistry.googleapis.com`—Artifact Registry
- `run.googleapis.com`—Cloud Run

You can enable the services with this command:

```
gcloud services enable cloudfunctions.googleapis.com
gcloud services enable cloudbuild.googleapis.com
gcloud services enable artifactregistry.googleapis.com
gcloud services enable run.googleapis.com
```

Now create an environment variable for the name of the function to deploy (e.g., `tag-updater`):

```
export CLOUD_FUNCTION_NAME=[CLOUD_FUNCTION_NAME]
```

To deploy this code as a Cloud Function, you can use the following gcloud command:

```
gcloud functions deploy $CLOUD_FUNCTION_NAME \
    --gen2 \
    --runtime=go120 \
    --region=$REGION \
    --trigger-http \
    --no-allow-unauthenticated \
    --env-vars-file env.yaml
```

Here you are using the following flags:

`--gen2`
 Deploys a Cloud Function using generation 2

`--runtime=go120`
 Uses the Go 1.20 runtime

`--region=$REGION`
 Deploys to this region

`--trigger-http`
 The function should be triggered by an HTTP request

`--no-allow-unauthenticated`
 The function should not be publicly accessible

`--env-vars-file`
 Uses the environment variables in the *env.yaml* file

Executing the command will take a few minutes as it works through building, deploying, and testing that the function is healthy. When it has completed, you will see a URI for the function that looks like this: `https://$CLOUD_FUNCTION_NAME-something.a.run.app`.

You can retrieve this using:

```
gcloud functions describe $CLOUD_FUNCTION_NAME --gen2 --region=$REGION \
--format='value(serviceConfig.uri)'
```

If you open this URI in a web browser, you will see a permission denied message. This is a good thing; it means an unauthenticated person cannot trigger the function.

You can also check that the function has been deployed using the command:

```
gcloud functions list
```

This should show a result similar to this, with the state showing active:

```
NAME         STATE    TRIGGER       REGION        ENVIRONMENT
tag-updater  ACTIVE   HTTP Trigger  europe-west2  2nd gen
```

You can then run the function using:

```
gcloud functions call $CLOUD_FUNCTION_NAME --gen2 --region=$REGION
```

You should see a result like this:

```
63653 tags retrieved and written to skillsmapper-tags as tags.csv
```

To check the logs for the function to see more details, use the following command:

```
gcloud functions logs read $CLOUD_FUNCTION_NAME --gen2 --region=$REGION
```

This will give you more detailed logs, including the system logs when the function was deployed.

Using a Service Account

By default, the Cloud Function will have used the default service account for the project `service-ACCOUNT_ID@PROJECT_ID.iam.gserviceaccount.com`. This is not a great idea, as it gives broad access to all resources in the project.

You can create a new service account that has the minimum permissions required for the function to work and no more. Specifically, the service account needs the following permissions:

- Execute BigQuery queries using the `bigquery.jobUser` predefined role.
- Write to Cloud Storage using the `storage.objectAdmin` predefined role, as it will need to be able to both create new objects and delete previous ones.

Create an environment variable to hold a service account name (e.g., `tag-updater-sa`):

```
export SERVICE_ACCOUNT_NAME=[SERVICE_ACCOUNT_NAME]
```

Then create the service account with the following command:

```
gcloud iam service-accounts create $SERVICE_ACCOUNT_NAME \
--display-name "${CLOUD_FUNCTION_NAME} service account"
```

You can check that it has been created using:

```
gcloud iam service-accounts list
```

When created, the service account has the format *[SERVICE_ACCOUNT_NAME]@[PROJECT_ID].iam.gserviceaccount.com*. This is how you reference it.

Now grant the service account the permissions it needs.

Add the BigQuery job user role:

```
gcloud projects add-iam-policy-binding $PROJECT_ID \
  --member=serviceAccount:$SERVICE_ACCOUNT_NAME@$PROJECT_ID.iam.gserviceaccount.com \
  --role=roles/bigquery.jobUser
```

Add the Cloud Storage objectAdmin role:

```
gsutil iam ch serviceAccount:$SERVICE_ACCOUNT_NAME@$PROJECT_ID.iam.gserviceaccount.com:objectAdmin \
gs://$BUCKET_NAME
```

Now you can redeploy the Cloud Function, specifying that the newly created service account is used with the `--service-account` flag:

```
gcloud functions deploy $CLOUD_FUNCTION_NAME \
--gen2 \
--runtime=go120 \
--service-account="${SERVICE_ACCOUNT_NAME}@${PROJECT_ID}.iam.gserviceaccount.com" \
--trigger-http \
--no-allow-unauthenticated \
--env-vars-file env.yaml
```

When the command completes, it will show the URI of the Cloud Function. Store this in an environment variable so you can reference it later:

```
export CLOUD_FUNCTION_URI=$(gcloud functions describe $CLOUD_FUNCTION_NAME \
--gen2 --format='value(serviceConfig.uri)')
```

You are now ready to test the Cloud Function.

Testing with cURL

Your Cloud Function is secure in that it can only be evoked by an authenticated user with the correct permissions. If you try to invoke it using cURL, you will get a 403 Forbidden error:

```
curl $CLOUD_FUNCTION_URI
```

This is a good thing, as it means that not just anyone can invoke the function and cause it to run. However, there is a way to test it by passing an authentication token to the function:

```
curl -H "Authorization: Bearer $(gcloud auth print-identity-token)" $CLOUD_FUNCTION_URI
```

This will use the permissions of the current user to invoke the function. Again, you should see a message:

```
63653 tags retrieved and written to skillsmapper-tags as tags.csv
```

Cloud Scheduler

You can now schedule the Cloud Function to run every Sunday at midnight.

First, you need to enable Cloud Scheduler:

```
gcloud services enable cloudscheduler.googleapis.com
```

Create an environment variable for the name of the job (e.g., `tag-updater-job`):

```
export JOB_NAME=[JOB_NAME]
```

Unfortunately, Cloud Scheduler will not be able to trigger the Cloud Functions at the moment; the function does not allow unauthenticated invocations.

You need to create another service account for the scheduler (e.g., `tag-updater-invoker-sa`):

```
export INVOKER_SERVICE_ACCOUNT_NAME=[INVOKER_SERVICE_ACCOUNT_NAME]

gcloud iam service-accounts create $INVOKER_SERVICE_ACCOUNT_NAME \
       --display-name "${CLOUD_FUNCTION_NAME} invoker service account"
```

Now grant the new service account the `run.invoker` role. Note that, as this is a 2nd gen Cloud Function, the permission to invoke the function is granted on the underlying Cloud Run service:

```
gcloud run services add-iam-policy-binding $CLOUD_FUNCTION_NAME \
  --member=serviceAccount:$INVOKER_SERVICE_ACCOUNT_NAME@$PROJECT_ID.iam.gserviceaccount.com \
  --role='roles/run.invoker'
```

By default, Cloud Scheduler will retry a job three times if it fails. You can change this using the `--max-retry-attempts` flag.

You authenticate with an OIDC token, which is linked to the service account that has the invoker role.

Use the following command to create the job:

```
gcloud scheduler jobs create http ${JOB_NAME} \
--schedule="0 0 * * SUN" \
--uri=${CLOUD_FUNCTION_URI} \
--max-retry-attempts=3 \
--location=${REGION} \
--oidc-service-account-email="${INVOKER_SERVICE_ACCOUNT_NAME}@${PROJECT_ID}.iam.gserviceaccount.com" \
--oidc-token-audience="${CLOUD_FUNCTION_URI}"
```

Check the status of the job in the job list:

```
gcloud scheduler jobs list --location=${REGION}
```

You should see that the job is enabled and scheduled to run each Sunday at midnight:

```
ID               LOCATION  SCHEDULE (TZ)        TARGET_TYPE  STATE
tag-updater-job  us-west2  0 0 * * SUN (Etc/UTC)  HTTP         ENABLED
```

To test the job, you can trigger it manually, overriding the schedule:

```
gcloud scheduler jobs run $JOB_NAME --location=$REGION
```

Check the status of the job:

```
gcloud scheduler jobs describe $JOB_NAME --location=$REGION
```

You will see a `lastAttemptTime`, which corresponds to when you triggered the job.

Check the log of the Cloud Function:

```
gcloud functions logs read ${CLOUD_FUNCTION_NAME} --gen2 --region=${REGION}
```

Alternatively, you can stream logs directly from the underlying Cloud Run service:

```
gcloud beta run services logs tail ${CLOUD_FUNCTION_NAME} --project ${PROJECT_ID}
```

Now check the data of the file in Cloud Storage as you did when running at the command line:

```
gsutil cat gs://$BUCKET_NAME/$OBJECT_NAME | wc -l
```

If all is well, you should see over 65,000 tags in the file.

Terraform Implementation

As you can see, although the solution is simple, there are still many steps to set it up.

In Chapter 12, you will see how Terraform can be used to fully automate this type of deployment; in the Appendix, the deployment for the whole of Skills Mapper has been automated. For now, here is a peek at how to do the same with Terraform.

To use this Terraform implementation, you need to have Terraform installed and configured, and you also need to have created a Google Cloud project, as described in Chapter 4. Use a new project so as not to conflict with what you have set up in this chapter.

Enable the required APIs using the following commands:

```
gcloud services enable cloudfunctions.googleapis.com
gcloud services enable cloudbuild.googleapis.com
gcloud services enable artifactregistry.googleapis.com
gcloud services enable run.googleapis.com
gcloud services enable cloudscheduler.googleapis.com
```

Now you can deploy the solution using Terraform. From the *terraform* directory, run the following command, providing the PROJECT_ID environment variable of the project to deploy to:

```
terraform apply -var project_id=${PROJECT_ID}
```

To clear everything up, run the following command:

```
terraform destroy
```

The reason to introduce this here is that you may be getting put off by all the gcloud commands. They are useful for learning but not essential. When you want to move to a reproducible environment, Terraform will come to your rescue.

Evaluation

Now let's look at how the solution will scale and how much it will cost.

How Will This Solution Scale?

The scaling of this solution is not a great concern, as it is a single task that runs weekly. It is also very unlikely that there will be a significant change in the number of tags to retrieve from the Stack Overflow dataset.

However, if you did want to schedule the task more frequently or even add tasks to collect data from other sources, you could easily do so by adding more Cloud Functions and changing the frequency of the Cloud Scheduler jobs.

How Much Will This Solution Cost?

The costs of this solution are very close to zero (and I mean close). The cost will likely be less than $0.01 per month:

- *Cloud Storage* data is charged at $0.026 per GB/month. This solution uses less than 1 MB of storage, so the cost is negligible.

- *Cloud Functions* are charged at $0.0000002 per GB/s. This solution uses less than 256 MB of memory for less than a minute per month, so the cost is negligible.

- *Cloud Scheduler* is charged at $0.01 per 100,000 invocations. This solution uses less than five invocations per month, so the cost is negligible too.

- *BigQuery* queries are charged after the first 1TB of data is scanned per month. This solution uses less than 10 MB of data per month, so there will be no cost.

- You will also be charged for moving around small amounts of data between services, but again, this is negligible.

This is the type of service that makes a lot of sense in a cloud native environment. A task that may previously have needed a dedicated server can now be run for virtually nothing.

Summary

You have built a solution that can be highly reliable and will run for minimal cost. This service should be able to sit in the background running for years uninterrupted, if needed.

The following are Google Cloud Services used in the solution:

- gcloud CLI is used for interacting with the Google Cloud API.
- bq is used for working with BigQuery at the command line.
- gsutil is used for working with Cloud Storage.
- BigQuery is used for querying the Stack Overflow public dataset.
- Cloud Storage is used as a simple way of storing the list of tags.
- Cloud Functions is used as a high-level abstraction to run code serverlessly.
- Cloud Scheduler is used as the mechanism scheduling runs of the job.

In the next project, you will take the list of tags that this service has provided and make it available for a user to select skills from.

CHAPTER 6

Project 2: Skill Service with Cloud Run

In Chapter 5, you used a Cloud Function to collect Stack Overflow tags from the Big-Query public dataset and store the results as an object in Cloud Storage. In this chapter, you will use these tags to develop an interactive service that offers skill suggestions to users as they type.

 The code for this chapter is in the `skill-service` folder of the GitHub repository (*https://oreil.ly/6kKB8*).

Requirements

Let's explore what's needed for this project.

User Story

The user story for this piece of functionality is shown in Figure 6-1.

As a contributing user, I want a skill search feature with real-time suggestions as I type, so that I can quickly find and select the most relevant skill for my profile.

Figure 6-1. Project 2 user story

Elaborated Requirements

This project also has the following specific requirements:

- Suggestions should be presented when a user types three or more characters.
- 95% of suggestion requests should return suggestions in less than 500 ms as, anything longer than this may be perceived as slow.
- The solution should be reliable and low cost.
- The solution should scale to thousands of simultaneous requests without desegregation.

Solution

What is required here is a reliable and scalable solution for looking up skills from a list of tags. Given the relatively small size of the data and the need for rapid response times, you'll keep this data in an in-memory trie data structure.

Summary of Services

Here is a summary of the Google Cloud services you will be using in this solution.

Cloud Storage

In Chapter 2, you collected tags from BigQuery's Stack Overflow dataset and stored them as an object in Cloud Storage. Now, you'll retrieve that object and use it to populate the skills that your service will use to generate suggestions for the user.

Cloud Run

You previously used Cloud Functions as the runtime for your application. However, while Cloud Functions are great for occasionally running code triggered by events, they are not intended to be used for long-running services. As the service will need to set up the trie data structure in memory, you don't want to have to do that each time there is a request. Instead, the requirement is for a long-running service, or at least one that can handle a large number of requests once started.

As you want a service that is long-running and can scale dynamically, you will use Cloud Run. In Cloud Run, instances are referred to as services rather than functions in Cloud Functions.

Cloud Run is the underlying technology of the Cloud Function you used in Chapter 5. Here, using it directly gives us more control of the container and how it runs. Specifically, you can scale the service to handle thousands of simultaneous requests.

If Cloud Run was a means of transport, it would be like a rental car; you have more flexibility than a taxi, but you have to drive it yourself. However, you still don't have to worry about the maintenance and upkeep of the car.

Cloud Run can scale in different ways:

Multiple instances
> Cloud Run automatically scales up the number of container instances based on the number of requests by monitoring an internal request queue. It can also scale down to zero when no requests are pending. This follows the 12-factor principle of favoring scaling horizontally rather than vertically.

Concurrency
> For languages with good concurrency support like Go or Java, it is possible to have multiple requests handled by a single instance rather than in Cloud Functions, where a function handles a single request at a time.

Resources
> As with Cloud Functions, you can vertically scale an instance, allocating more memory and CPU.

However, Cloud Run cannot scale infinitely and there are limits on the number of instances and the amount of memory and CPU available. For example:

- Concurrency is limited to a maximum of 1,000 simultaneous requests per instance.
- Memory is limited to 32 GB per instance.
- File system is limited to 32 GB per instance.
- CPU is limited to 8 vCPUs per instance.
- The number of instances is limited to 100 per region.
- For larger CPU and memory, the number of instances is limited to a lower amount, and this varies depending on the capacity in the Google Cloud region.

See Cloud Run Quotas and Limitations documentation (*https://oreil.ly/dCrDT*) for more details.

A single Cloud Run request is limited to 60 minutes of execution time. However, when Cloud Run does not receive requests, it will throttle down to 0 CPU and will terminate the instance after 60 minutes of inactivity.

Although Cloud Run does have limits, they are generous, and it should be possible to build many services within the restrictions. Cloud Run is a great service to use if you can; it is cost-effective since you are allocating resources directly from Borg only when you need them and not paying for them when you don't.

When I first used Cloud Run, I tried to deploy a containerized version of the Ghost blogging platform with it, thinking if it did not receive much traffic, it would scale to zero, and this would be a cost-effective way of running it.

However, my Ghost instance had a significant startup time, upward of a minute. When the instance terminated after inactivity, the next request would be met with a "Preparing Ghost" message while it started up again. This is understandable, as Ghost was designed to run on a server as a long-running task and not a serverless platform. While Cloud Run is great for many use cases, it is not suitable for all applications.

However, if you reach limitations or if you are using an existing application that does not fit with the constraints of Cloud Run, it may be necessary to consider a lower-level service like GKE Autopilot. You will have an opportunity to look at this option in Chapter 14.

In this case, even if Cloud Run scales down and requires a new instance to serve requests, the instance should be ready quickly, and the user should not notice a significant impact.

Implementation

The code for this project is in the *skill-service* directory of the book's repository. It is implemented in Go. While this may not be a language you have used before, it is worth taking a look at the code to see how it works.

The actual code for storing and retrieving the data is in the `internal/skill/autocomplete` package and is not specific to Cloud Run.

The *main.go* file is the entry point for the application and is where the Cloud Run-specific code is located. In the `init` function, the configuration the service needs is loaded from environment variables and instances of Google Cloud-specific clients are created to interact with the Cloud Storage and Cloud Logging services. It is good to initialize these clients once and reuse them rather than creating them each time a request is received.

The `main` function sets up an HTTP server with three endpoints. This is using the popular Gorilla Mux (*https://oreil.ly/yMYzZ*) library for routing requests. The three endpoints are:

GET /readiness
This is used by Cloud Run to determine if the service is healthy. It returns a 200 status. If it fails to return, Cloud Run will assume the instance has failed, terminate it, and start a new one.

`GET /liveness`

This is used by Cloud Run to determine if the service is ready to receive requests. It returns a 200 status code only after a flag is set when the trie data structure has been loaded into memory. This is to ensure the service is not sent requests by Cloud Run until it has the data it needs to respond to them.

`GET /autocomplete`

This is the endpoint that returns the suggestions to the user. It takes a query parameter `query` which is the text the user has typed so far. It returns a JSON array of strings that are the suggestions. This is the only endpoint that will ultimately be exposed to the user.

It is good to understand that Cloud Run just needs to provide an HTTP (or gRPC) endpoint running on port 8080 by default. There is no need to use a specific framework or library or even provide a specific entry point as with Cloud Functions. The point is, you can use whatever you want to build your service, and I am sure you will have your preferences.

Another piece of functionality in the `main` function of note is code to deal with a graceful shutdown. This is important, as Cloud Run will send a SIGTERM signal to the container when it is scaling down or terminating the instance. This is the disposability principle from the 12 factors. Applications should expect to be terminated at any time and should handle this gracefully. Here it is done by listening for the SIGTERM signal and then calling the `Shutdown` method on the HTTP server. This will allow any in-flight requests to be completed before the instance is terminated. In Chapter 3, I talked about services being largely stateless, but temporary state is acceptable. This is the time to clear up that temporary state.

The `populate` function retrieves the *tags.csv* file, created by the Tag Updater function from Chapter 5. It accesses Cloud Storage using the `storage` client. It then loads the data into a trie data structure. This is a treelike data structure that is optimized for searching for strings. The trie is stored in memory and is used to respond to requests.

Getting Ready for Deployment

Before getting hands-on, make sure you have a gcloud CLI either on your local machine or in Cloud Shell, and ensure you are using the same Google Cloud project as in Chapter 5, using the command:

```
gcloud config get project
```

You can set a `PROJECT_ID` environment variable again to make it easier to copy and paste commands:

```
export PROJECT_ID=$(gcloud config get-value project)
```

If you are not using the correct project, set it using this command:

```
gcloud config set project $PROJECT_ID
```

Deploy with Cloud Run

You can use the defaults of Cloud Run to deploy directly from the command line to ensure it works. This will create a container and put it into the Artifact Registry, a Google service for storing arifacts, like containers.

The service is using a Go application with no dependencies, so Cloud Run allows you to build directly from the source code alone.

Set an environment variable for the service name (e.g., `skill-service`):

```
export SKILL_SERVICE_NAME=[SKILL_SERVICE_NAME]
```

Following the 12-factor principle of storing configuration in the environment, you will use an environment variable file to pass the configuration to the service.

If you have created *.env* files, use this command and apply both the local and parent environment variables again:

```
set -a; source ../.env; source .env ;set +a
```

Create a file called *.env.yaml* from *env.yaml.template*. This command will substitute values from your environment variable, including those set in Chapter 5:

```
envsubst < env.yaml.template >.env.yaml
```

Then run the following command to deploy the service to Cloud Run:

```
gcloud run deploy $SKILL_SERVICE_NAME --source . \
  --env-vars-file=.env.yaml \
  --allow-unauthenticated
```

If you are asked to create an "Artifact Registry Docker repository to store built containers," select yes. This is where the container will be stored.

You are deploying the service from the source code in the current directory and passing an environment variable file, as you did in Chapter 5 with Cloud Functions.

This command is a shortcut for two commands. The first command is:

```
gcloud builds submit --pack image=[IMAGE] .
```

This builds a container using a buildpack using Cloud Build. A buildpack is a concept that existed in both the Heroku and Cloud Foundry platforms. It automatically identifies the application's language, installs the necessary dependencies, and packages it all up into a container. Cloud Run is using what is effectively version three of the buildpack concept, Cloud Native Buildpacks (*https://buildpacks.io*).

The buildpack to use is determined automatically; in this case, the presence of `go.mod` will be enough to determine that the Go Buildpack should be used and the `main.go` built. It then stores the container image in Google Artifact Registry, where [IMAGE] would be the name for the image. In the shortcut command, the image name is automatically generated.

If there were a Dockerfile in the current directory, it would use that to build the container in preference to the buildpack, meaning you could use a custom container.

This is one way of adding more flexibility if you need that customization, but the good thing about Cloud Run is that you don't need to worry about how the container is built if you don't want to.

The second command is:

```
gcloud run deploy $SKILL_SERVICE_NAME --image [IMAGE]
```

This deploys the container to Cloud Run. If you run this command, you will be prompted to Allow unauthenticated invocations to [SERVICE-NAME]?. Select `Y for this for now, but we will come back to the significance of this later.

As with Cloud Functions, the command will take about a minute to complete. When the service deploys successfully, you will see a message like this:

```
Building using Buildpacks and deploying container to Cloud Run service [skill-service] in project
[skillsmapper-org] region [us-central1]
  ✓ Building and deploying... Done.
  ✓ Uploading sources...
  ✓ Building Container... Logs are available at [https://console.cloud.google
    .com/cloud-build/builds/77c7c356-5269-445b-a013-12c70f542684?project=577723215354].
  ✓ Creating Revision...
  ✓ Routing traffic...
  ✓ Setting IAM Policy...
Done.
Service [skill-service] revision [skill-service-00002-lac] has been deployed and is serving 100
percent of traffic.
Service URL: https://skill-service-j7n5qulfna-uc.a.run.app
```

Use the following command to store the URL of the service in an environment variable:

```
export SKILL_SERVICE_URL=$(gcloud run services describe $SKILL_SERVICE_NAME \
  --format='value(status.url)')
```

You could then open the service in a browser if you wanted, querying for skills starting with "java":

```
open "${SKILL_SERVICE_URL}/autocomplete?prefix=java"
```

Smoke Testing

Rather than using a browser, however, you can test the service using cURL to test the basic functionality of the service. As the service is unauthenticated, you can use a GET request like this, requesting suggestions for the word java:

```
curl -X GET "${SKILL_SERVICE_URL}/autocomplete?prefix=java"
```

All being well, you should get a response like this:

```
{"results":["java","java-10","java-11","java-12","java-13","java-14","java-15",
"java-16","java-17","java-18"]}
```

This verifies the service is working correctly.

Running the Service Locally

Cloud Run, like many of the Google services you will use in this book, has a local emulator. This is useful if you would like to test the application locally without having to deploy it to Cloud Run on the cloud:

```
gcloud beta code dev
```

This will download and use the same container image that Cloud Build uses and run it locally, as well as containers that support Cloud Run itself. It may take a few minutes to download the images the first time you run the command.

In the background, *minikube*, a local Kubernetes, is being run. Although Cloud Run is a managed service in Cloud Run, it can also be run on a Kubernetes cluster, as in this case. If you have the kubectl CLI installed, you can see it running using this code:

```
kubectl get nodes
```

You should see a single Kubernetes node like this:

```
NAME              STATUS   ROLES           AGE   VERSION
gcloud-local-dev  Ready    control-plane   48m   v1.26.3
```

When the deployment completes, you will see a local URL where the service is available: by default, http://localhost:8080. You can then use 1cURL1 to test the service:

```
curl -X GET "http://localhost:8080/autocomplete?prefix=java"
```

In the background, this has all been deployed to the local Kubernetes. If you are interested to see how, run this command:

```
kubectl get pods
```

You will see something similar to this:

```
NAME                              READY   STATUS    RESTARTS   AGE
pod/skill-service-67dc67b44f-vwt9v  1/1     Running   0          83s
```

This is the pod, the Kubernetes component that contains the running skill-service container.

Securing

As in Chapter 5 with Cloud Functions, this Cloud Run service is currently using a default service account with broad permissions.

Cloud Run is also allowing unauthenticated invocations of the service. This may be OK for testing, but in a production environment, you would want to secure the service, and you will see how to do that in Chapter 11.

However, ultimately, the combination of risks means you have code that can be called by anyone on the internet using a service account with permissions that could do damage if code with security vulnerabilities was accidentally or maliciously deployed.

For safety, you can create a new service account with the minimum permissions required to run the service. In this case, that will be permission to read the object from Cloud Storage and nothing more. This is the principle of the least privilege which was not one of the original 12 factors, as those principles did not have much to say about security. However, security was emphasized when the 12 factors were revisited, and the principle of the least privilege is a good practice recommended by all cloud providers.

Create a Service Account

Create an environment variable to hold a service account name (e.g., `skill-service-sa`):

```
export SKILL_SERVICE_SA=[SKILL_SERVICE_SA]
```

Then create the service account with the following command:

```
gcloud iam service-accounts create ${SKILL_SERVICE_SA} \
  --display-name "${SKILL_SERVICE_NAME} service account"
```

Now grant the service account the permissions it needs by adding the Cloud Storage `objectViewer` role. This allows the service account to read objects from Cloud Storage, but not write; that would be more than the minimum privileges needed:

```
gsutil iam ch serviceAccount:$SKILL_SERVICE_SA@$PROJECT_ID.iam.gserviceaccount \
.com:objectViewer gs://$BUCKET_NAME
```

You also need to give the service account permission to write logs to Cloud Logging, Google Cloud's aggregated logging service:

```
gcloud projects add-iam-policy-binding $PROJECT_ID \
  --member=serviceAccount:$SKILL_SERVICE_SA@$PROJECT_ID.iam.gserviceaccount.com \
  --role=roles/logging.logWriter
```

You can then update the service to use the new service account using the `gcloud run services update` command rather than redeploying the service:

```
gcloud run services update $SKILL_SERVICE_NAME --service-account \
$SKILL_SERVICE_SA@$PROJECT_ID.iam.gserviceaccount.com
```

The service will still have the same URL after the update, so check it is still working using:

```
curl -X GET "${SKILL_SERVICE_URL}/autocomplete?prefix=java"
```

Congratulations, the skill-service is now more secure.

Performance Testing

Previously, you saw how you could test the service using cURL. This is a good way to test the basic functionality of the service, but it is not a good way to test the performance.

A better option is to use the Apache Bench tool to make a single request too. This is a command-line tool that can be used to test the performance of an HTTP request. Installation instructions were shown in Chapter 4. This command will make a single request to the service:

```
ab -n 1 -c 1 -rk "${SKILL_SERVICE_URL}/autocomplete?prefix=java"
```

You will see a detailed response, including the time taken to process the request:

```
Connection Times (ms)
              min  mean[+/-sd] median   max
Connect:       77   77   0.0      77     77
Processing:   150  150   0.0     150    150
Waiting:      150  150   0.0     150    150
Total:        227  227   0.0     227    227
```

The output provides various measurements:

Connect
    The time taken to establish the network connection to the server

Processing
    The time taken by the server to process the request and generate a response

Waiting
    The time the client had to wait before receiving the response

Total
    The total time from the initiation of the request until the receipt of the response

In this case, the total time is 227 ms, which is good, as it is below the target of 500 ms for the service. The *connect* time of 77 ms depends on your network conditions and isn't something your service has control over. The *processing* time of 150 ms is the actual time spent by the skill-service handling your request, which is an indicator of the service's performance.

However, this is just one query. You can test the performance of the service by sending multiple requests sequentially to see how the response varies.

This command will send 100 requests (-n) from a single user (-c) to the service:

```
ab -n 100 -c 1 -rk "${SKILL_SERVICE_URL}/autocomplete?prefix=java"
```

The response will look something like this:

```
Percentage of the requests served within a certain time (ms)
  50%    144
  66%    146
  75%    147
  80%    148
  90%    160
  95%    288
  98%    323
  99%    345
 100%    345 (longest request)
```

The results look OK, with the average request time of 144 ms and the longest request taking 345 ms. Most important for us is the 95% percentile, which is 288 ms. This means that 95% of the requests are completed in less than 288 ms, which is under the target of 500 ms.

Now let's try 100 requests from 10 concurrent users using the following command:

```
ab -n 100 -c 10 -rk "${SKILL_SERVICE_URL}/autocomplete?prefix=java"
```

This has very different results with the 95% percentile now being 1,669 ms in this case. This means that 95% of the requests are completed in less than 1,669 ms which is way over the target of 500 ms. Everyone is having a bad experience.

Let's see if it is possible to understand what is going on by looking into the logs.

Logging

By default, anything logged to stdout will appear in Cloud Logging as INFO and anything logged to stderr as WARNING. You can look at the logs for the service to see the requests being handled by the service:

```
gcloud beta run services logs read $SKILL_SERVICE_NAME
```

However, Cloud Logging, the Google logging service, supports structured logging, which provides much richer information. To see an example of structured logging, let's look at the last log message for the Cloud Run service:

```
gcloud logging read "resource.labels.service_name: ${SKILL_SERVICE_NAME}" --limit 1
```

You will see that a single log message looks like this:

```
httpRequest:
  latency: 0.189538428s
  protocol: HTTP/1.1
  remoteIp: 82.xx.xx.xx
  requestMethod: GET
  requestSize: '372'
  requestUrl: https://skill-lookup-xfefn34lsa-nw.a.run.app/autocomplete?prefix=java
  responseSize: '755'
  serverIp: 216.239.34.53
  status: 200
  userAgent: ApacheBench/2.3
insertId: 63ed415f0005bb0d6ea1fbd0
labels:
```

```
    instanceId: 00f8b6bdb81dec1b6587a81c09bcb444c2c83222fc91d65eb71e410c99d852a51d68bbbb5bc93185f6
      ca718ffe4bbcd8d0e08ef1f2e15a6a63664e2cd1921a
logName: projects/p1-tag-updater-manual/logs/run.googleapis.com%2Frequests
receiveTimestamp: '2023-02-15T20:32:31.669398873Z'
resource:
  labels:
    configuration_name: skill_service
    location: europe-west2
    project_id: p1-tag-updater-manual
    revision_name: skill_service-00019-tan
    service_name: skill_service
  type: cloud_run_revision
severity: INFO
spanId: '8866891408317688295'
timestamp: '2023-02-15T20:32:31.375565Z'
trace: projects/p1-tag-updater-manual/traces/b50ba47749e17f15efa689cehf05h4hd
```

This provides a comprehensive, structured log entry with levels of severity and labels. Structured logging is a way of logging that makes it easier to filter and search logs. It is also easier to parse logs and extract information from them.

You can create structured logging using the Cloud Logging client libraries in your service. Before doing this, the service account your service runs with needs to be granted the `logging.logWriter` role.

You can add this role to the service account using the following command:

```
gcloud projects add-iam-policy-binding $PROJECT_ID \
  --member=serviceAccount:$SERVICE_ACCOUNT_NAME@$PROJECT_ID.iam.gserviceaccount.com \
  --role=roles/logging.logWriter
```

Now you can use the structured logging in the service. In the case of Go, the service uses the `cloud.google.com/go/logging` package. In the init function, it initializes the logging client, as it does for the Cloud Storage and BigQuery clients previously. It then creates a logger for the service:

```
ctx := context.Background()
loggingClient, err := logging.NewClient(ctx, projectID)
if err != nil {
        log.Fatalf("failed to create client: %v", err)
}
logger = loggingClient.Logger(serviceName)
```

Logging is then added to record the time taken to populate the trie from the cloud storage object and the time taken to search the trie using structured log statements like this:

```
logger.Log(logging.Entry{
        Severity: logging.Debug,
        Payload:  fmt.Sprintf("populate took %v", duration)})
```

After updating the service, we can look at the logs again to see the structured logging. For example, you can look at the logs:

- For your service
- With the `textPayload` containing "populate took"

- In the last minute; `freshness 1m`
- Limiting the results to five

Use this command:

```
gcloud logging read "resource.labels.service_name: ${SKILL_SERVICE_NAME} \
textPayload: populate tags took" --limit 5 --freshness 1m
```

And you can just return the `textPayload` field (the one you are interested in) using this command:

```
gcloud logging read "resource.labels.service_name: ${SKILL_SERVICE_NAME} \
textPayload: populate tags took" --limit 5 --freshness 1m --format="value(textPayload)"
```

This returns results like this:

```
populate took 1.004742261s
populate took 1.125826744s
populate took 1.007365607s
populate took 1.042601112s
populate took 1.018384088s
```

This shows us that it takes about a second to populate the trie from the cloud storage object. Similarly, you can look at the logs for the search function, which starts with a "autocomplete for" prefix using:

```
gcloud logging read "resource.labels.service_name: ${SKILL_SERVICE_NAME} \
textPayload: autocomplete for" --limit 5 --freshness 1m \
--format="value(textPayload)"
```

And you should get results like this:

```
autocomplete for java took 161.854392ms
autocomplete for java took 228.471095ms
autocomplete for java took 205.602819ms
autocomplete for java took 262.176097ms
autocomplete for java took 109.83006ms
```

This shows you that it takes between 100 ms and 250 ms to search the trie for the autocomplete results. Let's see if you can use this to improve the performance of the service.

Improving Performance

You have deployed to Cloud Run using the default settings, which are:

- 1 vCPU
- 512 MB memory
- Concurrency: 80
- Minimum instances: 0
- Maximum instances: 100

You can go to the Cloud Run console, to the default dashboard for the service, and look at the metrics for the service to see what is happening and how you could improve response time:

```
open \
"https://console.cloud.google.com/run/detail/${REGION}/${SKILL_SERVICE_NAME}/ ↩
metrics?project=${PROJECT_ID}"
```

There are two things to note. The first is that the `Container startup latency` is approximately two seconds. This means, if a container is not running, it takes about two seconds to start a new container. What you could do is set the minimum number of instances to 1 instead of 0 so that there is always one container running.

You may also notice that the CPU of the container gets high reaching above 80%. This means that the container is not able to process requests as fast as it could. Any requests that come in while the container is busy are queued and processed when the container is free.

You could increase the number of CPUs for a container from 1 to 2 or reduce the concurrency from 80 to 40 to reduce the number of requests that are processed at the same time.

The beauty of Cloud Run is that you can change these settings without redeploying the service. You can change the settings of the service using the `gcloud run serv ices update` command.

First, collect a baseline of the performance of the service:

```
ab -n 100 -c 10 -rk "${SKILL_SERVICE_URL}/autocomplete?prefix=java"
```

Just look at the value for 95%. In this case, 95% of requests were served within 1,912 seconds.

Then change the number of minimum instances to 1 using this command:

```
gcloud run services update $SKILL_SERVICE_NAME --min-instances 1
```

Run the `ab` command again; the request time should stay roughly the same. However, you will have eliminated the wait for a container to start up.

Then double the number of CPUs and run the `ab` command again:

```
gcloud run services update $SKILL_SERVICE_NAME --cpu 2
```

Run the `ab` command again, you should see the 95% request time is reduced, as each request is processed faster; but it may not make as much difference as you might expect.

Another thing to try is halving the concurrency to reduce the load on the service while returning the CPU to 1. This can be done using the following command:

```
gcloud run services update $SKILL_SERVICE_NAME --cpu 1 --concurrency 40
```

Rerunning the test of 100 requests from 10 concurrent users using the following command:

```
ab -n 100 -c 10 -rk "${SKILL_SERVICE_URL}/autocomplete?prefix=java"
```

You can see how this has made performance considerably worse. This is because the service is now only processing 40 requests at a time instead of 80. This means that the requests are queued and take longer to process.

These are examples of how tweaking Cloud Run can increase or decrease the performance of the service; however, it is haphazard, as we are only observing from the outside. We do not know easily what is happening inside the service or what is affecting the performance of the service from Cloud Run and Google's networking and load balancing.

In Chapter 13, you will learn how to add greater observability to the service so that you can see the impact of these changes on the performance of the service more systematically.

How Much Will This Solution Cost?

Now let's look at how much the solution will cost.

Cloud Run is charged based on three factors:

CPU and memory per 100 ms of execution
For example, 1 vCPU and 512 MB of memory for 1 second could be an execution unit. If you assigned 2 vCPUs and 1 GB of memory to a service, it would be charged four times the amount per 100 ms; but if the extra resources mean it completed in 500 ms instead of 1 second, you would only be billed twice the amount.

A cost per request
The first one million requests are free per month; then they are $0.40 per one million requests. Although this is a very small amount, it can add up, and in Chapter 14, we will look at scaling options when you have many million requests.

Network ingress and egress
As with most services in Google Cloud, there is also a charge for network ingress and egress. The requests and responses for this service are small, but again they can add up, and later in the book we will look at options for this too.

Summary

In this introduction to Cloud Run, you have learned how to deploy a service to Cloud Run and how to monitor the performance of the service. You have also seen how to tweak the performance of the service by changing the number of CPUs and the concurrency of the service, but this is not always straightforward.

For this project, you used the following Google Cloud services directly:

- Cloud Run is used as the container runtime to run the containerized service.
- Cloud Logging is used to provide logging for the service.
- Cloud Storage is used to retrieve the previously stored list on tags.

Behind the scenes, you have also been using Cloud Build and Artifact Registry to build and store the container images, respectively, and we will discuss these later.

In Chapter 7, you will step up the complexity again and look at another Cloud Run service that is used to provide a REST API and is backed by a relational database.

Project 3: Fact Service with Spring Boot, Cloud Run, and Cloud SQL

In previous chapters, you embraced cloud native development. You made full use of the convenience of serverless Cloud Functions and then Cloud Run. You used the Go programming language, which, due to its relatively light footprint and fast startup time, is ideal for Cloud Run and autoscaling in particular. However, this chapter includes a more traditional use case: a long-running REST API service that persists data to a relational database. If you are coming to the cloud from an enterprise environment, this type of service is likely your bread and butter.

Often, cloud native assumes you are starting from a blank slate. However, even if you are working on a green field project, you will typically inherit constraints such as the languages and frameworks your team is used to. In this case, you are going to use Java and Spring Boot, but you will see how you still have options for making this a cloud native application.

On the first cloud native project I worked on, we were using Amazon Web Services. One team dove straight in, using the recently released serverless AWS Lambda and switching to Node.js as their programming language. All of this was completely new to them, and they were learning on the job. They soon ran into trouble. If you don't have to change everything at once, often that is a better strategy.

For the next project, you are going to build the core of the Skills Mapper system, a REST API that allows users to add and remove skills use to build a profile. I will refer to pieces of information (e.g., "Bob is learning Java") as facts, hence the name, facts service. However, we are going to constrain ourselves to Java, Spring, and PostgreSQL to show that even when there are constraints, you can still make use of cloud native principles and services.

The code for this chapter is in the `fact-service` folder of the GitHub repository (*https://oreil.ly/Eaw6u*).

Requirements

Let's dive into the requirements for this project.

User Story

The user story for this piece of functionality is shown in Figure 7-1.

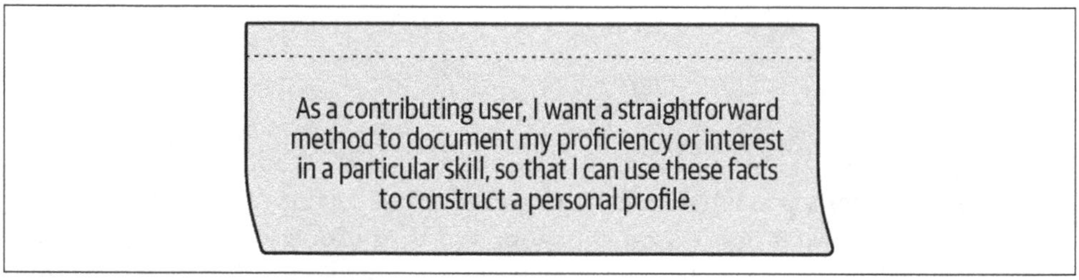

> As a contributing user, I want a straightforward method to document my proficiency or interest in a particular skill, so that I can use these facts to construct a personal profile.

Figure 7-1. Project 3 user story

Elaborated Requirements

This project also has the following specific requirements:

- A user should be able to add "facts," the level of interest or proficiency they have in a specified skill.
- A user should be able to retrieve all the facts they have added.
- The service must provide a REST API.
- The service must have a secure connection to a database.
- Credentials used to connect to the database must be stored securely.
- The service must securely and uniquely identify a user.
- The API should be highly available and be able to handle multiple simultaneous requests.
- The API should respond to requests within 500 ms, 95% of the time.
- Due to support requirements, the implementation should be in Java and Spring Boot, and the database should be a relational database that can be queried using SQL.

Solution

When choosing how to implement this requirement, you need to answer several questions:

Where to run the compute?

For this service, you have a long-running process, so it is not suitable for Cloud Functions. You will be using Java and Spring Boot in a container, so the startup time will be several seconds when using Cloud Run. This means it will not be able to cope well with on-demand requests within the required 500 ms. However, the autoscaling of Cloud Run will still be able to cope with unexpected demand and to be highly available. You will see how to make use of Cloud Run in a slightly different way to get the best of both worlds.

What type of database to use?

This service requires the use of a traditional relational database, or at least a service that appears as such to the application code. You will use Cloud SQL, as it is the simplest solution. Specifically, use Cloud SQL for PostgreSQL, as PostgreSQL is a de facto standard supported by several other database services on Google Cloud and other clouds. It gives you the option to switch to more powerful options later that also support PostgreSQL, if you need to. When architecting applications, keeping your options open like this is a good idea.

How to connect to the database?

You'll want to follow the 12-factor principles of externalizing configuration and storing any secrets securely. You will make use of Cloud Secret Manager for storing secrets and explore secure options for connecting to the chosen database.

How to identify a user?

You want to be able to authenticate users and link them uniquely to the facts they provide. Storing sensitive information like email addresses and passwords, creating a registration form, and changing and resetting passwords is a big headache you want to avoid if at all possible. You will use Identity Platform, a service that does the authentication and user management for you.

Summary of Services

Here is a summary of the Google Cloud services you will be using in this solution.

Spring Boot with Spring Cloud GCP

Spring is a popular Java framework for building web applications. It is a mature framework that has been around for a long time and has a large community. With the release of Spring Boot in 2012, it became even easier to get started with Spring, and it is now the most popular way to build Spring applications. I started using Spring in the mid-2000s, and I found it a very steep learning curve on par with the difficulty I had when learning Kubernetes for the first time. Spring Boot was a godsend in making Spring easy to adopt and be productive with.

One of the key features of Spring Boot is that it is opinionated. It makes a lot of decisions for you and provides a lot of defaults. However, it also provides abstractions over specific technologies, keeping options open, which is a great architectural principle that enables us to remain open to change. For example, Spring Boot provides abstractions over databases, messaging systems, caching, and security. Switching between different implementations of these technologies is often as simple as changing the configuration. A bit later you will see how this has been extended to the services provided by Google Cloud with Spring Cloud GCP (*https://oreil.ly/MkFwE*).

Identity Platform

In this service, a fact is made up by relating a person to a skill via a level of interest or proficiency. A skill is represented by a Stack Overflow tag you retrieved in Chapter 5 and made searchable in Chapter 6. However, you need a way of capturing the person it is associated with, and for that, you can use Identity Platform (*https://oreil.ly/X1UYp*). Identity Platform provides backend service, SDKs, and UI libraries that allow you to authenticate users. It is part of the Firebase app development platform (*https://oreil.ly/jR_6x*).

 Identity Platform is a fully managed service that handles user authentication and identity management on behalf of the application developer. Be careful not to confuse it with Google Cloud Identity which is a different service that enables you to use Google accounts for single sign-on, third-party applications.

Firebase began as a separate application development platform and was acquired by Google in 2014, with Firebase Authentication being one of the features. Firebase targets web and mobile development, and even now it feels one step removed from Google Cloud and not as strongly integrated as other services. Identity Platform supports a range of identity providers, including Google, GitHub, Twitter, and Microsoft accounts. This is great, as it offloads all the responsibility for account creation, storing sensitive information and managing accounts to these trusted providers. However, to get up and running and make testing straightforward, you will start with a simple username and password.

Cloud SQL

Cloud SQL (*https://oreil.ly/Hzpih*) is a Google service for providing managed relational databases in the cloud. It supports PostgreSQL, MySQL, and SQL Server. All three databases are SQL-compliant and are managed similarly. The main difference is the underlying technology used to provide the database.

I would not classify Cloud SQL as a cloud native database; rather than a database that has been designed specifically for the cloud, it is a traditional database hosted in the cloud. Cloud SQL is a fully managed service, so you don't need to worry about provisioning, patching, backups, high availability, or disaster recovery, but there are some limitations associated with the traditional databases it supports.

The most significant of these limitations is that you need to plan capacity up-front, and apart from automatically increasing storage, it struggles to scale up and down as scaling is only vertical, in that the machine hosting the database can be given more CPU and memory. Horizontal scaling, creating multiple instances, is limited to read replicas. The database also requires downtime for maintenance and restarts for many of the configuration changes. These are limitations that should be left behind in a true cloud native solution. However, the databases supported by Cloud SQL, especially PostgreSQL, are widely used technologies, and Cloud SQL can be low cost while providing reasonable resilience with a 99.95% SLA, and some configurations recently offering a 99.99% SLA. It is often going to be worth considering.

When using PostgreSQL, you can use the PostgreSQL protocol that is also supported fully or partially by Google's cloud native relational databases, AlloyDB and Spanner. This makes the transition straightforward when the limitations of Cloud SQL have been reached and 99.99%, or even 99.999%, availability and global scale are required. For that reason, you are going to choose Cloud SQL for PostgreSQL for this project.

Cloud Run

As you have seen in Chapter 6, Cloud Run is a flexible solution for running containers, and you will use it here again. My approach is to work my way down from the highest abstraction until I find a service that can work within the constraints I have identified, a process I call *progressive decomposition*, if anyone asks. This is not suitable for Cloud Functions, but Cloud Run seems like a good candidate. You will see in Chapter 14, where services like GKE Autopilot (Kubernetes) would be a better choice, but my principle is to start with the simplest solution and only introduce something more complicated when I reach a limitation. To quote the originator of the theory of constraints:

> Technology can bring benefits if, and only if, it diminishes a limitation.
> —Dr. Eliyahu M. Goldratt

In this case, you have not reached the limitation of Cloud Run, as it can be configured in a slightly different way to support the requirements of a highly available Java and Spring Boot service with fast response times.

Spring Cloud GCP

When working with Spring Boot on Google Cloud, you can use the Spring Cloud GCP libraries to make it even easier to consume Google Cloud services. You will use it to connect to Cloud SQL. Spring Cloud GCP provides familiar Spring abstractions over Google Cloud services. Although it forms part of the Spring Cloud, you can use just the GCP libraries in your application without having to use any of the other Spring Cloud features.

For example, you can use the Spring Data JPA library to access Cloud SQL; that is the approach you are going to take in this chapter. In this project, we will make use of Google Cloud APIs wherever possible. The code is going to "know" it is running Google Cloud. You will use Google APIs for logging and connecting to the database.

Table 7-1 includes a breakdown of the Google Cloud services supported by Spring Cloud GCP for Spring Boot applications. The services supported by Spring Cloud GCP nicely align with the "toolkit" of services used in this book. There are Spring starters for each service, a collection of managed libraries that provide all the required dependencies in your Maven or Gradle configuration.

Table 7-1. Spring Cloud GCP supported services

Category	GCP service	Spring abstraction	Spring starter
Databases	Cloud SQL (MySQL)	Spring JDBC template	`spring-cloud-gcp-starter-sql-mysql`
		Spring Data JPA	`spring-cloud-gcp-starter-sql-mysql`
Databases	Cloud SQL (PostgreSQL)	Spring JDBC template	`spring-cloud-gcp-starter-sql-postgres`
		Spring Data JPA	`spring-cloud-gcp-starter-sql-postgres`
	Cloud Spanner	Spring Data Spanner	`spring-cloud-gcp-data-spanner`
		Spring Data JPA with Hibernate	`spring-cloud-gcp-data-spanner`
	Cloud Firestore (Datastore mode)	Spring Data Datastore	`spring-cloud-gcp-data-datastore`
	Cloud Firestore (Firestore mode)	Spring Reactive Data Firestore	`spring-cloud-gcp-data-firestore`
Messaging	Cloud Pub/Sub	Spring Integration	`spring-cloud-gcp-starter-pubsub`
		Spring Cloud Stream	`spring-cloud-gcp-pubsub-stream-binder`
		Spring Cloud Bus	`spring-cloud-gcp-starter-bus-pubsub`
Configuration	Cloud Runtime Configuration	Spring Cloud Config	`spring-cloud-gcp-starter-config`
	Cloud Secret Manager	Spring Cloud Config	`spring-cloud-gcp-starter-secretmanager`
Storage	Cloud Storage	Spring Resource	`spring-cloud-gcp-starter-storage`

Category	GCP service	Spring abstraction	Spring starter
Cache	Cloud Memorystore	Spring Data Redis	`spring-boot-starter-data-redis`
Distributed tracing	Cloud Trace	Zipkin/Brave	`spring-cloud-gcp-starter-trace`
Centralized logging	Cloud Logging	SLF4J/Logback	`com.google.cloud:spring-cloud-gcp-starter-logging`
Monitoring metrics	Cloud Monitoring	Micrometer/ Prometheus	`spring-cloud-gcp-starter-metrics`
Security	Cloud Identity-Aware Proxy	Spring Security	`spring-cloud-gcp-starter-security-iap`

In this case, you just want to use Cloud SQL and Cloud Logging within Maven, so you need to include three dependencies: `spring-cloud-gcp-starter`, which is required to use any Spring Cloud GCP functionality, `spring-cloud-gcp-starter-sql-postgres` for Cloud SQL for PostgreSQL, and `spring-cloud-gcp-starter-logging` for Cloud Logging. These are added to the *pom.xml* file.

With the services and libraries you require in place, you can start implementation now.

Implementation

Let's get hands-on and implement this project.

Creating a New Spring Boot Project

To create a new Spring Boot project, you can use the Spring Initializr (*https://oreil.ly/lTwbz*). This is a web application that allows you to create a new Spring Boot project with several initial dependencies. You will use the following dependencies:

- Spring Cloud GCP
- Spring Web
- Spring Data JPA

You can use this cURL command to generate a template project for Maven. Download the generated zip, extract it, and then import it into your integrated development environment (IDE):

```
curl https://start.spring.io/starter.zip \
  -d type=maven-project \
  -d language=java \
  -d platformVersion=2.7.9 \
  -d name=fact-service \
  -d groupId=org.skillsmapper \
```

```
-d dependencies=cloud-gcp,web,data-jpa \
-o fact-service.zip
```

This is a great way of using Spring Boot and Spring Cloud GCP together to kickstart a new project and get you up and running quickly. In the example code, I have added standard Spring Controllers and a JPA repository to access the database. The code is available in the GitHub repository (*https://oreil.ly/P1kx-*).

Configuring Identity Platform

To authenticate users, you can use Identity Platform (*https://oreil.ly/lQ0VJ*).

This is one of the few services on Google Cloud that cannot be set up completely using the command line. So far in this book, you have used the command line wherever possible, as it easily automates the toil of typing commands later. For Identity Platform, however, the only option is to use the Google Cloud Web Console (*https://oreil.ly/Hcp6M*).

To begin, you will need to go to the Identity Provider page in the cloud console's marketplace (*https://oreil.ly/ZK_G2*) and click on the "Enable identity platform" button to enable the service.

This would be equivalent to the gcloud services enable command you have used for other services. Once the service is enabled, you will be taken to the Identity Platform onboarding page.

On the left-hand menu, select Providers, as shown in Figure 7-2, and then click on the Add a Provider button in the toolbar at the top. This will display a list of available providers; you can add many providers to your application, but for now, you will just add a simple one: Email / password, which you can select near the bottom of the list. Toggle the enable control, accept the default settings, and click the Save button.

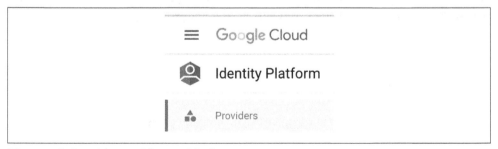

Figure 7-2. Providers in Identity Platform

Create environment variables to store the username and password for the test user, as you will use that later:

```
export TEST_EMAIL=[EMAIL]
export TEST_PASSWORD=[PASSWORD]
```

Even for test situations like this, it is a good idea to use a good password. You can use a password manager like 1Password or LastPass to generate a secure password for you and then copy and paste it into the console. For the email address, you can use the domain example.com, which is reserved for testing purposes (e.g., user@example.com).

Now, on the left-hand menu, select Users and then click on the Add User button. This will allow you to create a new user. Enter an email address and that password as you provided to the environment variables and click on the Save button. This will create a new user in the Identity Platform.

Now that you have authentication configured, you can start getting the application ready for deployment.

Building the Container

With the Spring Boot application written, you need to package it into a container. In Chapter 10, I will cover more options for automating this process; however, for now, I will introduce Jib (*https://oreil.ly/Kb3Xs*), a Google open source project that allows you to build containers for a Java application without a Dockerfile.

Jib uses a plugin with either Maven or Gradle to build the container without needing Docker installed. Ultimately, a container is just a layered archive file, and all Jib does is insert a layer containing the application code and dependencies. In this case, Jib is enabled by adding the following to the plugins section of the *pom.xml* file:

```
<plugin>
    <groupId>com.google.cloud.tools</groupId>
    <artifactId>jib-maven-plugin</artifactId>
    <version>3.3.1</version>
</plugin>
```

Adding this plugin to the *pom.xml* file will cause Jib to build a container when you run the mvn package command. The container will be tagged with the name fact-service and the version number from the *pom.xml* file. You could then push the container to the Google Container Registry (GCR) using the gcloud command-line tool:

```
gcloud container images push gcr.io/${PROJECT_ID}/${SERVICE_NAME}:${VERSION}
```

However, it is easier to just let Cloud Run do all this work; you will see how to do that later. For now, you need to set up a database for the service to connect to.

Creating a Cloud SQL Instance

You can use a Cloud SQL instance to host the database. First, you need to enable the sqlamin service in the project using:

```
gcloud services enable sqladmin.googleapis.com
```

First, there are some environment variables to set:

```
export INSTANCE_NAME='facts-instance'
export DATABASE_TIER='db-f1-micro'
export DISK_SIZE=10
```

Here is a command to create a new instance of PostgreSQL on Cloud SQL. One instance can host multiple databases:

```
gcloud sql instances create $INSTANCE_NAME \
    --database-version=POSTGRES_14 \
    --tier=$DATABASE_TIER \
    --region=$REGION \
    --availability-type=REGIONAL \
    --storage-size=$DISK_SIZE
```

Here, you have specified the instance name, the database version, the tier, the region, the availability type, and the disk size.

The tier is the machine type and the disk size is the amount of storage. Setting the tier to db-f1-micro defines the amount of CPU and memory of the machine that will be used to host the instance. This is a very small machine intended only for development.

You can also set the disk size to 10 (GB), the smallest allowed. This keeps costs to around 1–2 cents per hour. You can increase these values later if needed.

Using small machines has implications for the number of concurrent connections that can be made to the database. For example, this minimum configuration supports a maximum of 25 connections, which is less than the default of 100 normal for PostgreSQL. Higher tiers intended for nondevelopment use provide at least 100 connections by default.

The database version is the version of PostgreSQL that will be used. The region is the region where the database is deployed. Make sure this is the same region as the Cloud Run service to get the best performance.

The *region* denotes the geographical location in which the database is deployed. It's crucial to ensure that your database and Cloud Run service are in the same region to optimize performance due to reduced network latency.

Regarding availability, opt for a regional database, which provides replication across multiple zones within the chosen region. This enhances the database's availability, making it resistant to zone-specific failures. By default, regional databases are selected because they typically suit most use cases. They come with a 99.95% service-level agreement (SLA), which translates to expected downtime of fewer than five hours per year.

It may surprise you to learn that the size of your disk space can directly affect the number of input/output operations per second (IOPS) your system can handle. IOPS is a common performance measurement used to benchmark computer storage devices like hard disk drives (HDD), solid-state drives (SSD), and storage area networks. The more IOPS your system can handle, the faster it can read and write data, which can significantly improve the performance of data-heavy applications.

This relationship might seem counterintuitive at first, but here's how it works: a larger disk size allows for more potential input and output operations. For instance, a minimum disk size of 10 GB provides 300 IOPS. This capacity scales linearly, so with each additional 10 GB of disk space, you gain another 300 IOPS. Therefore, a 100 GB disk size would grant you 3,000 IOPS.

This understanding is critical when configuring your systems because it means that, even if your data storage needs are relatively small, you might still need to opt for a larger disk size to achieve the performance level you need. This often overlooked aspect can have significant implications for the speed and efficiency of your applications, so it's essential to take it into account when planning your system architecture.

On the other hand, you can choose a zonal database that operates within a single zone. Though this option is more affordable (half the price), it lacks the redundancy provided by multizone replication in a regional database. It's important to note that while a single-zone deployment still carries a 99.95% SLA, the practical reliability of a regional database—with its three replicas—is likely superior. However, Google's financial compensation only comes into play if availability falls short of the 99.95% SLA, regardless of the database type.

Behind the scenes of creating a PostgreSQL instance, a process akin to setting up a virtual machine is underway. This process involves installing and configuring PostgreSQL on this virtual infrastructure. While this is a highly automated process, it's a bit more complex and time-consuming than deploying a service designed from the ground up to be cloud native. This explains why the setup process takes several minutes, as the system needs to establish and configure a virtual environment capable of running a full-fledged PostgreSQL database server instance.

Creating a Database and User

Let's establish a new database within the instance. Set a variable for database name (e.g., facts):

```
export DATABASE_NAME='facts'
```

Then use the following command to create the database, referencing the instance you previously created:

```
gcloud sql databases create $DATABASE_NAME \
    --instance=$INSTANCE_NAME
```

Set environment variables for username (e.g., fact-user) and a randomly generated password that the fact service will use to authenticate with the database:

```
export FACT_SERVICE_DB_USER='[FACT_SERVICE_DB_USER]'
export FACT_SERVICE_DB_PASSWORD='[FACT_SERVICE_DB_PASSWORD]'
```

Now create a user for the fact service to use with the command:

```
gcloud sql users create $FACT_SERVICE_DB_USER \
    --instance=$INSTANCE_NAME \
    --password=$FACT_SERVICE_DB_PASSWORD
```

Your PostgreSQL database is now configured and ready for use.

Test Deploying to Cloud Run

Just like with the Go service in Chapter 6, you can indirectly use Cloud Build to build the container, push it to Google Container Registry, and then deploy it to Cloud Run. However, this time Cloud Build will use Jib to build the container, as it will detect the Jib Maven plugin:

```
gcloud run deploy ${FACT_SERVICE_NAME} --source . \
--set-env-vars PROJECT_ID=$PROJECT_ID,SERVICE_NAME=$FACT_SERVICE_NAME,SPRING_PROFILES_ACTIVE=h2 \
--allow-unauthenticated
```

Here, environment variables are being passed to the container using `--set-env-vars` instead of an *env.yaml* file.

This will deploy the service in a test mode by using the h2 in-memory database. The service will start in response to requests but will take a few seconds to start up, and when it is not being used, it will be shut down. This is a great way to test the service and make sure it is working as expected.

Having `spring-cloud-gcp-starter-sql-postgresql` in the classpath Spring will automatically enable Cloud SQL, and you will likely get the error `A database name must be provided`. This is avoided by putting `spring.cloud.gcp.sql.enabled=false` in the *application.properties* file to disable it by default and enabling it with `spring.cloud.gcp.sql.enabled=true` in the *application-gcp.properties* file.

You can get the URL of the service using:

```
export FACT_SERVICE_URL=$(gcloud run services describe $FACT_SERVICE_NAME --format='value(status.url)')
```

Then use a cURL command to test the service:

```
curl -X GET ${FACT_SERVICE_URL}/api/facts
```

At the moment, you will get a 401 Unauthorized error, as you have not configured authentication, but it does prove the service is running.

Creating a Secret in Secret Manager

Before establishing a connection between the Cloud Run service and the Cloud SQL database, it's necessary to create a secret in Secret Manager to safely store the database user's password.

Secret Manager is a secure and convenient solution provided by Google Cloud for managing sensitive information like passwords, API keys, and other secrets. It ensures that these secrets are accessible only to authenticated services and users, thereby helping to keep your application secure. It also offers versioning and audit logging, enabling you to keep track of who accessed what secret and when.

By using Secret Manager to store the database password, you are making sure that it's kept safe and can be accessed securely by your Cloud Run service when it needs to connect to the database.

As with any Google Cloud service, you first need to enable the Secret Manager service for your project using the following command:

```
gcloud services enable secretmanager.googleapis.com
```

Once the service is enabled, create an environment variable to hold the secret name (e.g., fact_service_db_password_secret):

```
export FACT_SERVICE_DB_PASSWORD_SECRET_NAME=[FACT_SERVICE_DB_PASSWORD_SECRET_NAME]
```

You can then create the secret using:

```
gcloud secrets create $FACT_SERVICE_DB_PASSWORD_SECRET_NAME \
    --replication-policy=automatic \
    --data-file=<(echo -n $FACT_SERVICE_DB_PASSWORD)
```

Here, you are taking the database password stored in the environment variable and passing it to the gcloud command using the <(echo -n $DATABASE_PASSWORD) syntax.

It is important to use the -n option to echo to avoid storing a new-line character at the end of the password, making it invalid.

You now have a secret to which you can give a service account access, rather than sitting unencrypted in an environment variable. You will then use that service account with the Cloud Run service.

Creating a Service Account

In line with the principle of least privilege, you can now create a dedicated service account that has only the necessary permissions to perform its tasks.

Create an environment variable for the service account name (e.g., `fact-service-sa`):

```
export FACT_SERVICE_SA=[FACT_SERVICE_SA]
```

Then create the service account using:

```
gcloud iam service-accounts create $FACT_SERVICE_SA \
    --description="${FACT_SERVICE_NAME} service account"
```

To enable your service account with the access it needs, you need to assign it two specific roles.

The first role is the Cloud SQL Client. This role grants the service account the necessary permissions to connect and interact with the Cloud SQL database. It's like giving the service account the keys to the database room.

The second role is the Secret Manager Secret Accessor. This role allows your service account to access and retrieve the secret you stored in the Secret Manager. Think of this as giving your service account the combination to the safe where you keep your most valuable secrets.

By assigning these roles, you empower your service account to perform its tasks, while still adhering to the principle of least privilege.

Use this command to add the Cloud SQL Client role:

```
gcloud projects add-iam-policy-binding $PROJECT_ID \
  --member=serviceAccount:${FACT_SERVICE_SA}@${PROJECT_ID}.iam.gserviceaccount.com \
  --role=roles/cloudsql.client
```

Then use this command to give the service account access to the secret in Secret Manager:

```
gcloud secrets add-iam-policy-binding $FACT_SERVICE_DB_PASSWORD_SECRET_NAME \
  --member=serviceAccount:${FACT_SERVICE_SA}@${PROJECT_ID}.iam.gserviceaccount.com \
  --role=roles/secretmanager.secretAccessor
```

You now have a service account with the permissions the Cloud Run service needs and no more.

Deploying to Cloud Run Connecting to Cloud SQL

To deploy for real, the fact service needs to connect to the Cloud SQL PostgreSQL database. There are several options for connecting to a Cloud SQL database from Cloud Run. In this case, as you are using the Spring Cloud GCP starter for Cloud SQL to connect to a Cloud SQL database using the Cloud SQL Proxy, as shown in Figure 7-3.

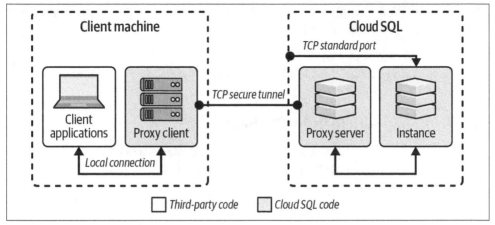

Figure 7-3. Cloud SQL Proxy

The Cloud SQL Proxy is a binary that normally runs as a sidecar container to the main application container. This is a proxy client that creates a connection via a secure tunnel to a corresponding proxy server on the machine the Cloud SQL database is running on, and then forwards the connection to the application container. If you were using Kubernetes, you could use a sidecar container to run the Cloud SQL Proxy, but as you are using Cloud Run, you need to use a different approach.

Fortunately, there is a mechanism in Cloud Run to provide the Cloud Proxy for you using the Cloud SQL Proxy as a Cloud Run service and then using the `--add-cloudsql-instances` option to connect to the Cloud SQL Proxy service, specifying the connection name of the Cloud SQL instance.

You can update the Cloud Run service to switch to using the Cloud SQL database by adding the `--add-cloudsql-instances` option and using the service account to run the Cloud Run container, so it has the correct permissions.

At this point, you also switch to passing environment variables in a file using `env-vars-file` and pass the secret containing the database password using `--update-secrets`.

First generate the *env.yaml* file using:

```
envsubst < env.yaml.template > env.yaml
```

Then run this command to update the fact service:

```
gcloud run services update $FACT_SERVICE_NAME \
    --service-account ${FACT_SERVICE_SA}@${PROJECT_ID}.iam.gserviceaccount.com \
    --add-cloudsql-instances ${PROJECT_ID}:${REGION}:${INSTANCE_NAME} \
    --env-vars-file=env.yaml \
    --update-secrets=DATABASE_PASSWORD=${FACT_SERVICE_DB_PASSWORD_SECRET_NAME}:latest
```

This will take a few seconds to redeploy the service. Once it is deployed, you can test it using the same cURL command as before:

```
curl -X GET ${FACT_SERVICE_URL}/api/facts
```

This time, it will be using the Cloud SQL database instead of h2, but you should still see the 401 Unauthorized error.

Authentication with Identity Platform

The service uses authentication so that only authenticated users can add facts. If you try to add a fact using the cURL command, you will get a 401 Unauthorized error:

```
curl -X POST \
  -H 'Content-Type: application/json' \
  -d '{ "skill": "java", "level": "learning" }`' \
  ${FACT_SERVICE_URL}/api/facts
```

You will get a 401 Unauthorized error like this:

```
{"timestamp":"2023-07-24T17:27:07.872+00:00","status":401,"error":"Unauthorized","path":"/api/facts"}
```

This is because the service is expecting a valid token in the `Authorization` header. This token would normally be provided by the user's browser when they log in to the application using a UI. However, for testing, you can use the command line to log in and retrieve the token. To do this, you need the API key from Identity Platform. This API key would also be used when calling the Identity Platform API from the client application.

Go to the Identity Platform providers page in the Cloud console (*https://oreil.ly/lVu05*) and click the link for `APPLICATION SETUP DETAILS`.

First, copy the value from the apiKey field and store it in an environment variable using the following command:

```
export API_KEY=[apiKey]
```

Next, use this API key along with the test username and password to retrieve an ID token. This ID token serves as a credential that allows the user to access resources:

```
export ID_TOKEN= \
$(curl "https://www.googleapis.com/identitytoolkit/v3/relyingparty/verifyPassword?key=${API_KEY}" \
-H "Content-Type: application/json" --data-binary \
"{\"email\":\"${TEST_EMAIL}\",\"password\":\"${TEST_PASSWORD}\",\"returnSecureToken\":true}" \
| jq -r '.idToken')
```

Now, with the ID token, you can make authenticated requests to your service. In this case, use the token in the Authorization header of the cURL command to add a fact:

```
curl -X POST \
  -H "Authorization: Bearer ${ID_TOKEN}" \
  -H 'Content-Type: application/json' \
  -d '{ "skill": "java", "level": "learning" }`' \
  ${FACT_SERVICE_URL}/api/facts
```

This will return a 201 Created response like this:

```
{"id":3,"timestamp":"2023-03-15T19:59:09.82879",
"userUID":"v9qeph7MLBf5EgFYlUCKMTYwQ6i1","level":"learning","skill":"java"}
```

You can also use the cURL command to retrieve the facts to see that the fact has been added again, providing the token in the Authorization header:

```
curl -X GET ${FACT_SERVICE_URL}/api/facts \
  -H "Authorization: Bearer ${ID_TOKEN}"
```

This will return a list of all facts added by the user to which the token belongs.

In the same way, you can use the token to authorize deleting the fact again:

```
curl -X DELETE \
  -H "Authorization: Bearer ${ID_TOKEN}" \
  ${FACT_SERVICE_URL}/api/facts/1
```

You now have a secured service that can create, retrieve, and delete from the database using the API.

Improving the Startup Time

At the moment, Cloud Run will shut down running containers when there are no requests. This means when a new request comes in, it needs to be started up again.

You can try this by running Apache Bench to send three requests to the service after not accessing it for a while:

```
ab -n 3 -H "Authorization: Bearer ${ID_TOKEN}" ${FACT_SERVICE_URL}/api/facts
```

You should see that the first request takes a few seconds to return (in my case 25 seconds) but the subsequent requests are much faster (259 ms). This is because the service has been started up to serve the first request but is still running for subsequent requests.

This is known as the *cold start problem* and is a common issue with serverless platforms, especially when using a language like Java where startup times are relatively slow. In a language like Go, it would be less of a problem, as Go starts relatively quickly compared to Java; however, the first request would still be slower than subsequent requests.

The way to avoid this is to keep at least one instance of the service running all the time. You can do this by setting the --min-instances option to 1 to ensure that at least one instance is always running.

You can also set the --max-instances to allow the service to scale up to handle more requests. However, you don't want it to scale to the default of 100 replicas. Remember, you only have a limited number of database connections, so you need to be careful not to scale up too much, as each instance is configured to keep five connections in its connection pool. This is one limitation of using a noncloud native database like

PostgreSQL with a serverless application. It is manageable, but it is something to be aware of.

This is the command to update the service with minimum and maximum instances specified:

```
gcloud run services update $FACT_SERVICE_NAME \
    --service-account ${FACT_SERVICE_SA}@${PROJECT_ID}.iam.gserviceaccount.com \
    --add-cloudsql-instances ${PROJECT_ID}:${REGION}:${INSTANCE_NAME} \
    --env-vars-file=env.yaml \
    --update-secrets=DATABASE_PASSWORD=${FACT_SERVICE_DB_PASSWORD_SECRET_NAME}:latest \
    --min-instances=1 \
    --max-instances=3
```

If you think of Cloud Run as a taxi, transport on demand, this is a bit like always having a taxi waiting outside your house ready to take you to the airport. It is more expensive, but it is much more convenient.

If you try the Apache Bench command again, you should see that the first request is much faster:

```
ab -n 3 -H "Authorization: Bearer ${ID_TOKEN}" ${FACT_SERVICE_URL}/api/facts
```

In my test, the fastest response was 240 ms and the slowest 235 ms, a great improvement in consistency and below the 500 ms that you require.

Evaluation

Now let's look at how the solution will scale and how much it will cost.

How Will This Solution Scale?

This solution is designed with scalability in mind.

First, the service itself has been designed to handle vertical scaling. This means that each instance's capacity can be increased by augmenting memory and CPU resources. This is done by adjusting the `--memory` and `--cpu` parameters during service deployment. Changing these parameters allows the service to handle a larger number of requests.

The solution also supports horizontal scaling. It can dynamically adjust—scale up or down—to handle fluctuations in the volume of requests. Even though it currently maintains a minimum of one running instance, this baseline could be raised to swiftly respond to traffic surges.

On the other hand, the database presents a slightly different story. It primarily supports vertical scaling, which means its capacity can be increased by adjusting the `--tier`, or the machine's specification on which the database operates. However, this process isn't automated and necessitates a database restart. This can result in a brief downtime period, which isn't ideal.

Moreover, there's another crucial aspect to bear in mind. The database can handle only a limited number of connections, dependent on the machine's size. Therefore, it's important to ensure that the total number of connections, which is the number of instances multiplied by the connections in each pool, doesn't exceed the available connections. This careful management of resources contributes to the overall robustness and efficiency of the solution.

How Much Will This Solution Cost?

Cloud Run is billed based on the number of requests and the amount of memory used by the service. The first two million requests are free and after that, it is $0.0002 per request. The memory is billed at $0.00001667 per GB per hour at the time of writing.

As the service needs to always be responsive, you will keep at least one instance running all the time. This is going to be the most significant cost. However, you can minimize this by setting the CPU and memory to the minimum required to run the service and allowing more instances to be scaled up to handle more requests.

Another significant cost is going to be the database, as it will be running all the time. The database is billed based on the amount of storage used and the tier the machine is running on. At the moment, you are using the smallest available database and storage amount, which keeps costs to a minimum. In Chapter 14, you will see how using other more cost-effective services where possible can help us keep the cost of this database down.

 Be aware that there is a charge per request; even though it may not seem significant when services are receiving millions of requests per month, it may start to become significant. At that point, GKE Autopilot, covered in Chapter 14, might be worth considering from a cost point of view alone.

The database is billed based on the amount of storage used and the tier of the machine it is running on. With the minimal configuration currently in use, the cost should be less than $10 per month.

Summary

You have created a REST service using Spring Boot and deployed it to Cloud Run. You have also added authentication using Identity Platform and a database backend using Cloud SQL. You have followed cloud native principles and made good use of the features of the Google Cloud Platform without getting too tied to it.

For this project, you used the following services directly:

- Cloud Run is used as the container runtime to run the container
- Cloud SQL is used as the database backend for the application
- Cloud Secrets Manager is used to securely store the database password
- Identity Platform is used to authenticate users

In Chapter 8, you will create a service to respond asynchronously when the facts change.

Project 4: Profile Service with Pub/Sub and Firestore

This chapter delves into the creation of a cloud native, event-driven microservice: the profile service. This profile service will build and continuously update user profiles based on changing facts from the fact service. The architecture will employ Google Pub/Sub for event notifications, Firestore as a serverless database to store user profiles, and Cloud Run for hosting the service.

 The code for this chapter is in the `profile-service` folder of the GitHub repository (*https://oreil.ly/m-4le*).

Requirements

Let's go straight into the requirements.

User Story

Figure 8-1 is the user story you will be focusing on.

Figure 8-1. Project 4 user story

Elaborated Requirements

It is safe to assume that the system has many users and most are not going to make frequent changes to their skills. This means it is more likely for there to be a request for a profile than for facts to be edited.

You can take advantage of this by storing the profile indefinitely once it's generated and only updating it when a change is made to the facts. This has the advantage of not needing to access the PostgreSQL database every time a profile is requested, meaning you can keep the instance size small and reduce the cost of the facts service.

Therefore, the requirements are as follows:

- The service should be triggered every time there's a change in the user facts stored in the fact service.
- The service should generate a user profile as a single JSON document that can be stored and later retrieved on demand.
- Since the profile service is triggered by fact changes and does not require an immediate response to the caller, it can operate asynchronously.
- The service must be able to scale to meet the demands of the system, managing large numbers of profile requests and updates.
- The service should be designed for high availability, ensuring that it's always ready to respond to change notifications and serve profiles.
- The service should be low cost and require minimal maintenance, leveraging serverless technology to minimize the need for server management and capacity planning.

By designing the service to meet these requirements, you can ensure it will efficiently and reliably manage user profiles, providing up-to-date information for users to share. The remainder of this chapter will guide you through how to build and deploy a service that fulfills these needs.

Solution

Again, it is possible to produce a low-cost solution to these requirements using Google Cloud Services.

Summary of Services

To build the profile service that meets these requirements, you are going to make use of a few key Google Cloud services. Let's take a closer look at each of them.

Google Firestore

Firestore is a NoSQL document database that is built for automatic scaling, high performance, and ease of application development. Given the small amounts of data you'll be storing for each user profile, Firestore is an excellent choice for your needs. Its serverless nature allows it to scale automatically according to demand, making it highly available and fault-tolerant.

While Firestore does require usage of a Google Cloud-specific API, and thus might not be ideal for all projects, it fits the current use case perfectly. The fact that it requires minimal configuration compared to other database services, such as Cloud SQL, significantly simplifies the maintenance of your service.

Google Pub/Sub

This service needs to know when a change has been made to the facts provided by a user. You can get the fact service to report changes by publishing an event to Google Pub/Sub.

Google Pub/Sub is a fully managed event ingestion and delivery system. It supports both event streaming similar to Apache Kafka and queue-based messaging similar to a message queue like RabbitMQ. It is a one-stop event and messaging system. This differs from AWS, for example, where queue (SQS), notifications (SNS), and event bus (Amazon EventBridge) features are provided by separate services. It is a highly available and fault-tolerant service that is scalable, serverless, and cost-effective.

In this project, you will be using Pub/Sub to push a notification to the profile service of changes to facts. The profile service will then update the profile of the user.

Cloud Run

For your profile service, you'll write the code in Go and host it on Cloud Run. Go's quick start-up time makes it ideal for situations where a service needs to start quickly in response to an event, do its work, and then shut down. This is an excellent use case for Cloud Run, which can start and stop instances rapidly, charging only for the time during which the service is running.

With these services, you will have a profile service that is responsive to changes, highly available, and cost-effective. Let's dive into how to use these services to build the solution.

Implementation

It is time to get hands-on and implement the service.

Storing Data in Firestore

The profile service uses Firestore, or more precisely Firestore in Firestore Native mode, to store profiles, each profile being a JSON document. Firestore is part of Firebase and was originally designed for simultaneous connection from many mobile clients. The other mode available is Datastore mode which supports Datastore, a previous Google Cloud service.

Ensure you are in the correct project with:

```
gcloud config set project $PROJECT_ID
```

Then, to use Firestore, you need to enable the Firestore API with this command:

```
gcloud services enable firestore.googleapis.com
```

Create the Firestore database with `--type=firestore-native` to use Firestore Native mode:

```
gcloud alpha firestore databases create --location=$REGION --type=firestore-native
```

Notice that this command has the alpha flag. This is because Firestore, like Firebase authentication, is not fully integrated with Google Cloud, and the command is not yet available in the main gcloud commands at the time of writing.

It used to be that you could only have one Firestore or Datastore database per project, and if you wanted to use Firestore in a different project, you would need to create a new project. In the case of this service, only one database is needed, so the default database is being used. However, during the writing of this book, the restriction was lifted and it is now possible to create multiple Firestore databases in a single project.

Sending Events to Pub/Sub

The next thing to do is revisit the earlier fact service and add the ability to publish a message to Pub/Sub when a fact is added or deleted. To do this, you need to include the Spring Cloud GCP Pub/Sub Starter and the Spring Integration in the *pom.xml* file:

```
<dependencies>
...
    <dependency>
      <groupId>com.google.cloud</groupId>
      <artifactId>spring-cloud-gcp-starter-pubsub</artifactId>
    </dependency>
    <dependency>
      <groupId>org.springframework.integration</groupId>
      <artifactId>spring-integration-core</artifactId>
    </dependency>
...
</dependencies>
```

Google Pub/Sub is a robust, fully managed service that enables real-time messaging between applications. However, when integrating Pub/Sub into your Spring applications, you might not want to deal with the specifics of the Pub/Sub API directly. This is where the Spring Cloud GCP library comes into play.

Spring Cloud GCP provides a channel adapter for Spring Integration, allowing Pub/Sub to be used as a message channel in your application. What this means is that you can interact with Pub/Sub using familiar Spring Integration paradigms, effectively abstracting away the underlying Pub/Sub API details. The beauty of this approach lies in its flexibility—while your application benefits from Pub/Sub, it isn't tightly coupled to it. This makes your code more portable and easier to maintain.

In practical terms, you can leverage the @ServiceActivator annotation from Spring Integration to define a method that will act as a message handler. This method is triggered when a message arrives on the subscribed channel.

For instance, if you have a Pub/Sub topic named factchanged, the name of this topic can be supplied by an environment variable (pubsub.topic.factchanged). This environment variable is set in the *env.yaml* file used during the Cloud Run deployment.

In the fact service in the code that accompanies this book, the following code has been added to FactApplication to enable this:

```
@Bean
@ServiceActivator(inputChannel = "pubsubOutputChannel")
public MessageHandler messageSender(PubSubTemplate pubsubTemplate) {
  return new PubSubMessageHandler(pubsubTemplate, env.getProperty("pubsub.topic.factchanged"));
}

@MessagingGateway(defaultRequestChannel = "pubsubOutputChannel")
public interface PubsubOutboundGateway {
  void sendToPubsub(String payload);
}
```

Here, a MessageHandler bean is being defined, which will handle outgoing messages to the Pub/Sub service. The @ServiceActivator annotation is used to specify that this handler will be listening on the pubsubOutputChannel for any messages.

The MessageHandler is configured with a PubSubTemplate, which is a helper class provided by the Spring Cloud GCP library to interact with Pub/Sub. The topic to which the messages will be sent is set to the value of the `pubsub.topic.factchanged` environment variable.

Additionally, a `PubsubOutboundGateway` interface is defined. This interface is marked with the `@MessagingGateway` annotation, which indicates it's a gateway to the messaging system. The method `sendToPubsub(String payload)` will send a message to the `pubsubOutputChannel`, effectively pushing the message to the configured Pub/Sub topic.

In the code then, you can use the `PubsubOutboundGateway` to send a message to Pub/Sub. For example, following is the code added to the `FactController` to send a message. This is called when a fact is added or deleted, sending an updated list of all facts for the user serialized as JSON.

Then the following method has been added to the `FactController` class:

```
public void factsChanged(Fact fact) {
  List<Fact> facts = factRepository.findByUser(fact.getUser());
  FactsChanged factsChanged = new FactsChanged(fact.getUser(), facts, OffsetDateTime.now());
  try {
    String jsonString = objectMapper.writeValueAsString(factsChanged);
    logger.info("Sending message to Pub/Sub: {}", jsonString);
    messagingGateway.sendToPubsub(jsonString);
  } catch (JsonProcessingException e) {
    logger.error("Error serializing message send to Pub/Sub: {}", e.getMessage());
  }
}
```

This method is called when a fact is added or deleted. It fetches the updated list of facts for the user and creates a new `FactsChanged` object. This object is then converted into a JSON string and sent to the Pub/Sub topic through the `sendToPubsub(String payload)` method of the `PubsubOutboundGateway`. If there's an error in the JSON serialization process, it will be logged.

This approach allows your application to send messages to Pub/Sub without being tightly coupled to Google Cloud–specific implementations, making your code more portable and easier to maintain.

Configuring Pub/Sub

While the fact service can now theoretically deploy to a Pub/Sub topic, that topic does not yet exist. To use Pub/Sub, you first need to enable the Pub/Sub API with this command:

```
gcloud services enable pubsub.googleapis.com
```

Now create an environment variable for the name of the topic you want to create (e.g., `fact-changed`):

```
export FACT_CHANGED_TOPIC=[FACT_CHANGED_TOPIC]
```

You can now create a topic to send the "fact-changed" event to:

```
gcloud pubsub topics create $FACT_CHANGED_TOPIC
```

It is also a good idea to create a second topic to act as a dead letter queue. A dead letter queue is a place to capture messages that can't be delivered. This is useful as it means you can retry sending the message later or use the failed messages for debugging if there was a problem with the message content. You can create a dead letter topic like this:

```
gcloud pubsub topics create $FACT_CHANGED_TOPIC-deadletter
```

With topics set up, you now need to connect them to the services with those services.

Configuring Service Accounts

As should be familiar by now, you need to add permissions to the service account that the fact service uses to allow it to publish messages to Pub/Sub. In this case, you need to add the `roles/pubsub.publisher` role to the service account like this:

```
gcloud pubsub topics add-iam-policy-binding ${FACT_CHANGED_TOPIC} \
  --member=serviceAccount:${FACT_SERVICE_SA}@${PROJECT_ID}.iam.gserviceaccount.com \
  --role=roles/pubsub.publisher
```

 In general, if something isn't working in Google Cloud, a good first step is to check for missing permissions on a service account, especially if you are using a service account other than the default. You can do this by going to the IAM & Admin section of the console and checking the permissions for the service account. Checking logs for Cloud Run for the service will also help to identify any issues.

You will also need a service account for the profile service itself. As the service will have events pushed to it, it does not need any permissions to access PubSub; however, it will need permissions to read and write to Firestore and to write logs.

Create an environment variable to hold a service account name (e.g., `profile-service-sa`):

```
export PROFILE_SERVICE_SA=[PROFILE_SERVICE_SA]
```

Then create the service account with the following command:

```
gcloud iam service-accounts create ${PROFILE_SERVICE_SA} \
  --display-name "${PROFILE_SERVICE_NAME} service account"
```

Give the service account permission to write logs to Cloud Logging:

```
gcloud projects add-iam-policy-binding $PROJECT_ID \
  --member=serviceAccount:$PROFILE_SERVICE_SA@$PROJECT_ID.iam.gserviceaccount.com \
  --role=roles/logging.logWriter
```

Also, give the service account permission to read and write to Firestore:

```
gcloud projects add-iam-policy-binding $PROJECT_ID \
  --member=serviceAccount:$PROFILE_SERVICE_SA@$PROJECT_ID.iam.gserviceaccount.com \
  --role=roles/datastore.user
```

You now have a service account to use when deploying the profile service a little later.

Receiving Pub/Sub Events

With the fact service now set up to publish events about user fact changes, let's focus on the profile service. The profile service's task is to subscribe to the fact service's topic and update the relevant user profile when a message is received.

You could consider using the Go Pub/Sub client to pull messages from the topic, but it's not ideal for this setup. Why? Because it would require the Cloud Run service to be run all the time, causing unnecessary resource consumption and increased costs. It could be scheduled to run at certain times, but this would mean there would be a significant delay in updating profiles.

Instead, you can adopt a more cloud native approach. Since the profile service is another Cloud Run service, you can set up an HTTP endpoint for Pub/Sub to push messages. When Pub/Sub pushes a message to this endpoint, it triggers an instance that processes the message in the HTTP request's body. This approach relieves the profile service from maintaining a connection with Pub/Sub, allowing it to focus solely on updating user profiles. Furthermore, it optimizes resource usage as service instances are created and billed only when a message needs processing.

If you have created *.env* files, use this command to apply the environment variable again:

```
set -a; source ../.env; source .env ;set +a
```

Create a file called *env.yaml* from *env.yaml.template*, substituting values from your environment variable, including those set in the previous chapters:

```
envsubst < env.yaml.template > env.yaml
```

As with the skill service, Cloud Build will use a buildpack to create a container for the profile service and deploy it to Cloud Run in a single command:

```
gcloud run deploy $PROFILE_SERVICE_NAME --source . \
  --service-account $PROFILE_SERVICE_SA@$PROJECT_ID.iam.gserviceaccount.com \
  --env-vars-file=env.yaml \
  --allow-unauthenticated
```

Again, the environment variables the service needs (the project ID and the Service Name) are stored in the *env.yaml* file.

With the service deployed, set the PROFILE_SERVICE_URL environment variable to the URL of the service, as you will need that to define where Pub/Sub should deliver events:

```
export PROFILE_SERVICE_URL=$(gcloud run services describe $PROFILE_SERVICE_NAME \
  --format='value(status.url)')
```

You are now ready to create a subscription to the topic that the fact service is publishing. A subscription is a way of linking events with a service. This subscription will be configured to send messages to the profile service.

Creating a Subscription

Even though messages are being published and the profile service is there waiting, nothing will happen until you create a subscription to the topic.

Create an environment variable for the name of the subscription to be created (e.g., `fact-changed-subscription`):

```
export FACT_CHANGED_SUBSCRIPTION=[FACT_CHANGED_SUBSCRIPTION]
```

At the moment, Pub/Sub will be able to invoke the Cloud Run profile service as it allows unauthenticated requests; however, you will turn this off later for security reasons. This means you need to create a service account for the subscription to use to be able to invoke the profile service. You can create the service account with this command:

```
gcloud iam service-accounts create ${FACT_CHANGED_SUBSCRIPTION}-sa \
  --display-name="${FACT_CHANGED_SUBSCRIPTION} service account"
```

Then give the service account the `roles/run.invoker` role to allow it to invoke the profile service:

```
gcloud run services add-iam-policy-binding $PROFILE_SERVICE_NAME \
--member=serviceAccount:${FACT_CHANGED_SUBSCRIPTION}-sa@${PROJECT_ID}.iam.gserviceaccount.com \
--role=roles/run.invoker
```

Now you are ready to create the subscription itself with this command:

```
gcloud pubsub subscriptions create ${FACT_CHANGED_SUBSCRIPTION} \
  --topic=${FACT_CHANGED_TOPIC} \                                                              ❶
  --push-endpoint=${PROFILE_SERVICE_URL}/factschanged \                                        ❷
  --max-delivery-attempts=5 \                                                                  ❸
  --dead-letter-topic=$FACT_CHANGED_TOPIC-deadletter \
  --push-auth-service-account=${FACT_CHANGED_SUBSCRIPTION}-sa@${PROJECT_ID}.iam.gserviceaccount.com ❹
```

❶   `--topic` is the name of the topic to which the fact service is publishing.

❷   `--push-endpoint` is the URL of the profile service with the `/factschanged` path appended. This is the URI where the profile service will accept messages.

❸   `--max-delivery-attempts` is set to 5. This means that if the profile service returns a non-2xx response code, Pub/Sub will retry sending the message up to five times.

❹   `--push-auth-service-account` is the service account you just created that the subscription will use to authenticate with the profile service.

This last setting is useful as it means that if the profile service is temporarily unavailable for any reason, the message will be retried later. However, after that, the message will be sent to the dead letter topic.

From now on, each time a message is received by the profile service, it will update the profile of the user. The profile service will also log the message it receives to the console. Each message is an invocation of the profile service and will be billed as such. That is why it is useful to limit the number of retries so it does not keep invoking the service forever. If you did notice that was happening, though, you can always delete the subscription while you debug, using:

```
gcloud pubsub subscriptions delete $FACT_CHANGED_SUBSCRIPTION
```

Testing the Profile Service

To test the profile service, you can use the `gcloud pubsub` command to publish a message to the topic. This will trigger the profile service to update the profile of the user.

First, retrieve an ID token for the test user from Identity Platform:

```
export ID_TOKEN=$(curl "https://www.googleapis
.com/identitytoolkit/v3/relyingparty/verifyPassword?key=${API_KEY}" \
-H "Content-Type: application/json" \
--data-binary "{\"email\":\"${TEST_EMAIL}\",\"password\":\"${TEST_PASSWORD}\"
\"returnSecureToken\":true}" | jq -r '.idToken')
```

The token that is returned is a JSON Web Token (JWT). Encoded in it is the user ID. Normally, the server side would verify the signature with Identity Platform before trusting any information in it. However, you can extract the user ID locally and store it in a `$USER_ID` environment variable using a command like this, assuming you have `jq` installed, as mentioned in Chapter 4:

```
payload=$(echo $ID_TOKEN | cut -d"." -f2)
decoded=$(echo $payload | base64 -d 2>/dev/null || echo $payload | base64 -di)
export USER_ID=$(echo $decoded | jq -r .user_id)
```

The payload of Pub/Sub messages is JSON. You can build an example fact-changed event using the template in the *examples/fact-changed.json.template* file:

```
envsubst < examples/fact-changed.json.template > examples/fact-changed.json
```

Now publish the example fact-changed event for the test user using:

```
gcloud pubsub topics publish $FACT_CHANGED_TOPIC --message "$(cat examples/fact-changed.json)"
```

You can then check the log for the profile service to see the message it received:

```
gcloud beta run services logs read $PROFILE_SERVICE_NAME
```

You will see a POST with a 200 status to the `/factschanged` path like this:

```
2023-04-24 19:58:37 POST 200 https://profile-builder-j7n5qulfna-uc.a.run.app/factschanged
```

Then a log message that the profile has been updated like this:

```
Updated profile: &{CPK4AwHuxTX900uAirPCTwcdTy63 Profile [Python] [JavaScript] [] []}
```

You can also check the Firestore database to see that the profile has been updated.

The URL of the console includes `-default-`, as you will be using the default database:

```
open \
"https://console.cloud.google.com/firestore/databases/-default-/ ↩
data/panel/profiles?project=${PROJECT_ID}"
```

You can do this by going to the Firestore console and selecting the `users` collection. You should see a document with the `id` of the user you published the message for. The document should have a `facts` field with the fact you published.

You can also retrieve a profile for the current user. You can then use this token to access the API:

```
curl -X GET -H "Authorization: Bearer ${ID_TOKEN}" ${PROFILE_SERVICE_URL}/api/profiles/me
```

This will return a JSON file representing the profile for the test user with the facts added:

```
{"User":"CPK4AwHuxTX900uAirPCTwcdTy63","Name":"Profile","PhotoURL":"","Interested":["Python"],
"Learning":["JavaScript"],"Using":null,"Used":null}
```

If this were a user with a profile like Google Cloud, the code would also retrieve the real name of the user and even a URL to their photo to show in the profile. You will learn how to do this in Chapter 11.

Evaluation

Let's evaluate the solution in terms of cost.

Overall, this is a low-cost solution; it is taking good advantage of cloud native services. The costs are broken down as follows.

Firestore

Firestore is a relatively cheap way to store data, as you are not paying for compute resources and are only storing small amounts of data. Billing is based on the following:

- The number of documents you read, write, and delete
- The number of index entries matched by aggregation queries
- The amount of storage that your database uses, including overhead for metadata and indexes
- The amount of network bandwidth that you use

However, there are generous free tiers for all of these, and you will need to have over 50,000 reads and 20,000 writes per day and store over 1 GB of data before the costs start kicking in. As this service is storing small profiles, the cost of storing the data is likely to be negligible.

Cloud Run

The cost of Cloud Run is also likely to be small; the service is written in Go with minimal resource requirements and only executes for a small amount of time in response to an event. As the free tier allows for 2 million requests per month and 400,000 GB seconds per month, the cost of running the service is likely to be negligible.

Cloud Pub/Sub

Pub/Sub has the following components in its cost:

- Throughput costs for message publishing and delivery
- Egress costs associated with throughput that crosses a Google Cloud zone or region boundary
- Storage costs for snapshots, messages retained by topics, and acknowledged messages retained by subscriptions

As you are not retaining messages or crossing boundaries, the cost of using Pub/Sub is limited to the costs for message publication and delivery.

The cost of message publication is based on the number of messages published and the size of the messages. The free tier for Pub/Sub is 10GiB per month, so as it stands, the volume of messages would need to be considered before this service-occurred cost is high.

Summary

Although a simple example, this is representative of true cloud native service. The service is event-driven and stateless. It is written in a cloud native language (Go) and uses a cloud native storage service (Firestore). It also uses a serverless runtime (Cloud Run), and it is not running all the time and only executes when an event is triggered. The service is also scalable; it is scaled up or down as required. As a result, the service is highly available and fault-tolerant, but also so cost-effective that it is almost free. This is the type of service that made me excited when I first started using the cloud—services that can be run for next to nothing but can perform in a way that would have previously needed a lot of hardware.

For this project, you used the following services directly:

- Cloud Pub/Sub is used to store the profiles.

With all the services in place, in Chapter 9, you will be bringing them together into a single API and providing a UI interface for users to interact with.

Project 5: API and User Interface with API Gateway and Cloud Storage

In previous chapters, you developed three separate Cloud Run services that collectively constitute the backend for the Skills Mapper application. While the benefit of this arrangement is that each service can be individually maintained and scaled, it has led to a somewhat fragmented system. Navigating this structure currently requires an understanding of which functionality is provided by each distinct service. To recap, these three services are:

Skill service
> This service offers suggestions of skills that can be added to the fact service.

Fact service
> This is responsible for maintaining the facts necessary for constructing a profile.

Profile service
> This updates user profiles as the associated facts evolve.

One significant challenge that needs to be addressed is unauthenticated invocation. Currently, these Cloud Run services expose their APIs to the internet without any authentication, which makes them susceptible to attacks.

To secure the system and streamline its operation, unifying these services under a single, secure API is the subject of this chapter. Additionally, you will deploy a user interface, providing users with a secure and consolidated point of access to the Skills Mapper application's functionality.

The code for this chapter is in the user-interface folder of the GitHub repository (*https://oreil.ly/sadOe*).

Requirements

Let's look at the requirements for this final project. The user story for this functionality is shown in Figure 9-1.

As a contributing user, I want a single access point through a secure API, so that I can seamlessly interact with all functionalities of the system from an intuitive user interface, enhancing my overall user experience.

Figure 9-1. Project 5 user story

Solution

This solution mainly introduces some of Google Cloud's powerful networking services.

User Interface

So far, you have used Cloud Run to host backend services. You can also use it to host the UI using the same approach as you did for the backend services. You can use Cloud Build to create a container for the UI and deploy it to Cloud Run. However, as the UI is a static website, you will see there is an alternative approach using Cloud Storage and Cloud CDN that will be a little simpler and a lot more cost-effective.

OpenAPI

To bring together multiple services under a single API, you can define a common API using the OpenAPI specification. You can then use that as the configuration for a Google Cloud API Gateway.

Although OpenAPI is at version 3.1.0 (*https://spec.openapis.org/oas/latest.html*) at the time of writing this book, the API Gateway only supports version 2.0, better known as Swagger 2.0 (*https://swagger.io/specification/v2/*).

The great thing about using an OpenAPI specification is that only the specific endpoints explicitly defined will be exposed via the API Gateway. This has a security benefit; it means that any endpoints not defined in the specification will not be exposed.

For example, with the profile service, there is the endpoint that Google Pub/Sub uses to deliver events to the service. As this endpoint is not defined in the specification, it will not be exposed publicly via the API Gateway, meaning there is no way for an attacker to send a potentially damaging message to the service via that route.

API Gateway

Google API Gateway is a managed service that is intended to allow you to expose your APIs to the internet. It is a fully managed service that handles the scaling and load balancing of your APIs. It also provides several features such as authentication, rate limiting, and monitoring.

You will use the API Gateway to expose Skills Mapper's API to the internet. The API Gateway will be configured from the OpenAPI 2.0 specification you create.

Global HTTP Load Balancer

In Chapter 11, the API Gateway and the UI will be fronted by a Global HTTP Load Balancer. This is a managed load balancer that is available in all regions. Again, it is a fully managed service. You will be able to provide a custom domain name and generate an SSL certificate to secure the connection.

Figure 9-2 includes a diagram of the solution.

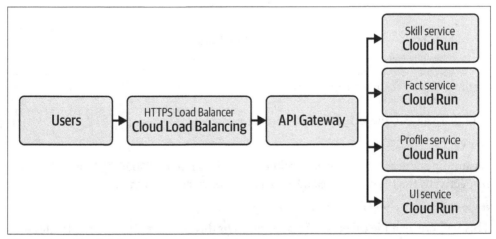

Figure 9-2. Citadel design

Implementation

Once again, let's roll up our sleeves and move onto the implementation.

Hosting the UI on Cloud Run

The user interface for Skills Mapper is built using HTML, the Materialize UI framework (*https://materializecss.com*), and JavaScript. As a result, it is a static website.

You can use Cloud Build to create a container for it and deploy it to Cloud Run. However, there is a little configuration to do first. Since you are using Identity Platform for authentication, you need to configure the UI to use the correct client ID. This is done by creating a file called *config.js* directory.

You need to populate the file with the values of the project ID and the API Key from the Identity Platform configuration.

If you haven't already set the PROJECT_ID environment variable, you can do so now:

```
export PROJECT_ID=$(gcloud config get-value project)
```

Then go to the Identity Platform configuration page (*https://console.cloud.google.com/customer-identity/providers*) (see Figure 9-3) for the project and copy the API Key. Click `Application Setup Details` and copy the value of the `apiKey` field.

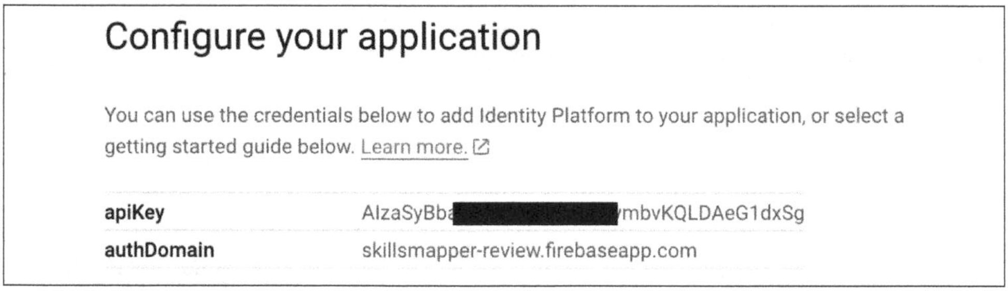

Figure 9-3. Application setup details

Add that value to the API_KEY environment variable:

```
export API_KEY=<API_KEY>
```

Assuming these are stored in environment variables named PROJECT_ID and API_KEY, respectively, the file can be created by using the `envsubst` command:

```
envsubst < config.js.template > src/js/config.js
```

This will create a file called *config.js* in the *src/js* directory, replacing the placeholders in *config.js.template* with environment variables. Check that the generated file has values substituted for the placeholders.

Creating a Dockerfile

The initial step in deploying the UI as a container is creating a Dockerfile. This file serves as a blueprint for Cloud Build to generate a container for the UI. Within the project directory, you'll find the Dockerfile named `Dockerfile`, with the web content located in the *src* directory. The Dockerfile is straightforward as Dockerfiles go and contains the following:

```
FROM nginx                                                    ❶
COPY src /usr/share/nginx/html                                ❷
COPY nginx/default.conf /etc/nginx/conf.d/default.conf  ❸
```

❶ This tells Docker to use the NGINX image as the base image. This is a widely used open source web server.

❷ This copies the contents of the *src* directory into the */usr/share/nginx/html* directory in the container, the directory that NGINX uses to serve static content.

❸ This copies a configuration file *default.conf* file into the */etc/nginx/conf.d* directory in the container.

This is all the configuration that is needed to create a container for the UI.

Creating a container with Cloud Build

In previous chapters, you used Cloud Build to create containers for your backend services. You built the containers directly from Go source code using a buildpack in the background. You built Java containers using Jib via a Maven plugin. In this case, you are building a container from a Dockerfile using Cloud Build. The process is not much different from before; Cloud Build will automatically detect that you have a Dockerfile and use the Docker builder rather than looking for Jib or resorting to buildpacks.

First, create an environment variable for the UI service name (e.g., *ui-service*):

```
export UI_SERVICE_NAME=[UI_SERVICE_NAME]
```

To build a container for the UI, run the following command to submit a build to Cloud Build:

```
gcloud builds submit --tag gcr.io/${PROJECT_ID}/${UI_SERVICE_NAME}
```

This will cause Cloud Build to build the container and push it to the Container Registry in the project, but not deploy it to Cloud Run.

Deploying the UI Container to Cloud Run

As the user interface container does not need any configuration, you do not need to configure any environment variables. It will also run without needing any additional permissions, so you do not need to configure any IAM roles. However, by default, it will use the default service account for the project which has more permissions than is needed. You can create a new service account with the minimum permissions needed and use that instead to follow the security principle of least privilege.

Therefore, create a new service account for the UI with the following command, but do not give it any permissions:

```
gcloud iam service-accounts create ${UI_SERVICE_NAME}-sa \
--display-name "${UI_SERVICE_NAME} service account"
```

You can then deploy the service to Cloud Run using the resulting container and the new service account with this command:

```
gcloud run deploy $UI_SERVICE_NAME \
    --image gcr.io/${PROJECT_ID}/${UI_SERVICE_NAME} \
    --service-account ${UI_SERVICE_NAME}-sa@${PROJECT_ID}.iam.gserviceaccount.com \
    --allow-unauthenticated
```

You can then retrieve the URL of the service with the following command and open it in a browser:

```
open $(gcloud run services describe ${UI_SERVICE_NAME} --format 'value(status.url)')
```

This will open the UI in a browser; however, it will not be able to talk to the API, as the API is not yet deployed. This is one way of hosting the UI, and it may be useful for testing purposes. However, Cloud Run is relatively expensive in this case as you are paying for compute when you don't need to; the website is static.

If you would like to remove the UI service, use the command:

```
gcloud run services delete ${UI_SERVICE_NAME}
```

Hosting the UI in a Cloud Storage Bucket

While you can use Cloud Run to host the UI, there is an easier and cheaper alternative; keeping to cloud native principles, you should always be considering simpler and more cost-effective alternatives when available. You can host the UI in a Cloud Storage bucket.

Creating a Cloud Storage bucket

Now create a new Cloud Storage bucket with the `gsutil` command. As cloud storage buckets must be globally unique, use the globally unique project ID as a prefix for the name:

```
gsutil mb -p ${PROJECT_ID} -c regional -l ${REGION} gs://${PROJECT_ID}-ui
```

The storage class `-c` is `regional` and the `-l` location is the same as the region you are using for the project.

Uploading files to the UI storage bucket

Then upload the static files to the new bucket:

```
gsutil -m cp -r ./src/* gs://${PROJECT_ID}-ui
```

Now grant everyone `objectViewer` (yes, everyone) read permissions to the bucket. This is normally a bit scary, as anyone on the internet will be able to read the files. However, since you are hosting a website that is exactly what you want, so run the following command:

```
gsutil iam ch allUsers:objectViewer gs://${PROJECT_ID}-ui
```

Configuring the bucket as a website

Finally, enable the `Website` feature on the bucket, using `index.html` as the default web page and `404.html` as the error page:

```
gcloud storage buckets update gs://${PROJECT_ID}-ui \
--web-main-page-suffix=index.html --web-error-page=404.html
```

Viewing the website

You will then be able to view the UI at the bucket's URL:

```
open https://storage.googleapis.com/${PROJECT_ID}-ui/index.html
```

When you use a Google Cloud Storage bucket to host a static website, the files are cached by the Cloud Storage network. This is a good thing, as it means the files are served nearer to your users. However, by default, the cache is set to 1 hour. This means that if you make a change to the website, it may take up to an hour for the change to be visible to users, so it is not practical for rapid development. To avoid this, you can set the cache to 0 seconds, which will cause the files to be reloaded from the bucket every time they are requested. This is not recommended for production use but is useful for development. You can set the cache to 0 seconds with the following command:

```
gsutil setmeta -h "Cache-Control:public, max-age=0" \
gs://${PROJECT_ID}-ui/index.html
```

Another option is using the Cloud Run deployment method for development and the Cloud Storage method for production.

How much will this cost?

Cloud Storage offers a highly cost-effective option for hosting static websites because it charges only for storage (which is minimal for static sites) and network egress. Cloud Storage is designed to provide high scalability and availability, making it a great choice for serving high-traffic websites.

If you were to use Cloud Run, you would still be paying for egress costs, but you would also be paying for compute time, which is not needed for a static website.

Although storage costs will be negligible, check the Cloud Storage pricing site (*https://oreil.ly/9DgFU*) for current pricing, especially of data egress, as the files are served to your users.

Configuring the API

A template OpenAPI configuration is in the project directory named *api.yaml.template*. This contains placeholders for project-specific information such as the project ID and the URLs of the Cloud Run services.

First set two environment variables: an API name (e.g., `skillsmapper`) and a domain that you will make the application available at eventually. In my case, I have `skillsmapper.org`:

```
export API_NAME=['API_NAME']
export DOMAIN=['DOMAIN']
```

Then set these environment variables using the following commands:

```
export FACT_SERVICE_URL=$(gcloud run services describe ${FACT_SERVICE_NAME} \
--format 'value(status.url)')
export SKILL_SERVICE_URL=$(gcloud run services describe ${SKILL_SERVICE_NAME} \
--format 'value(status.url)')
export PROFILE_SERVICE_URL=$(gcloud run services describe ${PROFILE_SERVICE_NAME} \
--format 'value(status.url)')
```

To substitute these to generate an *api.yaml* file for deployment using the `envsubst` command, as you did for the UI configuration, the following command is used:

```
envsubst < api.yaml.template > api.yaml
```

If you open the *api.yaml* file, you will see several endpoints and other configurations.

The first is the security definition. This is used to configure the authentication for the API using the Identity Platform you set up in Chapter 7. The configuration is as follows:

```
ssecurityDefinitions:
  firebase:
    authorizationUrl: ""
    flow: "implicit"
    type: "oauth2"
    x-google-issuer: "https://securetoken.google.com/${PROJECT_ID}"
    x-google-jwks_uri:
```

```
"https://www.googleapis.com/service_accounts/v1/metadata/x509/securetoken@system.gserviceaccount.com"
    x-google-audiences: ${PROJECT_ID}
```

The project ID is substituted for the placeholder ${PROJECT_ID} in two places that are used to create the JWT that is used for authentication. The x-google-issuer is the issuer of the JWT and the x-google-audiences is the audience of the JWT. Both of these contain the project ID.

A JWT is created by the Identity Platform and is passed to the API Gateway. The API Gateway will validate the JWT using the x-google-jwks_uri value. In a JWT, you will see them in fields like this:

```
"iss": "https://securetoken.google.com/[PROJECT_ID]",
"aud": "[PROJECT_ID]"
```

This is to ensure that the JWT has been issued by the correct project (the iss value in the JWT) and is the intended audience (the aud value in the JWT) is the same project.

The other Google Cloud–specific configuration in the *api.yaml* file is the x-google-backend configuration. This is used to configure the Cloud Run services that the API Gateway will proxy requests to. For example, the x-google-backend configuration for the GET /skills/autocomplete endpoint is as follows:

```
/skills/autocomplete:
  get:
    summary: Autocomplete skills
    operationId: skillsAutocomplete
    description: Returns a list of skill suggestions based on the provided prefix
    x-google-backend:
      address: ${SKILL_SERVICE_URL}/autocomplete
```

For endpoints that take parameters in the path, you need to use the path_transla tion: APPEND_PATH_TO_ADDRESS option. For example, the GET /api/facts/{id} endpoint is configured as follows:

```
/api/facts/{id}:
  get:
...
      x-google-backend:
        address: https://fact-service-<instanceid>.a.run.app
        path_translation: APPEND_PATH_TO_ADDRESS
        jwt_audience: https://fact-service-<instanceid>.a.run.app
```

By default, the API Gateway will pass the {id} parameter as a query parameter, and the service will not know how to deal with it, so you need to use the path_transla tion option to ensure the parameter is passed in the path. With this in place, the underlying Cloud Run service will receive the request at the URL https://fact-service-<instanceid>.a.run.app/api/facts/{id} with the {id} parameter in the path, as expected.

When authenticating with the Cloud Run alone, the JWT of the authenticated user is passed in the Authorization header. When using the API Gateway, the Authorization header contains a JWT for the service account the API Gateway uses.

This is because the API Gateway is not able to validate the JWT of the user, as it does not have the public key to validate the JWT. The API Gateway will validate the JWT of the service account and then pass the JWT of the user in the x-forwarded-authorization header to the Cloud Run service. In the services previously created, the code checks both the Authorization and x-forwarded-authorization headers for the JWT of the user.

With the API configuration complete, you can deploy it to the API Gateway.

Deploying the API to API Gateway

To deploy the API to the API Gateway, you first need to enable the API Gateway API and service control in the project. Service Control is used to control the rate of requests to the API Gateway. You can enable these with the following commands:

```
gcloud services enable apigateway.googleapis.com
gcloud services enable servicecontrol.googleapis.com
```

Now an environment variable for the API Gateway file name:

```
export API_SPEC_FILE=api.yaml
```

At the moment, Cloud Run services can be called directly from the internet, but as previously discussed, this is not good for security. It is much better if calling them can only be done from the API Gateway. To do this, you need to create a service account for the API Gateway:

```
gcloud iam service-accounts create "${API_NAME}-gateway-sa" \
    --display-name "Service account to invoke ${API_NAME} services"
```

Then give the service account permission to invoke each of the Cloud Run services in turn with the following commands.

For the fact service:

```
gcloud run services add-iam-policy-binding $FACT_SERVICE_NAME \
    --role roles/run.invoker \
    --member "serviceAccount:${API_NAME}-gateway-sa@${PROJECT_ID}.iam.gserviceaccount.com"
```

For the skill service:

```
gcloud run services add-iam-policy-binding $SKILL_SERVICE_NAME \
    --role roles/run.invoker \
    --member "serviceAccount:${API_NAME}-gateway-sa@${PROJECT_ID}.iam.gserviceaccount.com"
```

For the profile service:

```
gcloud run services add-iam-policy-binding $PROFILE_SERVICE_NAME \
    --role roles/run.invoker \
    --member "serviceAccount:${API_NAME}-gateway-sa@${PROJECT_ID}.iam.gserviceaccount.com"
```

With the configuration and service account created, you can now create an API Gateway configuration using the following command:

```
gcloud api-gateway api-configs create ${API_NAME}-config \
    --api=${API_NAME} \
    --openapi-spec=${API_SPEC_FILE} \
    --project=${PROJECT_ID} \
    --backend-auth-service-account=${API_NAME}-gateway-sa@${PROJECT_ID}.iam.gserviceaccount.com
```

This uses the API configuration file you generated earlier to create the API Gateway configuration.

You can now create the API Gateway service using the following command:

```
gcloud api-gateway gateways create ${API_NAME}-gateway \
    --api=${API_NAME} \
    --api-config=${API_NAME}-config \
    --location=${REGION} \
    --project=${PROJECT_ID}
```

With the API Gateway service created, you can then access the services via the API Gateway. Retrieve the URL of the API Gateway with the following command:

```
export GATEWAY_URL=$(gcloud api-gateway gateways describe skillsmapper-gateway \
    --location=${REGION} \
    --project=${PROJECT_ID} \
    --format 'value(defaultHostname)')
```

With the API Gateway set up with its own URL, you are now ready for testing.

Testing the API Gateway

Testing the gateway is as simple as making a request to the gateway URL in preference to the Cloud Run service URL. For example, to test the GET /skills/autocomplete endpoint, you could use the following command to call Cloud Run directly:

```
curl -X GET "${SKILL_SERVICE_URL}/autocomplete?prefix=java"
```

In the same way, you can now test the API Gateway by calling the same endpoint using the API Gateway URL:

```
curl -X GET "https://${GATEWAY_URL}/api/skills/autocomplete?prefix=java"
```

You should see the same response from both calls.

Disabling Unauthenticated Access to Cloud Run Services

With the API Gateway working, you can now remove unauthenticated access to the Cloud Run services by revoking the roles/run.invoker role from allUsers from the Cloud Run service.

When you list Cloud Run services with gcloud, it does not show if the service allows unauthenticated access, by default. In the example, code is a small script name check-services-unauthenticated.sh that will check that for you:

```
#!/bin/bash
SERVICES=$(gcloud run services list --platform managed --project $PROJECT_ID \
    --region $REGION --format 'value(metadata.name)')

for SERVICE in $SERVICES
do
  echo "Checking service $SERVICE..."
  POLICY=$(gcloud run services get-iam-policy $SERVICE --platform managed \
    --project $PROJECT_ID --region $REGION)
  if echo "$POLICY" | grep -q "allUsers"; then
    echo "$SERVICE is publicly accessible"
  else
    echo "$SERVICE is not publicly accessible"
  fi
done
```

For each service, the script uses gcloud to check the policy applied. You should see currently that all three services are publicly accessible:

```
Checking service fact-service...
fact-service is publicly accessible
Checking service profile-service...
profile-service is publicly accessible
Checking service skill-service...
skill-service is publicly accessible
```

This is a great reason for using the gcloud command-line tool, as it makes it easy to script things like this.

To revoke the roles/run.invoker role from allUsers for the skill service, you can use the following command:

```
gcloud run services remove-iam-policy-binding $SKILL_SERVICE_NAME \
    --role roles/run.invoker \
    --member "allUsers"
```

And similarly for the other services:

```
gcloud run services remove-iam-policy-binding $FACT_SERVICE_NAME \
    --role roles/run.invoker \
    --member "allUsers"

gcloud run services remove-iam-policy-binding $PROFILE_SERVICE_NAME \
    --role roles/run.invoker \
    --member "allUsers"
```

Run the check-services-unauthenticated.sh script again, and you should see that the services are no longer publicly accessible:

```
Checking service fact-service...
fact-service is not publicly accessible
```

```
Checking service profile-service...
profile-service is not publicly accessible
Checking service skill-service...
skill-service is not publicly accessible
```

Now, when you try to call the Cloud Run service directly, you will get a 403 Forbidden error as you no longer have permission to call the service anonymously:

```
curl -X GET "${SKILL_SERVICE_URL}/autocomplete?prefix=java"
```

However, you can still call the Cloud Run service via the API Gateway:

```
curl -X GET "https://${GATEWAY_URL}/api/skills/autocomplete?prefix=java"
```

This is because the API Gateway has the `roles/run.invoker` role to call the Cloud Run service on your behalf. This will also be the case for the other services you added to the API Gateway.

Summary

You've successfully configured and exposed your Cloud Run services in a secure manner via an API Gateway. Furthermore, you've leveraged Cloud Storage to host the user interface.

For this project, you used the following services directly:

- OpenAPI is used to design and define the structure of the API, setting clear standards for its behavior.
- Cloud Run is used to host the UI in an NGINX container.
- Cloud Build is used to build the backend services for the UI via a Dockerfile, although you did not use it directly.
- Cloud Storage is used to host the static website content.
- API Gateway allowed you to expose the API to the internet securely and efficiently, enabling robust access to the backend services.

Coming Next

Now that all components of the Skills Mapper application are deployed, Part III introduces you to the key facilities. These include the laboratory, citadel, factory, and observatory. These facilities are vital for making an application like this manageable and operational.

In Chapter 11, you'll discover how both the API and UI from this chapter can be fronted by a Global HTTP Load Balancer. This strategy will provide a unified, secure URL for accessing your application, thus enhancing its accessibility and usability.

You'll also go on to explore how to address the inherent complexity of the system by automating the deployment process further. In addition, you will delve into ways to enhance observability, ensuring that you have clear insight into your application's performance. Finally, I'll discuss how to make your system production-ready, focusing on stability, performance, and security. Get ready for making your application robust, resilient, and production-worthy.

PART III

The Facilities

In this part, you'll discover how to streamline your development and operations processes using Google Cloud services.

CHAPTER 10

Laboratory

The cornerstone of effective, scalable, cloud native development is establishing a personal *laboratory*, which is the focus of this chapter. This space serves as a secure playground for innovation. Your laboratory is your development environment, typically a local workstation or laptop, where you have the freedom to experiment, iterate, and rapidly observe the results. You may do this yourself, or if you are using pair programming, with a partner.

Given that your laboratory explorations will mainly involve coding, the quality of your developer experience (DX) can make a big difference. It plays a crucial role in streamlining work and driving productivity.

The primary objective of the laboratory in cloud native development is to produce a recipe for generating a containerized microservice. This recipe should be designed so that it can be seamlessly transitioned to the *factory*, preparing it for real-world, production deployment.

The secret to individual productivity and effective local development lies in optimizing *inner loop agility*. This term refers to the time taken between writing code and validating the results. The key is to minimize this duration as much as possible, allowing for rapid testing, feedback, and improvements. By enhancing your inner loop agility, you can quickly iterate and evolve your code, ultimately accelerating the pace of your cloud native development.

> The code for this chapter is in the `laboratory` folder of the GitHub repository (*https://oreil.ly/WUMt2*).

The Inner Loop

The software development process can be visualized as two distinct loops, both pivoting around the central act of *pushing* updates to source control.

The right diagram in Figure 10-1 represents the *outer loop*, which is initiated once the revised code is pushed to the source control system. This phase incorporates the integration of new code and its testing against the preexisting code base. I cover this in Chapter 12.

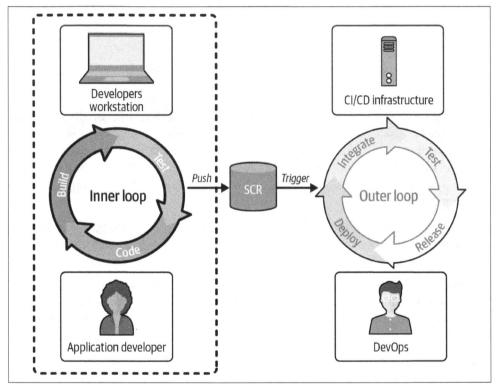

Figure 10-1. Inner loop

The *inner stage* is your day-to-day work. It consists of three steps: write code, build it to a testable state, and run the tests. The starting point might change if you're using test-driven development (TDD).

You write code, build it to a state where it can be tested, execute the test, and then repeat the test. Of course, in TDD, the starting point is a failing test rather than code, but the loop is the same either way.

You will likely go through these micro feedback loops hundreds of times daily as a developer. The shorter the loop, the more productive you will be. The better your tests are, the earlier you can run them and the earlier you find bugs. However, your tests must run fast, so your feedback loop remains short.

Let's see how Google Cloud helps us build a short inner loop that forms the laboratory's core.

 I find it liberating if my inner loop runs efficiently on a modest laptop. This means I can be productive wherever I am without worrying about my battery life. It is also great for that all-important carbon usage.

Containers in the Inner Loop

One of the foundations of cloud native is packaging code as containers. If you are used to developing in noncontainerized environments, you may already have a fast feedback loop. In noncompiled languages like Python or Node.js, getting feedback is a case of making a change and running the code. One of the strengths of Go, for example, is that even though it is a compiled language, it is fast to compile and run. When using Java with Spring Boot, it is also possible to have a rapid code, build, and testing of the local loop, especially when using Spring's developer tools.

So why slow everything down by adding the complication of containers to the inner loop? Isn't this colossal overhead? Whereas before you could just run the code, now you have to build a container, push it to a repository, and redeploy it after each code change. I have seen Java developers horrified when they are presented with Kubernetes and have their productivity destroyed as their inner loop goes from a few seconds to minutes due to all the extra steps that containers add.

There is an excellent reason to develop using containers, though; it eliminates the "it runs on my machine" issue. This is also the goal of the dev/prod parity principle of the 12-factor applications. A container is immutable; if it runs in one place, it will run everywhere. This is a valuable benefit because, as I said earlier, the sooner you can find an issue, the simpler it is to resolve. Fortunately, tools can automate and streamline the process, so the container overhead becomes insignificant.

To illustrate, let's take a Spring Boot development inner loop as an example (see Figure 10-2). Before containers, you would have had three steps: code, build, and test.

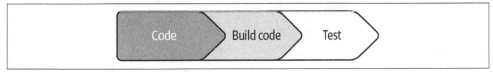

Figure 10-2. Spring Boot: code, build, test

Add containers, and you have to build a container image, tag the image, push the image to a container registry, patch the deployment to use the new container image, and redeploy with the new image before being able to test (Figure 10-3).

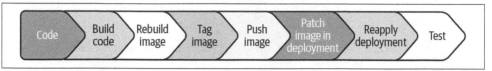

Figure 10-3. Spring Boot with Docker and Kubernetes

This is where Google provides tools to automate the extra steps and eliminate the overhead (Figure 10-4). The first is Skaffold; this tool automates most of these additional steps. The second is a tool needed for simplifying and automating building the container itself. For Spring Boot, Jib is a good choice, but I will cover more options later.

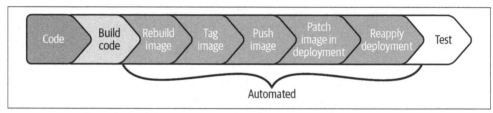

Figure 10-4. Jib and Skaffold providing automation

Tools like these form the basis of a laboratory as they allow cloud native developers to automate away the overhead of working with containers. Let's explore some more Google Cloud tools that fit together to support you.

Inside the Laboratory

A laboratory should provide everything needed to execute the inner loop automatically, from making a change in code to testing and getting feedback. You then break out of the loop by pushing changes into source control to be picked up by the factory's build and testing processes.

The laboratory needs the following:

- An IDE in which to write the code
- A way of building a container
- A place to store built containers
- A way of testing containerized microservices
- A way of testing dependent services

Choosing an IDE

When building a laboratory with Google Cloud, you don't need to give up the integrated development environment (IDE) you are familiar with—quite the opposite. Google offers extra open source tools to enhance your IDE and options for where your IDE runs.

Cloud Code

Cloud Code (*https://oreil.ly/bU3GP*) is a set of plugins for popular IDEs that makes it easier to develop applications for Google Cloud. It is a great building block for your laboratory and for getting that fast feedback during local development.

Cloud Code provides and manages Google Cloud SDK, Skaffold, Minikube, and kubectl. It also gives tools that help provide a smooth path from the laboratory to the factory and then help with debugging deployed applications.

Desktop IDE with Cloud Code

Cloud Code provides a plugin for many desktop IDEs:

- VSCode (*https://oreil.ly/THhba*)
- IntelliJ (*https://oreil.ly/3F0Rh*)
- PyCharm (*https://oreil.ly/t2G7M*)
- GoLand (*https://oreil.ly/XH7lf*)
- WebStorm (*https://oreil.ly/bZmqD*)
- Eclipse (*https://oreil.ly/22TzQ*)

Cloud Shell Editor

Cloud Code is also a Web IDE running entirely in a browser. The Cloud Shell Editor (*https://oreil.ly/sKXXA*) is based on Eclipse Theia (*https://oreil.ly/vZJcB*) with a user interface based on VSCode.

It is available anywhere you have a browser through the Google Cloud console. Although it is possible to use this as your primary IDE, I find it most handy for making quick changes.

Cloud Workstations

The newest option at the time of writing is Cloud Workstations (*https://oreil.ly/oWUw6*), and for me, this is the best of both worlds: a thin client application that behaves like a desktop IDE, but the backend runs in Google Cloud on a virtual machine. This means you can have anything from a modest to a mighty machine backing your IDE on Google Cloud and still use it as if it were a desktop IDE.

However, the real benefit of both the Cloud Shell Editor and Cloud Workstations is that you are working on Google Cloud and using the Cloud's ultrafast network. Operations that may be slow when working with a desktop IDE, like uploading a container to a container registry or accessing a Google Cloud service, are superfast, making for a great developer experience with a fast inner loop.

 In commercial environments, code exfiltration is a concern. This is where developers with source code on their laptops can accidentally or maliciously share it with someone they shouldn't. If this code is the company's IP from which they make their money, this can be a big problem. Using Cloud Shell Editor or Cloud Workstations rather than a traditional IDE means source code never leaves Google Cloud, removing that risk and reducing the headache of controlling source code.

Comparison of Cloud Code–Enabled IDEs

Table 10-1 summarized the difference between the IDE options.

Table 10-1. A Comparison of Cloud Code–enabled IDEs

IDE	Cost	Offline	Speed	Developer experience	Security
Desktop IDE	Low	Yes	Low	High	Low
Cloud Shell Editor	Low	No	High	Medium	High
Cloud Workstations	Medium	No	High	High	High

Skaffold

At the center of Cloud Code is Skaffold (*https://skaffold.dev*), a Google open source project that automates your inner loop, building, pushing, and deploying your containerized application. Skaffold aims to tighten and highly optimize your inner loop, giving you instant feedback while developing. It is a flexible tool for building a laboratory.

When configured and run, Skaffold takes the source code from your project, automatically builds the code, and packages the artifacts into a container using a mechanism of your choice. It then tags the container and makes it available for deployment. For a remote Kubernetes cluster, for example, this means automatically pushing the container to a remote repository. Skaffold then automates the task of redeploying the new container to the runtime, Kubernetes or otherwise.

Efficiently Building Containers

The most significant bottleneck in an inner loop with containers is building the container itself. Fortunately, Skaffold supports several options.

Using a Dockerfile

The most common way of building a container is to write a Dockerfile and use a Docker daemon on your local machine to create the container image. The problem with this is that adding this containerization step may add minutes to your inner loop, making it a disaster for productivity. The only time you used this in previous chapters was in Chapter 9 when you built a container for the UI. You want to keep the loop to seconds. Fortunately, there are other options available to streamline and automate the process.

Jib

If you are building applications in Java, Jib (*https://oreil.ly/s1vla*) is a Google open source project that lets you build OCI-compliant containers using a Maven or Gradle (*https://gradle.org*) plugin. You used this for the fact service in Chapter 7.

Jib does not require Docker to be installed and doesn't need a Dockerfile. By default, Jib uses an OpenJDK base container image containing a Java runtime, although you can specify any base container you like. Jib then adds layers containing your application, much like adding the filling to a sandwich. It also automates the step of pushing the new image to a repository.

When building a Java container using a Dockerfile, dependencies are downloaded and the entire application is rebuilt as one layer. The great thing about Jib is that it creates multiple layers for the application in the container. Jib is then smart enough to know which dependencies or classes have changed and swaps in a thin layer with the changes, leaving the rest of the container image as before. This means building containers is fast, and containers are not rebuilt unnecessarily.

Ko

Ko (*https://oreil.ly/UpZAu*) is a similar project for Go developers. Like Jib, Ko is a fast container builder. It is great if your application is a single Go executable without dependencies required in the base image. By default, Ko uses the minimal distroless (*https://oreil.ly/n1Yf0*) base image, although, like Jib, this can be changed. Again, it does not require Docker to be installed on your machine and supports multiplatform builds. You have not used Ko yet in this book, preferring to use buildpacks for the Go services; however, Ko is much faster than buildpacks.

Buildpacks

Cloud Native Buildpacks (*https://buildpacks.io*) are an evolution of the buildpacks technology that made developer-centric platforms like Heroku and Cloud Foundry so popular. By default, buildpacks allow you to supply your code and then "automagically" inspect it to identify a builder image that knows how to build the application. For example, a `pom.xml` may cause a Maven buildpack to be used. The resultant application is then packaged into a run image.

Buildpacks are another excellent option for speeding up your inner loop. The disadvantage of buildpacks is that they require a local Docker daemon and tend to be considerably slower to rebuild than a solution like Jib or Ko. However, they are smart enough to use caching of dependencies to avoid the complete rebuilds you would have when using a Dockerfile. The big advantage of buildpacks is that you just need to provide the code and they do the rest; you don't need to touch a Dockerfile, and buildpacks support a wide range of languages.

Comparison of Container Build Tools

Table 10-2 summarizes the difference between the container build tool options.

Table 10-2. A Comparison of container build tools

Tool	Language support	Requires Docker	Incremental build	Build from source code	Time to build
Dockerfile	All	Yes	No	No	High
Jib	Java	No	No	No	Low
Ko	Go	No	Yes	No	Low
Buildpacks	All	Yes	Yes	Yes	Medium

Deploy to a Development Container Runtime

Once the container is built and is available in a container registry, it can be redeployed to the container runtime for testing and verification. I will discuss the pros and cons of using the different container runtimes that Google Cloud uses in later chapters, but in the context of what is best for your inner loop, here are options that Skaffold supports.

Local Kubernetes

By default, Cloud Code comes with Minikube (*https://oreil.ly/a1dk4*), a local Kubernetes cluster. This is the easiest and quickest container runtime to deploy and test your containers. It is also used as an emulator for Cloud Run.

Alternatives for local Kubernetes include Kind (*https://oreil.ly/RNNe8*), k3d (*https://oreil.ly/Puken*), and Docker Desktop (*https://oreil.ly/MfG14*).

Using a local Kubernetes is great if you have poor internet access or work offline, as you don't need to wait for your container image to be uploaded to a remote repository. It is also likely the cheapest option. I like working on a modest laptop, and running local Kubernetes uses a lot of resources and battery, which is a downside.

Minikube is also included with the Cloud Console Editor and Cloud Workstations.

Shared GKE

If you work in a team, you could have access to a shared Google Kubernetes Engine (GKE) cluster (*https://oreil.ly/VaI0Z*). This could be centrally managed and shared by giving each developer their namespace to deploy to. While this may make sense for a team, it is likely not the best option for an individual developer as, most of the time, it will be idle but costing you money.

> Don't use GKE; use GKE Autopilot or Cloud Run, especially for development workloads.

GKE Autopilot

GKE Autopilot (*https://oreil.ly/4h8dV*) is an operating mode of GKE where Google manages the cluster. The significant advantage of this over normal GKE is that you only pay for the CPU, memory, and storage used when running on GKE Autopilot. For development, you only pay when your container runs, which will likely be a considerable saving to running a standard GKE cluster with idle capacity. You will get a chance to try GKE Autopilot in Chapter 14.

Cloud Run

The final option is Cloud Run (*https://oreil.ly/Msman*). This is an easier way of running a container than using Kubernetes. In Google Cloud, Cloud Run is a managed service built on Borg. However, in Google's on-prem Anthos offering, Cloud Run runs on Kubernetes. Cloud Run should be suitable for running nearly all containerized microservices and pay-per-use services, just like GKE Autopilot. Out of all the Google-hosted services, it is likely the most accessible and cheapest option for testing your container in development. You have already used Cloud Run a lot in this book, and hopefully, you understand its flexibility and why it is worth considering for most services.

Comparison of Development Container Runtimes

Table 10-3 summarizes the difference between the container runtime options.

Table 10-3. A comparison of development container runtimes

Runtime	Cost	Local overhead	Speed to redeploy
Local Kubernetes	Low	Yes	High
Shared GKE	High	No	Medium
GKE Autopilot	Medium	No	Medium
Cloud Run	Medium	No	Medium

Choosing a Container Repository

If you are working with a local Kubernetes cluster like Minikube, there is no need to push your container to a registry, as it is available on your machine after building. However, if you are using a separate GKE cluster, GKE Autopilot, or Cloud Run, you will need to push it to a container registry. As you are in Google Cloud, it makes sense to use the provided Artifact Registry, but there are other options.

Artifact Registry or Container Registry?

In Google Cloud, Artifact Registry is currently the recommended service for container image storage. You may see references to Container Registry, which is Artifact Registry's predecessor. There is no real reason to use Container Registry, as Artifact Registry has all the features of Container Registry, with extra features such as being able to store other types of artifacts and supporting both regional and multiregional hosts.

External Registry

You could alternatively use an external container registry such as docker.io (*https://docker.io*); however, this will require extra configuration for authentication. It will also be slower both for pushing containers and pulling containers for deployment, so it is one of those things where it only makes sense to use an external registry if you have a good reason.

Choosing an Integration Testing Method

When testing locally, your application is likely to make use of services like databases or messaging. In later chapters, as these services are introduced, I will explain the options for using or emulating them in your local loop. However, here are the high-level options.

Actual Service Instance

Using a real service for integration testing keeps to the 12-factor principle of dev/prod parity. Many services have the option to run at minimal capacity for testing. If you are working locally, there is the issue of network lag; however, if you are using one of the in-cloud options (Cloud Shell Editor or Cloud Workstations), this can work very well.

Local Emulator

Sometimes, it just may not be cost-effective or possible to use a genuine service for integration testing. An example is the Cloud Spanner database, which used to have a high minimal cost deployment, although the introduction of fractional deployments has mitigated this. However, another is not having an internet connection. For example, suppose you are developing on an airplane or on a cruise ship (as I did once). In this case, a local emulator is a good option.

Here are some examples of emulators of Google services used in this book:

Cloud Pub/Sub
 The Pub/Sub emulator (*https://oreil.ly/606j3*) provides an in-memory implementation of the API for local testing purposes.

Cloud Firestore
 The Firestore emulator (*https://oreil.ly/K3hs0*) is part of the Firebase Local Emulator Suite, which lets you run Firestore, Realtime Database, Firebase Authentication, Cloud Functions, and Cloud Pub/Sub locally.

Cloud Spanner
 The Cloud Spanner emulator (*https://oreil.ly/0AiFc*) provides a local, in-memory environment for development and testing.

Cloud Storage
 While not an emulator in the traditional sense, the *gsutil* tool can interact with the local file system in a way that emulates interaction with the Cloud Storage API.

Note that local emulators may not offer complete functionality or may behave differently than the actual services in some cases. Therefore, it's crucial to test your application in the actual Google Cloud environment before deploying it to production.

Local Container

In scenarios where official emulators are unavailable or access to the actual service is restricted, leveraging local containers can provide a robust alternative. One of the projects that facilitate this is the Testcontainers project (*https://oreil.ly/HePis*).

Testcontainers is a highly regarded Java library specifically designed for facilitating the use of Docker containers within automated testing environments. Its central purpose is to allow you to emulate various services in isolated, short-lived containers, ensuring your tests run against a fresh instance of the service every time. This attribute makes it an effective tool for improving the reproducibility and reliability of your automated testing pipeline.

The library is known for its extensive coverage, providing disposable containers for a broad range of services such as databases, web browsers (with Selenium), message queues, and more. It enables developers to execute integration tests against a wide variety of systems without needing to install them locally or on a shared test server.

In addition to its existing functionalities, Testcontainers has an active community contributing to its continuous improvement and expansion. New disposable containers mimicking different services are frequently added, further widening the spectrum of test scenarios it supports.

However, while local containers and emulators like those from Testcontainers can offer substantial benefits for local development and testing, they may not perfectly mirror the behavior of live services. Therefore, it's always important to run final validation tests on the actual production-like services whenever possible, ensuring that your application behaves as expected under real-world conditions.

Comparison of Service Integration Testing

Table 10-4 summarizes the difference between the integration testing options.

Table 10-4. A aomparison of service integration testing

Service	Cost	Local overhead	Realism
Actual service	Medium	Low	High
Local emulator	Low	Medium	Medium
Local container	Low	Medium	Medium
Mock service	Low	Low	Low

Building an Example Laboratory

Let's show how all this fits together with a simple example.

In this case, you'll use Cloud Code through the Cloud Shell Editor and use the provided Minikube for inner loop testing.

Because Cloud Code and Cloud Shell come with a local Minikube, you can work effectively locally. However, if you want to use a local IDE, you can use Cloud Workstations.

There is no charge for using the Cloud Shell Editor. It is essentially a free virtual machine with 5 GB of free persistent disk, so the state is stored between sessions.

It also provides a 2 vCPU, 4 GB RAM Minikube cluster included with the Cloud Shell instance, making this a zero-cost way of working with Kubernetes.

Start the Cloud Shell Editor

In your web browser, open Google Cloud console (*https://oreil.ly/2E3cx*), as shown in Figure 10-5. In the top right of the Console, click the Active Cloud Shell button to open Cloud Shell.

Figure 10-5. Activate Cloud Shell button

When Cloud Shell opens, click the Open Editor button to open the Cloud Shell Editor, as shown in Figure 10-6.

Figure 10-6. Open Editor button

Clone the Code

In the Cloud Shell Editor terminal, clone the Skills Mapper project using this git command:

```
git clone https://github.com/SkillsMapper/skillsmapper
```

Now in the Cloud Shell Editor, navigate to and open the cloned project; then go to the `fact-service` directory.

Enable Jib

You may remember this is a Java project that already uses *Jib* to build a container.

In the project, open the *pom.xml* and notice the Jib plugin in the `plugin` section:

```
<plugin>
    <groupId>com.google.cloud.tools</groupId>
    <artifactId>jib-maven-plugin</artifactId>
```

```
    <version>3.3.1</version>
</plugin>
```

Init Skaffold

To initialize Skaffold, enter this command in Cloud Shell:

```
skaffold init --generate-manifests
```

Skaffold attempts to detect how your container can be built. As the `pom.xml` has the Jib plugin included, `Jib Maven Plugin` will be shown as an option.

Select (`Jib Maven Plugin (org.skillsmapper:fact-service, pom.xml)`).

When you see the prompt `Select port to forward for pom-xml-image (leave blank for none)`, enter 8080. This will forward port 8080 of your local machine onto the Kubernetes service in the Minikube cluster, allowing you to connect.

The `--generate-manifests` argument causes Skaffold to generate Kubernetes manifests to use for deployment. As you do not have any at present, when prompted with `Do you want to write this configuration, along with the generated k8s manifests, to skaffold.yaml?`, enter y.

While the generated manifests are not ideal, especially as it generates default container names and labels to `pom-xml-image`, they are a good starting point.

In the Skills Mapper project, there is a modified *skaffold.yaml* file and a *deployment.yaml* for the fact service in the k8s directory:

```
apiVersion: skaffold/v4beta5
kind: Config
metadata:
  name: fact-service
build:
  artifacts:
    - image: fact-service
      jib:
        project: org.skillsmapper:fact-service
manifests:
  rawYaml:
    - k8s/deployment.yaml
```

In the build section, you have specified the `fact-service` image and the Maven project to build using Jib. The manifests section specifies the Kubernetes deployment to use to deploy to the local Minikube cluster.

Repeat for the Skill and Profile Services

The skill service and profile service are written in Go as opposed to Java but will behave in the same way in Skaffold.

Change to the `skill-service` directory and then again run:

```
skaffold init --generate-manifests
```

This time Skaffold will use buildpacks and generate a *skaffold.yaml* file similar to this:

```
apiVersion: skaffold/v4beta5
kind: Config
metadata:
  name: skill-service
build:
  artifacts:
    - image: skill-service
      buildpacks:
        builder: gcr.io/buildpacks/builder:v1
manifests:
  rawYaml:
    - k8s/deployment.yaml
```

However, the buildpack may take minutes to build, and that is not great for the inner loop, where speed is important. Instead, you can use the Go equivalent of Jib to get build times down to a couple seconds. In the project, there is a *skaffold.yaml* file that uses Ko to build the container:

```
apiVersion: skaffold/v4beta5
kind: Config
metadata:
  name: skill-service
build:
  artifacts:
    - image: skill-service
      ko:
        baseImage: gcr.io/distroless/static:nonroot
        importPath: github.com/SkillsMapper/skillsmapper/skill-service
manifests:
  rawYaml:
    - k8s/deployment.yaml
```

The skill service also requires environment variables to be set. For this, use a Kubernetes ConfigMap. In the *skill-service/k8s* directory, there is a *configmap.yaml.template* file that defines the ConfigMap. Run the following command to create the ConfigMap:

```
envsubst < k8s/configmap.yaml.template > k8s/configmap.yaml
```

The profile service follows the same pattern as the skill service. Repeat the steps in the `profile-service` directory to set up Skaffold and create the ConfigMap.

Start Minikube

You can now start the provided Minikube cluster by entering this command in Cloud Shell:

```
minikube start
```

Check that Minikube is running but connecting to it through the Kubernetes kubectl client:

```
kubectl get nodes
```

If everything is working correctly, you should see a response like this showing your single-node Kubernetes cluster is running:

```
NAME      STATUS  ROLES         AGE   VERSION
minikube  Ready   control-plane 44m   v1.26.3
```

Create a Secret for Service Account Keys

The skill service requires a Google Cloud service account key to access the Google Cloud Storage bucket.

You can retrieve a key for the skill service service account using the following command:

```
gcloud iam service-accounts keys create ${SKILL_SERVICE_SA}.json \
--iam-account ${SKILL_SERVICE_SA}@${PROJECT_ID}.iam.gserviceaccount.com
```

Then create a Kubernetes secret on the Minikube cluster containing the key using the following command:

```
kubectl create secret generic ${SKILL_SERVICE_SA}-key \
--from-file=${SKILL_SERVICE_SA}.json=${SKILL_SERVICE_SA}.json
```

When the service is created, the key will be mounted into the container at `/var/secrets/google/${SKILL_SERVICE_SA}.json` for the service to use.

To configure the profile and fact service, follow the same steps but using the `PROFILE_SERVICE_SA` and `FACT_SERVICE_SA` environment variable, respectively, in the place of `SKILL_SERVICE_SA`.

While you could configure the fact service in the same way, it has a default Spring Profile that does not use Google Cloud services, so it can be run without a service account. In a way, this is a good thing, as it means you can run the application locally without needing to connect to Google Cloud.

Build a Container with Skaffold

This is an example of the skill service, but the same applies to both the fact and profiles services as well.

In the `skills-service` directory, use Skaffold to build a container:

```
skaffold build
```

As this is the first time to build, it will take a few seconds.

Run Skaffold

There are now two options to deploy with Skaffold. To build and deploy the application once, use the command:

```
skaffold run --port-forward
```

When this command completes successfully, you will find your application running in your Minikube Kubernetes cluster. To check, use the command:

```
kubectl get pods
```

You should see your pod running like this:

```
NAME                          READY   STATUS    RESTARTS   AGE
skill-service-8f766466c-28589   1/1   Running   0          8s
```

In Kubernetes, a service is used to expose an application running in a pod outside the cluster. Skaffold would have also created a service. You can check this using:

```
kubectl get service
```

This will show the service running on port 8080:

```
NAME            TYPE        CLUSTER-IP   EXTERNAL-IP   PORT(S)    AGE
skill-service   ClusterIP   None         <none>        8080/TCP   16h
```

In this case, you have used the `--port-forward` flag to forward the local port 8080 to port 8080 on the Kubernetes cluster. This means that the skill service will be available at *http://localhost:8080*.

Open a second tab and enter:

```
curl -X GET "http://localhost:8080/autocomplete?prefix=java"
```

You should see the response:

```
{"results":["java","java-10","java-11","java-12","java-13",
"java-14","java-15","java-16","java-17","java-18"]}
```

You can also launch this in the browser in Cloud Shell by clicking the Web Preview button and then preview on port 8080.

Alternatively, if you would like the application to be deployed automatically every time you make a change, use the command:

```
skaffold dev
```

By doing this, Skaffold will monitor the source files for any changes. When detected, it will automatically rebuild and redeploy a new container. For Java applications, this may take a few seconds, so it is likely you will not want a deployment every time you make a change. However, knowing that, redeployment with `skaffold run` means that feedback is almost as fast as starting Spring Boot directly.

For Go applications like the skill service, the build time is so fast that you can use `skaffold dev` to get a great inner loop experience.

Another option is running the Skaffold debug command:

```
skaffold debug
```

This command starts the application in debug mode, so any breakpoints in the code will activate just as if the application was running in debug mode outside the Kubernetes cluster.

Summary

Choosing how to build a laboratory does depend on your needs, but the options are there to build a great developer experience by optimizing your inner loop.

Here are your variables:

- Which IDE option to use and where to run it
- How to build your containers
- Which container runtime to use to run your container
- How to test your application with dependent services

In Chapter 11, you will be creating the citadel to further protect the API and UI you deployed in Chapter 9.

Citadel

While the **API Gateway** is useful for providing a single entry point to your services, it is vulnerable to attack. In this chapter, you will learn how to secure the system from attackers using an HTTP(S) Load Balancer with an SSL/TLS certificate and Cloud Armor. Effectively, you will be building the wall (or more accurately, firewall) of the *citadel* to protect the application inside.

The code for this chapter is in the `citadel` folder of the GitHub repository (*https://oreil.ly/wrpIE*).

Securing from Attackers

In Chapter 9, you put services behind an API Gateway. In this chapter, you are going to protect them further.

Adding a Custom Domain

The Google API Gateway exposes a single URL to access the services behind the API. This is an HTTPS endpoint offering a secure connection. Similarly, putting the UI in a Cloud Storage bucket and exposing it as a website has provided a secure URL. However, it is more useful to put the API and the UI behind the same custom domain name. It is also useful to protect the API Gateway and UI behind a Global Load Balancer and provide your custom HTTPS URL with a valid SSL certificate. As part of Google's global networking infrastructure, a Global Load Balancer also provides additional benefits such as high availability and scalability, optional caching via a global content delivery network (CDN), and protection against distributed denial-of-service (DDoS) attacks.

Setting up a Global Load Balancer has many steps, and you will work through them in this chapter.

There are many resources created in the chapter that need a name. Create an environment variable with a prefix (e.g., `skillsmapper`) to help keep names consistent:

```
export PREFIX=skillsmapper
```

Reserving a Static IP Address

First, you need to reserve a static IP address for the Global Load Balancer. A static IP address remains consistent, so you can point a DNS entry at it and it will always be the same, as opposed to the default ephemeral IP address that can change.

IP addresses are provided by the compute API, so you need to enable that service:

```
gcloud services enable compute.googleapis.com
```

Then you can reserve the address with this command:

```
gcloud compute addresses create ${PREFIX}-ip --global
```

 There is a limited supply of IP addresses in the world; while there is no charge for a static IP address used with an HTTP/s Load Balancer, there is an hourly charge for static IP addresses that are unused, so you should delete it when you are finished with it. You can delete the address with this command:

```
gcloud compute addresses delete ${PREFIX}-ip
```

Creating an A Record to the Static IP Address

You can use the IP address to create an A record in your DNS provider. Get the IP address with the following command:

```
gcloud compute addresses describe ${PREFIX}-ip --global --format 'value(address)'
```

For example, I own the domain `skillsmapper.org` provided by Google Domains (*https://oreil.ly/2dv0D*), so I would create an A record for `skillsmapper.org` pointing to this IP address.

Creating an SSL Certificate

To provide a secure connection to your domain, you need to create an SSL certificate or, more accurately, have Google Cloud create one for you. Create an environment variable for the domain name you created an A record for (e.g., `skillsmapper.org`):

```
export DOMAIN=[DOMAIN]
```

Then use the following command to create the certificate:

```
gcloud compute ssl-certificates create ${PREFIX}-cert \
    --domains=$DOMAIN
```

Creating the certificate can take about an hour, in my experience. You can check the status of the certificate with the following command. Initially, the domainStatus will be PENDING, but when the status is ACTIVE, it is ready to use:

```
gcloud compute ssl-certificates describe ${PREFIX}-cert
```

While you are waiting for the certificate to be issued, you can continue to set up the load balancer.

Create a Load Balancer

To create a load balancer, there are several components you need to put into place in addition to the Cloud Run services and the API Gateway. Figure 11-1 shows the components you will create.

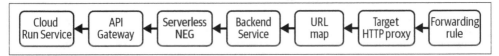

Figure 11-1. Overview of load balancer components

Work from left to right, starting from the API Gateway and working toward the forwarding rule. The forwarding rule will take the external IP address as input.

Network endpoint group

A network endpoint group (NEG) specifies a group of backend endpoints for a load balancer, as shown in Figure 11-2.

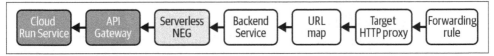

Figure 11-2. Serverless NEG

A serverless NEG is a type of NEG that is backed by serverless services like a Cloud Run service. However, as you are using the API Gateway, you need to create a serverless NEG that is backed by the API Gateway. You can create the NEG with the following command:

```
gcloud beta compute network-endpoint-groups create ${PREFIX}-api-gateway-serverless-neg \
    --region=${REGION} \
    --network-endpoint-type=serverless \
    --serverless-deployment-platform=apigateway.googleapis.com \
    --serverless-deployment-resource=${PREFIX}-gateway
```

At the time of writing, this is still a beta command, as the ability to create a serverless NEG backed by an API Gateway is relatively new; you will therefore need to include beta in the command.

Backend services

A backend service is typically a service in front of a group of backend instances that receive and process requests from a load balancer, as shown in Figure 11-3.

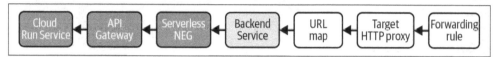

Figure 11-3. Backend service

However, in this case, you are using a serverless backend. You can create the backend service with the following command:

```
gcloud compute backend-services create ${PREFIX}-api-backend \
    --load-balancing-scheme=EXTERNAL \
    --global
```

Then connect the serverless NEG to the backend service using this command:

```
gcloud compute backend-services add-backend ${PREFIX}-api-backend \
    --global \
    --network-endpoint-group=${PREFIX}-api-gateway-serverless-neg \
    --network-endpoint-group-region=${REGION}
```

Create a backend bucket using the bucket you created to host the UI in Chapter 9:

```
gcloud compute backend-buckets create ${PREFIX}-ui \
    --gcs-bucket-name=${PROJECT_ID}-ui
```

Using the Google content delivery network

At this point, you could also decide to use a content delivery network (CDN) with this; Google Cloud's built-in CDN can be used. This uses Google's globally distributed edge points of presence to cache HTTP(S) load-balanced content close to your users. Caching content at the edges of Google's network provides faster delivery of content to your users while reducing serving costs. There is an extra storage cost as there is a data cache at each edge and network costs to get it there; however, because the UI is only a few small files, this will be negligible.

Enable CDN with this command:

```
gcloud compute backend-buckets update ${PREFIX}-ui --enable-cdn
```

URL map

A URL map routes incoming requests to the backend services you just created, as shown in Figure 11-4.

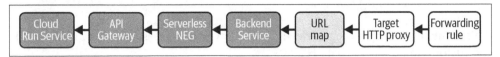

Figure 11-4. URL map

You can create the URL map and link it with the bucket you created to host the UI in Chapter 9 by default with the following command:

```
gcloud compute url-maps create ${PREFIX}-url-map \
    --default-backend-bucket=${PREFIX}-ui
```

Then add a path matcher to route requests to the API Gateway backend service:

```
gcloud compute url-maps add-path-matcher ${PREFIX}-url-map \
    --default-backend-bucket=${PREFIX}-ui \
    --path-matcher-name api-path-matcher \
    --path-rules "/api/*=${PREFIX}-api-backend"
```

In this case, any request that starts with /api/ will be routed to the API Gateway backend service. Anything else, such as the requests for the HTML, JavaScript, and CSS files, will be routed to the backend bucket by default.

Target HTTPS proxy

The URL map is now ready to be used by the target proxy, as shown in Figure 11-5. The target proxy is the component that receives the incoming request and routes it to the URL map.

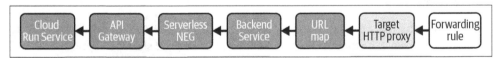

Figure 11-5. Target HTTPS proxy

Create a target HTTPS proxy to route requests to your URL map, providing the certificate you created earlier to encrypt the connection:

```
gcloud compute target-https-proxies create ${PREFIX}-https-proxy \
    --url-map=${PREFIX}-url-map \
    --ssl-certificates=${PREFIX}-cert
```

Forwarding rule

Finally, create a forwarding rule to route requests to the target HTTPS proxy, as shown in Figure 11-6.

Figure 11-6. Forwarding rule

This is the final piece of the puzzle and will allow you to access your API Gateway via the custom domain name over HTTPS:

```
gcloud compute forwarding-rules create ${PREFIX}-fw \
    --load-balancing-scheme=EXTERNAL \
    --network-tier=PREMIUM \
    --address=${PREFIX}-ip \
    --target-https-proxy=${PREFIX}-https-proxy \
    --global \
    --ports=443
```

This will create an entry point with the external IP address you reserved earlier. You can check the status of the forwarding rule with the following command:

```
gcloud compute forwarding-rules describe ${PREFIX}-fw --global
```

Make sure the `IPAddress` is the same as the IP address you created an A record for at your DNS provider earlier. When that DNS record propagates and your SSL certificate is issued, you will be in a position to test the UI.

Testing the UI

You can test the UI by visiting the domain name you created an A record for earlier. For example, I created an A record for `skillsmapper.org`, so you can visit *https://skillsmapper.org* in my browser and see the UI.

Testing the API

You can test the API in a similar way to how you tested the API Gateway, by visiting the domain name. For example, here is how you can test the skill lookup:

```
curl -X GET "https://${DOMAIN}/api/skills/autocomplete?prefix=java"
```

You will receive the same response as you did when you tested the API Gateway.

Authenticating Real Users with Identity Platform

In Chapter 7, you configured Identity Platform using an email and password provider for login. However, managing the passwords of many users can be a headache. Fortunately, Identity Provider also uses an external identity provider such as Google or Facebook. This is a common pattern for applications; it allows users to log in using their existing accounts.

Here is how you can configure Identity Provider to use Google as the identity provider. Go to the Identity Provider section (*https://oreil.ly/nOLci*) of the Google Cloud console and make sure you select Providers from the menu on the left. You should see the Email/Password provider you created earlier.

Click "Add a Provider" and select Google from the list of providers.

The page will guide you through setting up the Web SDK configuration, including collecting the Web Client ID and Web Client Secret A from elsewhere in the Google Cloud console.

On the right, you should also see a box labeled Authorized Domains. This is where you can add the domain name you created earlier. For example, I added skillsmapper.org to the list of authorized domains. Without doing this, you will not be able to use the Google login. With the configuration complete, click Save.

Finally, you need to go to visit the OAuth consent page:

```
open "https://console.cloud.google.com/apis/credentials/consent?project=${PROJECT_ID}"
```

Select the External option and complete the following:

- Give the user support email, to an email address you own.
- In authorized domain, add the value of the domain name you created earlier. For example, I added skillsmapper.org to the list of authorized domains.
- Provide the developer contact email, to an email address you own.

For the next two screens, accept the defaults, click "Save and Continue," and then on the summary tab, click "Back to Dashboard."

Testing the UI Authentication

With the Identity Platform set up, you can now test the UI authentication. You can do this by visiting the domain name you created earlier. For example, I created an A record for `skillsmapper.org` so you can visit `https://skillsmapper.org` in my browser and see the UI:

```
open "https://${DOMAIN}"
```

You should see a Skills Mapper page. Click "Sign in with Google" and you should be redirected to the Google login screen. Once you have logged in, you should be redirected back to the UI.

Evaluation

There are a lot of steps to successfully expose your API to the internet. However, once you have done it, you can reuse the same steps for any other API you create. The steps are also very similar to the steps you would take to expose an API to the internet using a traditional serverless platform such as AWS Lambda.

How Will This Solution Scale?

You can also use Apache Bench to test the API when accessing the service on Cloud Run directly:

```
ab -n 1000 -c 10 -rk "https://${DOMAIN}/api/skills/autocomplete?prefix=java"
```

This is a useful test; you may notice that the response time, especially the minimum time, is slower than going to the Cloud Run service directly due to the additional network hops required to access the service. However, the response time is still good, and the benefits of using a custom domain name and SSL certificate are worth the additional latency. You will also see in later chapters how using the load balancer opens up more features.

Enhancing Defenses with Cloud Armor

While Google's Global Load Balancer inherently offers a level of protection against DDoS attacks, you can strengthen your defenses further by integrating Google Cloud Armor with HTTP(S) Load Balancing. Cloud Armor allows you to establish IP allow/deny lists and create rules based on Layer 7 parameters, significantly enhancing the protection of your application.

For instance, if a DDoS attack originates from a specific IP address or range of address, Cloud Armor policies enable you to block the attacker(s) right at the network's edge, preventing the attack from reaching your application.

Blocking Specific Addresses

Here is a simple demonstration. First, find out your public IP address. I use the WhatIsMyIPAddress website (*https://oreil.ly/u90-g*) for this and add this to an environment variable called MY_IP:

```
export MY_IP=[YOUR_IP_ADDRESS]
```

Then create a security policy:

```
gcloud compute security-policies create "${PREFIX}-security-policy"
```

The rules within this security policy will dictate which traffic is permitted or rejected. You can create rules that allow or deny traffic based on the IP address or range (CIDR block) and IP protocol, among other parameters. The default rule is that all traffic is allowed.

To formulate a rule that denies traffic from a specific IP range, use a command like the following:

```
gcloud compute security-policies rules create 1000 \
  --security-policy "${PREFIX}-security-policy" \
  --action "deny-403" \
  --src-ip-ranges "${MY_IP}/32"
```

This denies requests from your IP. The `1000` is the priority of the rule, and the lower the number, the higher priority. For example, a rule with a priority `100` will be evaluated before a rule with a priority `1000`.

Before applying this security policy, verify that you can access the SkillsMapper API:

```
curl "https://${DOMAIN}/api/skills/autocomplete?prefix=java"
```

You should receive the expected response:

```
{"results":["java","java-10","java-11","java-12","java-13",
"java-14","java-15","java-16","java-17","java-18"]}
```

Now apply the policy to the API backend using this command:

```
gcloud compute backend-services update ${PREFIX}-api-backend \
  --security-policy "${PREFIX}-security-policy" \
  --global
```

Wait a minute or two for the policy to propagate. Then attempt to access the API once again:

```
curl "https://${DOMAIN}/api/skills/autocomplete?prefix=java"
```

You will see your request has been blocked:

```
<!doctype html><meta charset="utf-8">
<meta name=viewport content="width=device-width, initial-scale=1">
<title>403</title>403 Forbidden
```

To give yourself access again, remove the rule:

```
gcloud compute security-policies rules delete 1000 \
  --security-policy "${PREFIX}-security-policy"
```

This is a trivial example, but it could run the other way around. You could add a default rule to deny all IPs and then add a higher priority rule allowing only your IP. This would mean only you can access the API.

Rate-Limiting Calls to the API

Another use for Cloud Armor is to rate limit calls to the API.

Here is the Apache Bench command to make 1,000 requests with 10 concurrent connections:

```
ab -n 100 -c 10 -rk "https://${DOMAIN}/api/skills/autocomplete?prefix=java"
```

To protect the API, you can limit a single IP to 100 requests per minute:

```
gcloud compute security-policies rules create 100 \
    --security-policy "${PREFIX}-security-policy"      \
    --src-ip-ranges="0.0.0.0/0"       \
    --action=throttle      \
    --rate-limit-threshold-count=100 \
    --rate-limit-threshold-interval-sec=60 \
    --conform-action=allow        \
    --exceed-action=deny-429       \
    --enforce-on-key=IP
```

This rule restricts the API call rate to 10 per second. If a user from a single IP address exceeds this limit, they will receive a 429 overlimit error.

Here is a similar command to the `ab` command using a tool called siege, rather appropriate for attacking the citadel:

```
siege -c 10 -r 100 -v "https://${DOMAIN}/api/skills/autocomplete?prefix=java"
```

Siege will make 100 requests with 10 concurrent connections and list the response codes. You will see after a while that the requests are being rejected with a 429 overlimit error as the throttle limit is exceeded:

```
HTTP/1.1 200   0.48 secs:   110 bytes ==> GET  /api/skills/autocomplete?prefix=java
HTTP/1.1 200   0.47 secs:   110 bytes ==> GET  /api/skills/autocomplete?prefix=java
HTTP/1.1 429   0.46 secs:   142 bytes ==> GET  /api/skills/autocomplete?prefix=java
HTTP/1.1 429   0.46 secs:   142 bytes ==> GET  /api/skills/autocomplete?prefix=java
```

You can extend this to ban any IP that surpasses the limit excessively. For example, exceeding the limit of 100 requests in 60 seconds would result in a five-minute ban and a 403 Forbidden error would be returned instead of a 429 overlimit error:

```
gcloud compute security-policies rules create 100 \
    --security-policy "${PREFIX}-security-policy" \
    --src-ip-ranges="0.0.0.0/0" \
    --action=rate-based-ban \
    --ban-duration-sec=300 \
    --rate-limit-threshold-count=100 \
    --rate-limit-threshold-interval-sec=60 \
    --conform-action=allow \
    --exceed-action=deny-403 \
    --enforce-on-key=IP
```

Extending Cloud Armor Further

Though it's a step toward securing against DDoS attacks at a reasonable cost, Cloud Armor also offers a premium service known as Google Cloud Armor Managed Protection Plus (*https://oreil.ly/wX6bV*).

This service provides threat intelligence features, like automatically blocking a managed list of known malicious IP addresses and Adaptive Protection, which uses AI models to detect and block DDoS attacks. While this solution costs several thousand dollars monthly and necessitates a minimum commitment of one year, it is an example of a significant enhancement in application security that is available.

How Much Will This Solution Cost?

There are several charges associated with this solution. The main ones are:

- Forwarding rule for the Load Balancer. This will cost $0.025 per hour, which adds up to $18.00 per month.
- Data processed by the Load Balancer. This will cost $0.01 per GB.

- Cloud Armor policy with two rules enforcing a rate limit will cost $7 per month.

Adding these features is not free, but it is still very reasonable.

Summary

You have created a citadel with strong walls to protect the application using a Global Load Balancer with the default protection it provides and specific protection with Cloud Armor to protect against attack. As you can see, managing the system is becoming more complex as you add more layers. It is not trivial to set up everything or to tear everything down, and debugging any problems will get difficult quickly.

In this chapter, you used the following services directly:

- Global HTTP Load Balancer is used to route requests to the API Gateway from a domain name and provide an encrypted connection.
- Identity Platform is used to authenticate users using their Google account.
- Cloud Armor is used to protect the application from outside attacks and rate-limit individual IP addresses.

In the following chapters, you will look at how you can address the complexity you now have by automating the deployment further, providing observability and making the system more suitable for production.

CHAPTER 12

Factory

In previous chapters, you have been taking a largely manual approach to deploying both infrastructure and services. To be fair, leveraging the automation in the gcloud CLI and Cloud Run, in particular, has helped a lot, but it is still a manual process.

In Chapter 11, where you built the citadel (in particular, when configuring the API Gateway and Global HTTP Load Balancer), there was a lot of manual configuration and typing of commands. It was repetitive and error-prone, and if you wanted to deploy the application again, you would have to repeat the process.

Automating Build, Deployment, and Provisioning

This is a waste of time when you could be getting on with developing more features rather than fiddling with the command line. This type of work is known as "toil." Toil is bad; toil should be eliminated when you see it. Toil is a sign that you need to automate something. When I first learned about software development at school, I was taught that when you have to do something more than twice, you should write a program to do it for you. This is one of those times that advice applies.

In this chapter, you will look at how you can use Google Cloud to automate away the toil you have been increasingly experiencing in previous chapters. You will also learn how this can be done for provisioning the infrastructure too.

The code for this chapter is in the `factory` folder of the GitHub repository (*https://oreil.ly/fbB1L*).

Requirements

You can think of what you are doing in this chapter as building a washing machine factory, the sort of place Sir John Harvey-Jones from Chapter 1 would visit. There are two things the factory produces:

Applications
> The containerized services themselves. These can just be deployed in the citadel with everything in place they need. These are like the washing machine; you will create a pipeline that builds them and gets them ready to be delivered and plumbed in.

Infrastructure
> Washing machines need infrastructure to run. Connections to electricity and water and a space under the worktop in a kitchen or utility room (if you are British like me). With the infrastructure in place, the washing machine can just be delivered, connected to water, plugged into electricity, and away you go. Not only can the factory make the washing machine, it can also make the pipes and cables it needs too.

When you are building a factory, you want it to provide the following, as shown in Figure 12-1:

- Somewhere to store source code like a silo for raw materials
- An automated build pipeline that acts like a robotic assembly line
- Somewhere to store the finished products; in this case, containers, like a warehouse
- An automated deployment mechanism like a truck with an installation engineer

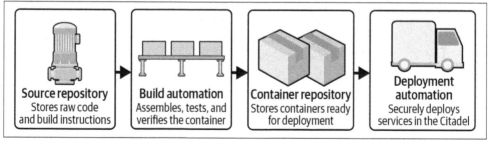

Source repository	Build automation	Container repository	Deployment automation
Stores raw code and build instructions	Assembles, tests, and verifies the container	Stores containers ready for deployment	Securely deploys services in the Citadel

Figure 12-1. The factory

The Outer Loop

In Chapter 10, you learned about the laboratory and how you could automate the process of build, deploy, and test for applications on your local machine to provide rapid feedback. This is known as the inner loop.

The *factory* is the automated process that builds and deploys the application to the cloud, as shown in Figure 12-1. The factory is the outer loop (see Figure 12-2). It is made up of two parts, the build pipeline (the assembly line) and the deployment pipeline (the delivery truck and installation engineer).

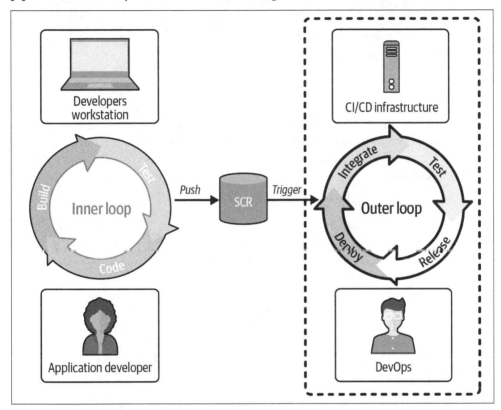

Figure 12-2. Outer loop

The build pipeline takes the raw materials and the source code and turns it into a containerized service. This means that whenever a developer commits a change to the source code repository, the build pipeline will automatically build, test, and store the containerized service.

The test suite will typically include all unit tests and, usually, integration tests. This is known as continuous integration (Figure 12-3). Building applications in this way means that you can get rapid feedback on the quality of the code and the impact of any changes; however, hopefully, you would have picked up most issues earlier by testing in the inner loop in the laboratory.

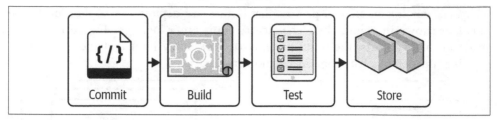

Figure 12-3. Continuous integration

By building and testing in a consistent and automated way, you can be confident that the application will work as expected when deployed. By adding security controls and checks on dependencies and the build process, you can also be confident that the application will be secure and reliable. This is known as securing the software supply chain and is discussed in depth at Supply-Chain Levels for Software Artifacts, or SLSA (*https://slsa.dev*).

This is similar to the goal of a real factory—to reliably produce a product of consistent quality.

The deployment pipeline takes the containerized service and deploys it to the cloud. This is known as continuous deployment if deployment to a production deployment is fully automated, as shown in Figure 12-4. If deployment is optional or deployment is only automatic to test environments, it is known as continuous delivery.

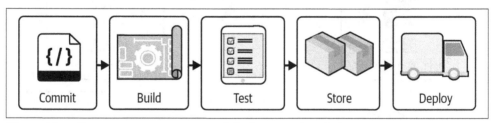

Figure 12-4. Continuous integration and deployment (CI/CD)

 In reality, continuous deployment to production is not always possible. For example, if you are deploying to a regulated environment, you may need to have a manual approval step. This is still continuous delivery but not continuous deployment. However, if the automated tests in your pipeline are comprehensive enough, you can be confident that the application will work as expected when deployed; therefore, continuous deployment is a useful tool.

Think of this again like buying a new washing machine. The machine is built and tested at a factory and stored in a warehouse. It is then delivered, and you have the choice to have it installed (deployed) at the same time or do it yourself later.

DORA Metrics

DevOps Research and Assessment (DORA) is an organization that researches the benefits organizations get from DevOps principles and practices like the ones discussed here.

From their research, DORA has identified four metrics that high-performers score well against for delivery and operational performance. They suggest using these metrics as goals for an aspirational organization. These metrics are:

Lead time for changes
> The amount of time it takes a commit to get into production; that is, how long it takes to go through the inner and outer loops. This includes both the development time (how long it takes to code the feature) and the wait time in various stages of the CI/CD pipeline.

Deployment frequency
> How often an organization successfully releases to production. This could be multiple deployments per day for high-performing organizations.

Change failure rate
> The percentage of deployments causing a failure in production. This could be defined as a service impairment or service outage. The key is to track when a failure requires remediation (like a hotfix, rollback, fix forward, or patch).

Time to restore serice
> How long it takes an organization to recover from a failure in production. This could be the time it takes to correct a defect or to restore service during a catastrophic event (like a site outage).

These four metrics provide a balanced view of not only how fast and frequently an organization delivers software efficiently but also how effectively they respond to problems in production. They are based on years of research and have been shown to be predictive of software delivery performance and organizational performance. The type of automation provided by the factory is the enabler of these metrics. The message is that just because automation is in place does not mean an organization will perform well, but organizations that do perform well are likely to have a factory in place.

For more information on DORA metrics, you can refer to the book *Accelerate: The Science of Lean Software and DevOps* (IT Revolution Press) by Nicole Forsgren, Jez Humble, and Gene Kim, which discusses these topics in detail.

Canary Releases

When deploying to production, you may want to do a canary release. This is where you deploy the new version of the application alongside the old version and gradually increase the traffic to the new version. This allows you to test the new version in production and roll back if there are any issues.

For example, you could choose to deploy the new version of a service to only 5% of users initially and then monitor the error rate and performance. If everything is working as expected, you can gradually increase the percentage of users until all users are using the new version. In Chapter 13 on observability and monitoring, you will look at how you can monitor the performance of your application and use this to make decisions about when to roll out new versions.

Summary of Services

To build this facility, you will use the following services:

Source repository—GitHub

The source code is the raw materials and blueprints for building containerized services. As you would expect, these are stored in a source code repository. Google Cloud has its own source code repository, Google Source Repositories (*https://oreil.ly/cRKc7*), which is Git-based. But for many people, GitHub will be the first choice. Fortunately, there are mechanisms for connecting to other Git providers in the Google Cloud ecosystem.

These include mirroring the GitHub repositories in Google Source Repositories, but you can also connect the build pipeline directly to several Git service providers, including GitHub and BitBucket. These connections can only be created via the console on Cloud Build (1st gen) but can be connected programmatically with the 2nd gen. Therefore, you will be using 2nd gen.

Build automation—Cloud Build

Cloud Build is the mechanism for creating a continuous integration pipeline, the automated assembly line for building and testing containerized services to store, ready for deployment. You have come across Cloud Build before, but this time you will be automating how it is triggered rather than using Cloud Run.

Container storage—Artifact Registry

When containers are assembled, they will automatically be stored in Artifact Repository until the automated deployment is ready for them. Think of Artifact Repository as the warehouse storing the containers ready for delivery. At this point, you can also publish a message saying a new container is available.

Deployment automation—Cloud Build or Cloud Deploy

When a container is ready for deployment, you need something to pick it up and deploy it into the citadel. In this chapter you will use Cloud Build again, but for more complex deloyments Cloud Deploy is also an option. Think of it as a skilled installer with a truck delivering and installing the new washing machine.

Implementation

You are now going to use the completed SkillsMapper code that accompanies this book as an example. The code is available on GitHub at SkillsMapper Repo (*https://oreil.ly/jbVj0*). If you have not already done so, you should fork the repository into your own GitHub account if you want to make any changes, but you can also use the original repository if you prefer, as it is public.

Creating the factory

The first step is to create the "factory," and for this, you will create a separate project from the one that is used for running the applications, the "citadel." All automation will be in a separate project from the applications themselves. Refer back to Chapter 4 if you need a reminder of how to create a project

A suggested naming convention is to use the same name as the citadel project but with -management appended. For example, if the citadel project is skillsmapper the management project would be skillsmapper-management.

Having a separate project for management is a good idea for several reasons. It allows you to:

- Separate the billing and budgeting for the citadel and the management infrastructure.

- Give different people access to the citadel and the management infrastructure.

- Delete the management infrastructure without affecting the citadel.

- Have multiple citadels for different environments (e.g., skillsmapper-development, skillsmapper-test, skillsmapper-production) and a single management project.

For the rest of this chapter, we will assume that the management project is called skillsmapper-management and refer to it as the management project, and the citadel project is a citadel project named skillsmapper-development and refer to it as the target project.

Create two environment variables for referring to these projects:

```
export MANAGEMENT_PROJECT_ID=[MANAGEMENT_PROJECT_ID]
export TARGET_PROJECT_ID=[TARGET_PROJECT_ID]
```

Connecting to the source code repository

When you have a management project, you can start to build the factory. Remember to switch your gcloud context to the management project using:

```
gcloud config set project $MANAGEMENT_PROJECT_ID
```

When in the management project, you will need to connect to the repository to be able to build the application. This is done using a Cloud Build connection. As is good practice, GitHub's credentials for the connection are stored in Secret Manager. As you are in a new project, you will need to first enable the services you are going to use, in this case, Cloud Build and Secret Manager:

```
gcloud services enable cloudbuild.googleapis.com
gcloud services enable secretmanager.googleapis.com
```

Next, permit Cloud Build to create secrets. The Cloud Build P4SA service account is a built-in product service account with a name in the format `service-[PROJECT _NUMBER]@gcp-sa-cloudbuild.iam.gserviceaccount.com`. Grant the P4SA service account permission to create secrets in Secret Manager using the following command:

```
gcloud projects add-iam-policy-binding $MANAGEMENT_PROJECT_ID \
--member='serviceAccount:service-'$(gcloud projects describe $MANAGEMENT_PROJECT_ID
--format='value(projectNumber)')'@gcp-sa-cloudbuild.iam.gserviceaccount.com' \
--role='roles/secretmanager.admin'
```

Create an environment variable to store a connection name (e.g., `skillsmapper-github-connection`):

```
export CONNECTION_NAME=[CONNECTION_NAME]
```

Then create the connection:

```
gcloud alpha builds connections create github $CONNECTION_NAME --region=$REGION
```

> At the time of writing, this functionality is still in preview, hence the use of the `alpha` command. The syntax may have changed by the time you read this.

This will give you a link that will open your browser and guide you through connecting to your GitHub account. When completed, check that the connection has been created successfully with this command:

```
gcloud alpha builds connections describe $CONNECTION_NAME --region=$REGION
```

Look for the value of `installationState`; the stage should show the value `COMPLETE`.

Now you can connect to the SkillsMapper GitHub repository. Set the `REPO_NAME` and `REPO_URI` as follows unless you are using your own fork, in which case you should use your own repository name and URI:

```
export REPO_NAME=skillsmapper
export REPO_URI=https://github.com/SkillsMapper/skillsmapper.git
```

Then run the following command to connect to the repository:

```
gcloud alpha builds repositories create $REPO_NAME --remote-uri=$REPO_URI \
--connection=$CONNECTION_NAME --region=$REGION
```

When this command completes with the `Created repository [SkillsMapper]` message, you will have a repository connection to use with Cloud Build as the source repository. These are the raw materials for the automated assembly line. You can check it using this command:

```
gcloud alpha builds repositories list --connection=$CONNECTION_NAME --region=$REGION
```

You will see the repository listed with the name you specified, mapping to the URI of the GitHub repository.

Creating a container repository

Next, you need to create a container repository to store the containers that are built by the assembly line.

Create an environment variable to store the name of the container repository:

```
export CONTAINER_REPO='skillsmapper'
```

Now use the following command to create the container repository:

```
gcloud artifacts repositories create $CONTAINER_REPO --repository-format=docker --location=$REGION
```

This will create a new container repository named `skillsmapper` to store the Docker format containers Cloud Build will create. You can check using the following command:

```
gcloud artifacts repositories list --location=$REGION
```

Notice `ENCRYPTION` is set to `Google-managed` key. Like most Google Cloud services, Artifact Repository encrypts data at rest by default.

Implementing continuous integration with Cloud Build

In previous chapters, you have been using Cloud Build behind the scenes whether you realized it or not. Every time you used `gcloud run deploy` or `gcloud functions deploy` you have been triggering a Cloud Build pipeline in the background using your local source code as the source.

Now you are going to use it to automatically trigger a build whenever there is a commit to the main branch of the GitHub repository. You will use the skill service as an example, but it will be a similar process to the other services. The build configuration will differ slightly for the fact service and the skill service, for example, as it is a Java application rather than Go. Cloud Build is very flexible and can be configured to build almost any type of application.

First, define some environment variables:

```
export TRIGGER_NAME='skill-service-trigger'
export BRANCH_PATTERN='^main$'
export BUILD_CONFIG_FILE='skill-service/cloudbuild.yaml'
```

This is setting the name of the trigger to `skill-service-trigger`, the branch pattern to `^main$` (i.e., only trigger when there is a commit to the main branch), and the build config file to a file in the skill service directory *skill-service/cloudbuild.yaml*.

The single SkillsMapper repository contains multiple services. What you don't want is for all services to be rebuilt and redeployed when there is a commit to the main branch. To only build and deploy the service that has changed, you can restrict the files that trigger a build with the `included-file` parameter. In the next example, only changes to files in the *skill-service* directory will trigger a build.

Then use the following command to create the trigger. Again, note this is a beta command at the time of writing:

```
gcloud beta builds triggers create github \
  --name=$TRIGGER_NAME \
  --repository=projects/$MANAGEMENT_PROJECT_ID/locations/$REGION/connections
/$CONNECTION_NAME/repositories/$REPO_NAME \
  --branch-pattern=$BRANCH_PATTERN \
  --build-config=$BUILD_CONFIG_FILE \
  --region=$REGION \
  --included-files="${SKILL_SERVICE_NAME}/**" \
  --substitutions=_REPOSITORY=$CONTAINER_REPO,_REGION=$REGION,
_SERVICE_NAME=$SKILL_SERVICE_NAME,_IMAGE_NAME=$SKILL_SERVICE_IMAGE_NAME
```

This will create a trigger that will build the skill service whenever there is a commit to the main branch of the GitHub repository. You can check that the trigger has been created successfully with the following command:

```
gcloud beta builds triggers list --region=$REGION
```

You should see the trigger listed with the name you gave it. The trigger runs on git commit, but you can also run it manually with the following command:

```
gcloud beta builds triggers run $TRIGGER_NAME \
  --region=$REGION \
  --branch=main
```

This will run the trigger on the main branch. The message returned will include a link to the build log in the `metadata.build.logUrl` field, which you can open in your browser to see progress.

To speed up the build process by excluding files that are not needed for the build process, you can create a `.gcloudignore` in the root of the repository to exclude files. This works in a similar way as a *.gitignore* file. For example, you can exclude all markdown files like *README.md* files with the following entry in the *.gcloudignore* file: `*/*.md`.

Now let's look at the details of the Cloud Build configuration file to understand what the build pipeline is doing.

Understanding Cloud Build configurations

The Cloud Build configuration is a YAML file, in this case, the *cloudbuild.yaml* file in the *skill-service* directory.

It is made up of one or more build steps. The build process starts with a workspace containing a fresh clone of the GitHub repository for each execution and then runs each step in turn.

In the case of the skill service, it is a Go application and there are multiple steps. Each step in the configuration file uses a container image and runs a specific commands as shown in Table 12-1.

Table 12-1. Skill service build steps

Step	Container	Command	Description
Go version	`gcr.io/cloud-builders/go:1.20`	`go version`	Check the version of Go as a smoke test
Download dependencies	`cloud-builders/go:1.20`	`go mod download`	Download dependencies specified in the *go.mod* file using Go version 1.20
Run linting checks	`golangci/golangci-lint`	`golangci-lint run`	Run a selection of Go linters to check the code
Run unit tests	`gcr.io/cloud-builders/go:1.20`	`go test`	Run all unit tests using Go version 1.20
Run security checkss	`securego/gosec`	`gosec`	Run security checks on the code
Build container image	`k8s-skaffold/pack`	`pack`	Build the container image using Buildpacks
Push container image	`cloud-builders/docker`	`push`	Push the container to artifact repository

This is a simple example, but there are many more steps you can add, such as running integration tests and building documentation.

You can use any container image you like, including your own custom images, as long as the Cloud Build service account can access them. Once you have set up steps in the configuration file, they will run automatically when the trigger is fired. You can be confident that the code is always built in the same way, and if you have a step to update your documentation, for example, it will always be up to date.

Cloud Build configurations support templating with substitutions of variables at run-time. You will see these being used a lot in the example configuration. Whenever you run a Cloud Build job, you have access to the following build-in variables:

$PROJECT_ID

The ID of the project running the build.

$BUILD_ID

The ID of the build.

$PROJECT_NUMBER

The number of the project running the build.

$LOCATION

The region associated with the build. This can be global if the build is not associated with a specific region.

These are provided automatically and cannot be overwritten.

There is also a set of built-in variables that are populated when the build is run from a trigger on Google Cloud. An example in use in this configuration is $COMMIT_SHA, as Cloud Build can access the Git repository and retrieve the hash of the commit in use.

This is useful as you can use it to tag the container and tie the container to the commit of the source code for debugging and tracing issues.

> Note that Artifact Registry supports tag immutability, meaning you cannot overwrite a tag once it has been created. If you try to push a container with the same tag as an existing container, for example latest, you will get an error. This is a security measure to prevent malicious actors from pushing a container with the same tag as a trusted container.

You can also use pass variables using the same substitution mechanism, but these must start with an underscore (e.g., _IMAGE_NAME) to distinguish them from built-in substitutions.

Testing a build with local code

What you are aiming for is to trigger a build from a commit to the GitHub repo. However, you can trigger the build manually. The build will still run on Google Cloud but will be using your local source code as input. There used to be the option of running a build locally using a Cloud Build Emulator, but this has been deprecated.

When you run using local code, the $COMMIT_SHA and other similar variables will not be set automatically. Instead, you can pass them in using the substitutions flag. This is the same mechanism for providing custom substitutions used in the build configuration file.

Here is the command to trigger the build locally from the root of the project with substitutions:

```
gcloud builds submit --config $SKILL_SERVICE_NAME/cloudbuild.yaml . \
  --substitutions=REPOSITORY=$CONTAINER_REPO,_REGION=$REGION,
_SERVICE_NAME=$SKILL_SERVICE_NAME,_IMAGE_NAME=$SKILL_SERVICE_IMAGE_NAME,
COMMIT_SHA=$(git rev-parse HEAD)
```

Here _REPOSITORY, _REGION, _SERVICE_NAME and _IMAGE_NAME are custom substitution variables and COMMIT_SHA is overriding a built-in variable. Running a build locally in this way is useful for testing that your *cloudbuild.yaml* is doing what you expect.

Adding continuous deployment to the Cloud Build pipeline

At the moment, the pipeline will build the container and push it to Artifact Registry. Although a new container is ready, it will not deploy to Cloud Run. The next steps handle that deployment, taking the pipeline from a continuous integration (CI) pipeline to a continuous deployment (CD) pipeline.

The final step in the pipeline is to deploy the container to Cloud Run. The step that does this from Cloud Build simply uses a container that includes the gcloud CLI cloud-builders/gcloud and then uses the same gcloud run deploy command you used to deploy manually in previous chapters.

As the deployment to Cloud Run will be to a different project than the one running the build, you will need to pass the --project flag to the gcloud run deploy command.

When deploying using Cloud Run, you have been passing a *.env.yaml* file with environment variables used by the service. However, as this may contain sensitive information, it will not be in the GitHub repo, so you can instead pass each environment variable as a substitution to the build. The full build step will look like this and is included in *cloudbuild.yaml*:

```
- id: 'Deploy to Cloud Run'
  name: 'gcr.io/cloud-builders/gcloud:latest'
  entrypoint: /bin/bash
  args:
    - '-c'
    - |
      gcloud run deploy ${_SERVICE_NAME} \
        --image ${_REGION}-docker.pkg
        .dev/$PROJECT_ID/${_REPOSITORY}/${_IMAGE_NAME}:$COMMIT_SHA \
        --project ${_TARGET_PROJECT_ID} \

        --region ${_REGION} \
        --update-env-vars PROJECT_ID=${_TARGET_PROJECT_ID}, \
          BUCKET_NAME=${_TARGET_PROJECT_ID}-tags,OBJECT_NAME=tags.csv, \
          SERVICE_NAME=${_SERVICE_NAME}
```

You will also need to use the TARGET_PROJECT_ID environment variable with the ID of the project you want to deploy to. This is the project you were working with in previous chapters, for example skillsmapper-development.

As the build will be running in the management prod project, you will need to grant to the Cloud Build service account in the management project the Cloud Run Admin role in the destination project.

First, get the email address of the Cloud Build service account in the management project:

```
export CLOUDBUILD_SA_EMAIL=$(gcloud projects describe $MANAGEMENT_PROJECT_ID \
--format='value(projectNumber)')@cloudbuild.gserviceaccount.com
```

Then grant the Cloud Build service account the Cloud Run Admin role in the destination project:

```
gcloud projects add-iam-policy-binding $TARGET_PROJECT_ID \
  --member=serviceAccount:$CLOUDBUILD_SA_EMAIL \
  --role=roles/run.admin
```

Now allow the Cloud Build Service to "impersonate" the Cloud Run service account:

```
gcloud projects add-iam-policy-binding $TARGET_PROJECT_ID \
  --member=serviceAccount:$CLOUDBUILD_SA_EMAIL \
  --role=roles/iam.serviceAccountUser
```

The Cloud Run service account also will need permission to retrieve containers from the management project's Artifact Registry. This is because the Cloud Run service account will be pulling the container from Artifact Registry and not the Cloud Build service account:

```
gcloud projects add-iam-policy-binding $MANAGEMENT_PROJECT_ID \
      --member='serviceAccount:service-'$(gcloud projects describe $TARGET_PROJECT_ID
    --format='value(projectNumber)')'@gcp-sa-cloudbuild.iam.gserviceaccount.com' \
    --role='roles/artifactregistry.reader'
```

Delete the existing trigger:

```
gcloud beta builds triggers delete $TRIGGER_NAME \
  --region=$REGION
```

Then create a new one using the new build configuration file and substitutions:

```
gcloud beta builds triggers create github \
  --name=$TRIGGER_NAME \
  --repository=projects/$MANAGEMENT_PROJECT_ID/locations/$REGION/connections
/$CONNECTION_NAME/repositories/$REPO_NAME \
  --branch-pattern=$BRANCH_PATTERN \
  --build-config=$BUILD_CONFIG_FILE \
  --region=$REGION \
  --included-files="${SKILL_SERVICE_NAME}/**" \
  --substitutions=_REPOSITORY=$CONTAINER_REPO,_REGION=$REGION,
_SERVICE_NAME=$SKILL_SERVICE_NAME,_IMAGE_NAME=$SKILL_SERVICE_IMAGE_NAME,
_TARGET_PROJECT_ID=$TARGET_PROJECT_ID
```

Trigger the build manually:

```
gcloud beta builds triggers run $TRIGGER_NAME \
  --region=$REGION \
  --branch=main
```

The result of this command will be a lot of YAML but will include a URL to the build log. You could also use the **open** command to open the log in a browser by getting the command to output YAML and then parsing it with yq to get the log URL:

```
open "$(gcloud beta builds triggers run $TRIGGER_NAME \
  --region=$REGION \
  --branch=main \
  --format=yaml | yq eval '.metadata.build.logUrl' -)"
```

Tricks like this are useful for automating what you do in the console.

For completeness, *cloudbuild.yaml* configurations are also included for the fact service and profile service in their respective directories in the code that accompanies this book.

Deploying Infrastructure

In the Appendix, there are instructions for deploying a complete version of the entire SkillMapper application using the Terraform and infrastructure as code tool. Almost everything that can be achieved on the gcloud CLI can be defined in code and applied automatically.

It is also possible to automate that deployment using Cloud Build, too, so any changes to the Terraform configuration are applied automatically by Cloud Build. This is a technique known as GitOps, as operations effectively become controlled by the content of a Git repository.

How Much Will This Cost?

Cloud Build has a free tier where builds are performed on a machine with 1 vCPU and 4 GB RAM. At the time of writing, builds are free for the first 120 minutes per day and $0.003 per minute after that. If you would like to speed up your builds, you can use a machine with more CPU and RAM. The cost of this will depend on the machine type you choose. You can find more information on the pricing page for Cloud Build (*https://oreil.ly/2lF_C*).

Artifact Registry has a free tier where you can store up to 0.5 GB of data and transfer a certain amount of data. After that, there are monthly costs for storage and data transfer. You can find more information on the pricing page for Artifact Registry (*https://oreil.ly/Hs9CV*).

Summary

In this chapter, you created a Cloud Build pipeline that builds a container and pushes it to Artifact Registry. You also added a step to deploy the container to Cloud Run.

To create this facility, you used the following services directly:

- Cloud Build (*https://oreil.ly/WEQCs*) is used to create pipelines for building and deploying services
- Artifact Registry (*https://oreil.ly/2-lRf*) is used to store the container images

While you now have the factory for building and deploying a Cloud Run service from a GitHub repo, you should also understand how it is running and how to debug it. In Chapter 13, you will learn how to monitor and debug services by adding the observatory.

Observatory

Every Saturday morning, I am in the habit of collecting metrics on a spreadsheet. I weigh myself, take my blood pressure, check my resting heart rate, and record how long I slept each night and how much exercise I have done. I also go for a 5 km run and record the time and how I feel. This acts as a system check. I have been doing this for several years and now I have a lot of data.

This data provides insights into what constitutes my "normal," allowing me to perceive shifts over time and detect any abnormalities. For instance, a gradual increase in my weight could prompt me to reevaluate my diet, while an elevated blood pressure might lead me to seek medical advice. The modest effort I invest each Saturday morning offers an enlightening view of my health and fuels my motivation to continually enhance my fitness.

Monitoring the System

With the factory and citadel in place, you have an automated system for safely deploying the application and an environment in which to securely run it. However, there are a lot of moving parts, and it is going to be tough to understand what is happening. It will be difficult to notice, let alone fix problems. This is the reason to start to collect metrics and logs and make them available in a central place, as I do with my spreadsheet. By understanding what is normal and what is changing over time and noticing any anomalies, you will understand the health of the system and identify opportunities for improvement.

In an on-premises environment, you have the advantage of physical access to the hardware for metric collection. However, this is not an option in Google Cloud or any other cloud environment, as the hardware is owned by the service provider. Fortunately, Google Cloud is engineered with built-in metrics, logging, and tracing from the ground up, and these signals are centrally aggregated. The platform automatically collects thousands of metrics, which you can supplement with custom metrics from your applications for a full picture.

The crux is, while most of the data is readily available, you need an *observatory*, a centralized point to monitor this vast data universe. This chapter will guide you in building that observatory.

 The code for this chapter is in the observatory folder of the GitHub repository (*https://oreil.ly/VFkXV*).

Site Reliability Engineering

Operating an application in a Cloud environment is a discipline in its own right. Site reliability engineering (SRE) is Google's preferred approach, and the tools supplied by Google Cloud (as you would expect) support SRE. There are three excellent free books on the subject available at the Google SRE website (*https://sre.google*). These O'Reilly books are also highly recommended: *Building Secure and Reliable Systems* by Heather Adkins et al. and *Observability Engineering* by Charity Majors et al.

This chapter will not delve into the mechanics of SRE per se. Instead, it will introduce you to a collection of tools specifically designed to monitor applications operating on Google Cloud. Gaining insights into your application's behavior is critical for identifying, debugging, and rectifying issues.

Golden Signals

That said, one of the SRE principles worth noting is the *golden signals*. These are four metrics that are the most important to monitor for any application:

Traffic
> The amount of demand the system is responding to, normally measured as the number of requests per second. Think of this as your heartbeat or pulse rate. Just as a heart rate measures the number of times your heart beats in a minute, traffic indicates how many requests your system is handling. A suddenly elevated heart rate might indicate stress or excitement, much like a surge in traffic might hint at increased user activity or a possible DoS attack.

Saturation

How much of the available capacity the system is using. This could be the percentage of CPU, memory, disk, and network capacity in use, for example. This can be likened to lung capacity when you're exercising. When you're at rest, you're using a small portion of your lung capacity; when you're running, you're pushing your lungs to use as much of their capacity as possible. Similarly, if your system's resources are being fully utilized, your system is "breathing heavily," potentially leading to exhaustion or slowdown.

Errors

The proportion of requests that fail or return an unexpected result in comparison to the total number of requests. This is a good indicator of the reliability and stability of a system. Imagine going for a health checkup and receiving some abnormal test results. These anomalies, like unusual blood work, might point toward specific health issues. Similarly, a higher rate of errors in a system could indicate underlying problems that need addressing.

Latency

The time to process and respond to a particular request. This is a good indicator of the performance of a system. This is akin to the reflex time of the human body. For instance, the time it takes for your hand to pull away from something hot. In an optimal state, you'd have a quick reflex, just as an efficient system would have low latency. Delays in reflex might suggest neurological concerns, just as high latency could point toward performance bottlenecks.

These are the metrics I will concentrate on in the system. The idea is that if you can monitor these four metrics, you will have a good understanding of the health of the system, much like I attempt to understand the health of my body.

Implementing Observability

Observability on Google Cloud is organized with Workspaces within the Cloud Monitoring service. These are dashboards that can be used to provide a "single pane of glass" to show what is happening in the whole system and give secure access to the information, some of which may be sensitive. Let's take the skill service from the Skills Mapper project and show how you can add useful metrics about its resources using a Workspace.

Monitoring Workspaces

In Google Cloud, a Workspace resides within a project and inherits its name. While it's tethered to one project, it can oversee resources from up to 100 different projects. For this chapter, you'll set up a Workspace in the management project, but it will monitor resources from the citadel project.

You might wonder, "Why not create the workspace directly in the citadel project?" There's a reason: if you were to ever remove the citadel project, especially if it's a temporary setup, the Workspace would vanish with it, so this is a better option.

By placing your Workspace in a distinct project, you also gain flexibility. Multiple environments—be it dev, test, qa, or prod—can all be under the watchful eyes of a single Workspace. It aligns with the vision of an observatory: a unified vantage point to gaze across your entire digital cosmos.

Configuring Cloud Monitoring

The project that you are in—in this case, the management project—is monitored automatically. You can expand the metrics scope by adding additional projects. To add the Citadel project to the current project, set environment variables for the management and monitored project ID (e.g., `skillsmapper-management` and `skillsmapper-development`, respectively):

```
export MANAGEMENT_PROJECT_ID=[MANAGEMENT_PROJECT_ID]
export MONITORED_PROJECT_ID=[MONITORED_PROJECT_ID]
```

Make sure that your current project is the management project:

```
gcloud config set project $MANAGEMENT_PROJECT_ID
```

Just as Firebase emerged as a standalone product before its integration with Google Cloud, Google Cloud Monitoring similarly began its journey under a different identity: Stackdriver. Originally developed as an independent monitoring solution, Stackdriver was acquired by Google and subsequently integrated into the Google Cloud suite.

Because of this historical evolution, certain aspects of Google Cloud Monitoring still bear remnants of its Stackdriver roots, especially in the tools provided for users to interact with it. Notably, the gcloud CLI, which is the primary tool for managing Google Cloud resources, doesn't fully encapsulate all the features of the monitoring service. Some of these commands, due to their transitional nature or a recent addition, are labeled as "beta," indicating that they might not be as stable as other well-established commands or could undergo further changes in subsequent releases.

Use this command to add the monitored project to the scope of the management project:

```
gcloud beta monitoring metrics-scopes create $MONITORED_PROJECT_ID
```

You will now be able to collect metrics from the monitored project as well as the management project.

Metrics

There are hundreds, if not thousands, of built-in metrics available for services in Google Cloud. These are collected automatically and can be viewed in the Google Cloud console. For example, you can view the metrics for a Cloud Run service by selecting the service and then selecting the Metrics tab. All these metrics are also available programmatically.

Google Cloud offers a vast array of built-in metrics across its myriad of services, with the numbers potentially reaching into the thousands. These metrics are seamlessly and automatically gathered, allowing users to gain insights into various aspects of their cloud infrastructure and applications.

To access these metrics via the Google Cloud console, it's quite intuitive:

- Navigate to the specific service section, such as Cloud Run.
- Choose the service instance of interest.
- Click on the Metrics tab to get a comprehensive view of its performance indicators.

Moreover, the flexibility of Google Cloud extends beyond just manual viewing. These metrics are also programmatically accessible, paving the way for automated analytics, integrations with other systems, or custom monitoring dashboards tailored to unique operational needs.

Dashboards

Dashboards are a way to visualize what is important and are formed from one or more charts. Each chart visualizes one metric of the monitored projects.

Google Cloud provides several built-in dashboards for specific services (e.g., Cloud Run, Cloud Storage, Cloud SQL, etc.), and you can view these at Google Cloud Dashboards (*https://oreil.ly/N3leT*).

As an example, Figure 13-1 includes the default Cloud Run dashboard for a running skill service.

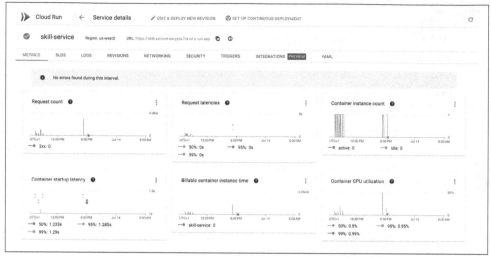

Figure 13-1. Cloud Run dashboard

Creating a Custom Dashboard

You can also assemble your custom dashboards from these metrics, such as the amount of memory a specific Cloud Run service is using or the number of Cloud Run instances that are running. You can build dashboards from the Google Cloud console, but to define dashboards programmatically, you can use YAML.

As you want to automate the creation of the observatory and maintain the configuration in version control, this is a more sustainable way of doing it. For example, this YAML will create a dashboard named Example Dashboard with a single widget that contains Hello World:

```
displayName: Example Dashboard
gridLayout:
  widgets:
  - text:
      content: Hello World
```

However, you will want something more substantial. The file *templates/service-dashboard.yaml.template* contains widgets for monitoring a Cloud Run service. Rather than just showing rudimentary metrics, it displays widgets that capture the essence of the golden signals. Let's take a look at the widgets and their significance.

The dashboard is made up of four widgets that map to the golden signals:

Container instance count
> At its core, this widget provides insights into the number of service instances that are currently active. Monitoring this count is crucial because it indicates the service's *saturation* level. If the number of instances suddenly spikes, it might suggest a surge in demand or potential inefficiencies that warrant attention.

Request latencies

This widget delves deep into the *latency* of service requests. By showing P50, P90, and P99 latencies, it offers a granular view of the service's responsiveness. Tracking these percentiles helps ensure that the vast majority of users experience optimal performance, and it also shines a light on outliers that might require further investigation.

Request Count

Keeping a tab on the *traffic* is fundamental. This widget counts the number of incoming requests, allowing teams to understand usage patterns, anticipate scaling needs, and even gauge the success of feature launches.

Percentage unsuccessful

Not all requests will be successful, and this widget is dedicated to shedding light on the *error* rate. It's paramount to understand why requests fail, as these errors can diminish user trust, affect revenue, and even signal deeper technical issues.

The dashboard also contains the logs from the service. This is useful for debugging and troubleshooting. The idea is that you have a single view of everything important about the service.

Use `envsubst` to populate it with the variables applicable to your project, specifically the service name (e.g., `skill-service`) and the ID of the monitored project (e.g., `skillsmapper-management`). Set an environment `SERVICE_NAME` environment variable to the value of `$SKILL_SERVICE_NAME`:

```
export SERVICE_NAME=$SKILL_SERVICE_NAME
```

```
envsubst < templates/service-dashboard.yaml.template > service-dashboard.yaml
```

Then ensure you are in the management project:

```
gcloud config set project $MANAGEMENT_PROJECT_ID
```

Now create a dashboard from the configuration file:

```
gcloud monitoring dashboards create --config-from-file=service-dashboard.yaml
```

You can then view the dashboard by selecting it in the Google Cloud console:

```
open 'https://console.cloud.google.com/monitoring/dashboards?project='$MANAGEMENT_PROJECT_ID
```

There is also a trick you can use in the Google Cloud console to create a dashboard and then export it to YAML.

In the Google Cloud console, note the dashboard ID in the URL and save it in an environment together with the number of the management project. For example, in the URL `https://console.cloud.google.com/monitoring/dashboards/builder/7fdd430f-4fa1-4f43-aea6-5f8bd9b865df` the dashboard ID will be `7fdd430f-4fa1-4f43-aea6-5f8bd9b865df`:

```
export DASHBOARD_ID=[DASHBOARD_ID]
```

Also, capture the project number of the management project:

```
export MANAGEMENT_PROJECT_NUMBER \
=$(gcloud projects describe $MANAGEMENT_PROJECT_ID --format='value(projectNumber)')
```

Then use the following command to export the dashboard to YAML:

```
gcloud alpha monitoring dashboards describe \
projects/$MANAGEMENT_PROJECT_NUMBER/dashboards/$DASHBOARD_ID > dashboard.yaml
```

You will then have a *dashboard.yaml* file to customize as you like. This gives you a head start in creating your own dashboards.

Logging

Google Cloud Logging is a centralized repository where logs and events from your applications and services are automatically collected, stored, and made available for analysis. As discussed in previous chapters, when you access the logs, you'll see a vast collection of logs from every service within the project by default. Given the massive scale of logs that could be generated, especially in large projects, filtering becomes an essential tool.

Log filters are powerful tools that help you focus on the specific logs you're interested in. Think of them as search criteria that can be customized to your needs.

The Google Cloud Logging query language (LQL) (*https://oreil.ly/Tn9Jy*) is the language you'd use to define these filters. LQL provides a versatile syntax that can be used to write expressions that match specific log entries. The documentation provides more details, and you can dive deeper into the LQL by following the link.

An essential concept when dealing with filters is labels. Labels are like tags, key-value pairs that can be associated with various resources to categorize or mark them. These labels are immensely beneficial when you want to create specific filters. For instance, Cloud Run, the serverless compute platform by Google Cloud, automatically labels each log with the associated service's name.

So, if you're trying to focus solely on logs from the skill service, you can utilize this automatic labeling. The filter to accomplish this would look something like:

```
export FILTER=resource.labels.service_name=skill-service
```

Set your project back to the project your application is running in:

```
gcloud config set project $MONITORED_PROJECT_ID
```

You can then use the filter with the `gcloud logging read` command to view the logs for the skill service. The limit is set to 10 to limit the number of log entries returned:

```
gcloud logging read $FILTER --limit=10
```

This will show just the last 10 logs for the skill service.

Then narrow it down further by matching the log entry that contains the text loaded and tags:

```
export FILTER='resource.labels.service_name=skill-service AND jsonPayload.message=~"loaded.*tags"'
```

The logs returned are structured logs, so you will see the full log messages as YAML. The actual log messages in this case are in jsonPayload.message. You can use the --format option to extract just the log messages:

```
gcloud logging read $FILTER --limit=10 --format='value(jsonPayload.message)'
```

For example, with the filter above, you will see the following if the service had started twice:

```
loaded 63653 tags
loaded 63653 tags
```

Google Cloud Logging is a comprehensive system that automatically consolidates, stores, and allows analysis of logs from all your applications and services. However, given the potentially massive scale of logs produced, particularly in larger projects, filtering these logs becomes paramount.

Creating filters through Google Cloud LQL empowers you to concentrate on specific logs of interest. These filters act as tailored search parameters, taking into account labels—key-value pairs tagged to different resources. This becomes particularly helpful in scenarios like focusing solely on logs from the skill service in a Cloud Run setup.

Log-Based Metrics

While Google Cloud offers many preconfigured metrics to monitor various aspects of your services, there will be times that you need more granularity or a focus on specific events. In such instances, Google Cloud provides the flexibility to define custom metrics. These can be broadly categorized into two types: log-based metrics and user-defined metrics.

Log-based metrics are derived directly from the logs your application generates. They allow you to quantify and monitor particular events or patterns that appear in your logs. For instance, as you just saw, each time the skill service initializes, it logs the number of tags loaded from the file stored in Google Cloud Storage. This action is logged, noting the exact count of tags loaded. With log-based metrics, you can create a custom metric that counts the number of times the tags are retrieved. You can also create another that monitors the number of tags loading, allowing you to notice if this number changes. If this number is significantly lower than the average, it is likely there is an issue that needs to be investigated.

Creating a counter metric from logs

As you just saw, there is a log entry created each time the skill service starts, logging the number of tags loaded from Cloud Storage. Similarly, there is a log entry created each time a request for a tag suggestion has been processed. Here is an example:

```
autocomplete for java took 84.714804ms
```

A custom counter metric will enable you to record the number of suggestions by all instances of the skill service. You cannot create this type of metric with a gcloud command alone; you need to define it in a file and then use the file to create the metric.

In the provided sample code, there's a template file named *templates/tag_suggestion_count.json.template* that serves as the blueprint for this metric. Use envsubst to create a JSON file from it, substituting in the monitored project ID:

```
envsubst < templates/tag_suggestion_count.json.template > tag_suggestion_count.json
```

Make sure that your current project is the monitored project:

```
gcloud config set project $MONITORED_PROJECT_ID
```

Then you can create the metric using this command:

```
gcloud logging metrics create tag_suggestion_count \
  --config-from-file=tag_suggestion_count.json
```

You have now created a user-defined, log-based counter metric. However, you will need to add it to a dashboard to see it. Before that, create another type of metric to show with it.

Creating a distribution metric from logs

It would also be useful to extract the time it took to make the suggestion from the log entry itself. This is possible with a distribution metric.

Instead of just counting the number of logs, you can extract the value from the log entry with a regular expression. Again, you will need to define it in a file and then use the file to create the metric with gcloud.

The file *templates/tag_suggestion_times.json.template* defines the metric. It is similar to the file used to create the counter metric. The main difference is the use of a regular expression to match the log entry and extract the time it took for the suggestion:

```
"REGEXP_EXTRACT(jsonPayload.message, \"took\\\\s(\\\\\d+\\\\\.\\\\\d+)\")"
```

Again, use envsubst to create a JSON file from it, substituting in the monitored project ID.

```
envsubst < templates/tag_suggestion_times.json.template > tag_suggestion_times.json
```

You can then create the metric with the following command:

```
gcloud logging metrics create tag_suggestion_times \
--config-from-file=tag_suggestion_times.json
```

To list the metrics, use this command:

```
gcloud logging metrics list
```

Note that metric data will only be collected from the point the metric was created. You will not see metrics from past logs. Therefore, at this point, generate some queries by calling the skill service using Apache Bench:

```
ab -n 100 -c 1 -rk "https://${DOMAIN}/api/skills/autocomplete?prefix=java"
```

These metrics will then be available to add to a dashboard, and there will be some data to display.

Creating a dashboard with user-defined metrics

To add the metrics to a dashboard, you will need to create a configuration file. The file *templates/tag-dashboard.yaml.template* is a template for the dashboard configuration file. It contains placeholders for the project ID and service name.

Make sure that your current project is the management project:

```
gcloud config set project $MANAGEMENT_PROJECT_ID
```

```
envsubst < templates/tag-dashboard.yaml.template > tag-dashboard.yaml
```

Now create a dashboard from the configuration file:

```
gcloud monitoring dashboards create --config-from-file=tag-dashboard.yaml
```

Go to the Google Cloud console using this URL:

```
open 'https://console.cloud.google.com/monitoring/dashboards?project='$MANAGEMENT_PROJECT_ID
```

You will see a new dashboard named "skills-service performance." Open this and you will see two charts, one visualizing the number of suggestions made per minute and the other showing the time taken to respond to the 50% percentile of requests.

Alerts

With metrics in place and an understanding of what is normal, you can create alerts to notify you when something appears wrong. With my personal metrics, if my heart rate suddenly goes to 200 bpm, that is not normal for me and I would want to know. Similarly, if the number of tags loaded is less than 60,000, instead of the normal number of around 63,000, that is not normal for the skill service. If 90% of responses to requests are taking over 1 second, that is also not normal, and it does not quickly resolve itself; it is a problem that needs investigation. This is what alerts are for.

Create the metric for an alert

For example, you could create an alert that triggers when the number of tags loaded is less than 60,000, as the skill service would be working, but since the number of tags is normally around 63,000, it would indicate a problem. The log message looks like this:

```
"loaded 63653 tags"
```

Again, in the provided sample code, there's a template file named *templates/tags _loaded_number.json.template* that extracts the number from the log message. Create a JSON file from it, substituting in the monitored project ID.

```
envsubst < templates/tags_loaded_number.json.template > tags_loaded_number.json
```

Make sure that your current project is the monitored project:

```
gcloud config set project $MONITORED_PROJECT_ID
```

Then you can create the metric using this command:

```
gcloud logging metrics create tags_loaded_number \
  --config-from-file=tags_loaded_number.json
```

Create a notification channel for alerts

Before you can create an alert, you need a channel to be notified on. Google Cloud supports many channel types, but in this case, you will be creating a channel for notification by email. Again, the configuration is defined in YAML and then applied with gcloud. In the provided example code, there is a file *templates/email_notification _channel.yaml.template*. This contains a placeholder for an email address.

Set the environment variable NOTIFICATION_EMAIL_ADDRESS to an email address where you would like to receive notifications:

```
export NOTIFICATION_EMAIL_ADDRESS=['NOTIFICATION_EMAIL_ADDRESS']
```

Now use envsubst to create a YAML file from the template:

```
envsubst < templates/email_notification_channel.yaml.template > email_notification_channel.yaml
```

Make sure you are in the management project:

```
gcloud config set project $MANAGEMENT_PROJECT_ID
```

Then create the notification channel from the configuration using gcloud:

```
gcloud alpha monitoring channels create --channel-content-from-file=email_notification_channel.yaml
```

This will create a channel with a unique ID. You will see this ID returned from the command. You can also you this command to set it to an environment variable, as long as there are not any other channels created already:

```
export NOTIFICATION_CHANNEL_ID=$(gcloud alpha monitoring channels list \
--format="value(name.split('/').slice(-1))")
```

You are now ready to create the alert policy.

Create an alerting policy

Once again, creating an alert policy is a case of defining the configuration in YAML and then applying it with gcloud. In the provided example code, there is a file *templates/tags_loaded_number_alert.yaml.template*. This contains placeholders for the project ID, metric name, and notification channel ID. The alert specifies that if the number of tags loaded is less than 60,000 then an alert should be triggered:

Use `envsubst` to create a YAML file from the template:

```
envsubst < templates/tags_loaded_number_alert.json.template > tags_loaded_number_alert.json
```

Create the alerting policy using the following command:

```
gcloud alpha monitoring policies create --policy-from-file=tags_loaded_number_alert.json
```

This will create the policy. Now if the number of tags loaded is ever below 60,000, you will receive a notification at the email you provided. You could test an alert by replacing the *tags.csv* file the skill service uses with one with less than 60,000 tags.

When the skill service is next loaded, the alert will be triggered, raise an incident, and send an email that will look like Figure 13-2. It also contains a link to the incident on Google Cloud and a description provided in the configuration to explain the alert and provide troubleshooting tips.

Figure 13-2. Alert email

In this case, the next time the tag updater runs on its weekly schedule, the *tags.csv* file will be updated. When the skill service next starts, it will load over 60,000 tags again, and the incident will be resolved.

User-Defined Metrics and Tracing

Rather than generating metrics by scraping logs, you can also create a custom metric from the application. Google provides a client library for many languages that you can use to create metrics from your application: OpenTelemetry (*https://oreil.ly/ TEoFI*).

OpenTelemetry is a set of open source tools for collecting telemetry data from your application and sending it to a monitoring system. At the time of writing, it is a CNCF incubating project and was formed by merging two earlier projects: OpenTracing for tracing and OpenCensus for metrics.

Once you use a solution like OpenTelemetry, you are treating traces, metrics, and logs as first-class citizens and designing them as part of your application rather than retrospectively by an operations team. This is a very cloud native approach and fits in well with SRE practices. As developers are thinking about the data, they will need to resolve problems, debug issues, and be able to design better applications.

As OpenTelemetry is a CNCF project, it does not lock you into Google Cloud. OpenTelemetry is supported by all the major cloud providers and many other products, so the work you do to instrument your application will be portable across providers. It supports many languages and frameworks, so you can use it with your existing applications.

At the moment, however, it is still in beta, and the documentation is not complete. The following sections are based on my experience of using it with the skill service. By the time you read this book, the official Google Cloud documentation is likely to have improved.

Tracing

The skill service receives a request, performs a lookup, and returns the results. From the outside, this is the latency of a single request, but internally it is made up of several steps. You can use tracing to see the latency of each step and to understand where the time is spent.

A trace describes how the system responds to a request. A trace is made up of spans, with a span representing a step to responding to the request. These concepts were first proposed in a paper on Dapper (*https://oreil.ly/bdIZu*), Google's internal distributed tracing system. By adding trace and span IDs to log messages, Google Cloud Trace and Google Cloud Logging will then be able to interpret the traces and display them in a dashboard. Traces are also useful for requests that span multiple services, as you can see the latency of each service as well as the individual step.

In the skill service, the trace will be at the request level where the prefix is submitted in the HTTP GET request, and the result will be returned.

While Google supplied a client library for tracing, it is now deprecated, and it is recommended to use OpenTelemetry instead.

Adding Trace and Span IDs to Logs

By default, all requests that are made to a Cloud Run HTTP endpoint already have tracing enabled, so you should already see traces in the Google Cloud Trace console.

For example, Figure 13-3 is a trace to the skill service. You can see there is a single span for the request, as no span has been specified. The overall request takes 4.6 seconds, but the actual processing time in the skill service is only 1.6 seconds. Here, the latency is due to the time taken to start the container and load the tags from Google Cloud Storage, as the skill service has not been used for a while and needs to cold start.

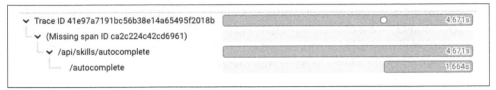

Figure 13-3. Google Cloud Trace

A trace ID is set in the X-Cloud-Trace-Context header for each request to enable tracking.

However, the default trace could be more useful, as currently it only shows the request to the skill service and not the internal steps. The skill service is already using the OpenTelemetry client library to generate traces. However, the service account needs to be granted the cloudtrace.agent role to be able to write traces to Google Cloud Trace.

In the skill service project, add the cloudtrace.agent role to the service account:

```
gcloud projects add-iam-policy-binding $PROJECT_ID \
  --member=serviceAccount:$SKILL_SERVICE_SA@$PROJECT_ID.iam.gserviceaccount.com \
  --role=roles/cloudtrace.agent
```

You can now see the traces in the Google Cloud Trace console in Figure 13-4. This gives an example of how traces can drill down into the code to show you where the time is spent. However, nearly all the time spent on the autocomplete function is in the search span, and this makes sense. You can see that the surrounding code that is not in the search span is not taking much time.

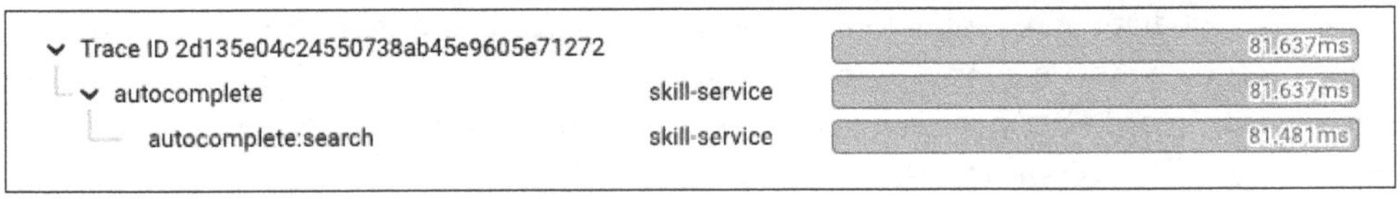

```
Trace ID 2d135e04c24550738ab45e9605e71272                          81.637ms
  autocomplete                          skill-service               81.637ms
    autocomplete:search                 skill-service               81.481ms
```

Figure 13-4. Google Cloud Trace with spans

The beauty of traces is that you can keep adding spans to drill down into the code to see where the time is spent. However, there is a lot more in the OpenTelemetry client documentation about how to build on this.

How Much Does It Cost?

The ingestion of the first 50 GiB of logs per month for a project is free; after that, it is $0.50/GiB, which includes 30 days of storage, (the default). You can increase the period for logs, but this will incur a storage cost.

There is also a free allotment of monitoring data per month, but charges apply after the first 150 MiB is ingested per billing account. Log-based metrics are also chargeable. This is all as of the time of writing. It is a good idea to keep an eye on the pricing page (*https://oreil.ly/-8RTP*) for changes, as when working at scale, these costs can add up once you have a lot of services and therefore a lot of data.

Summary

You have just dipped your toe into observability. As you may appreciate by now, it is a huge topic, and there is a lot more to learn. However, you have now seen how you can use the Cloud Logging and Cloud Monitoring services to capture logs and metrics and display them in dashboards. You have also seen how you can use alerts to notify you when something goes wrong.

To create this facility, you used the following services directly:

- Cloud Logging (*https://oreil.ly/Zllr1*) is used for capturing and aggregating logs in one place and making them searchable.
- Cloud Monitoring (*https://oreil.ly/U-f43*) is used for collecting and displaying metrics and creating alerts.
- OpenTelemetry (*https://oreil.ly/gSjsX*) is used for creating metrics and traces from your application to use in Cloud Monitoring and Cloud Trace.

It has been said, "You cannot improve what you cannot measure," a foundational principle that informed decisions rely on tangible data and observations. Without a clear understanding of a situation, making effective improvements becomes a shot in the dark. In Chapter 14, you'll look at the scalability of the system. Equipped with the right metrics, you can pinpoint inefficiencies, make informed choices, and optimize performance for better outcomes. You will learn about some of the options you have when scalability becomes an issue.

PART IV

Going Further

In this part, with the application developed and the facilities built, you'll delve into scaling options followed by resources to broaden your expertise in Google Cloud.

CHAPTER 14

Scaling Up

In Chapter 13, I touched on the four golden signals of monitoring: saturation, latency, traffic, and errors. In this chapter, you can use those to help scale and secure applications.

As the amount of traffic increases, you would expect resources to become more saturated and latency to increase. If you are not careful, this can lead to errors and even downtime. You can use the golden signals to help scale your applications to meet the demands of your users.

So far, you have used a core of services from Google Cloud to build services. However, as the demands on your services increase, there are other options; in this chapter, you will be introduced to some of these and the circumstances in which employing them would make sense.

The code for this chapter is in the `scaling` folder of the GitHub repository (*https://oreil.ly/nbNsV*).

Skill Service with Memorystore

At the moment, the skill service retrieves Stack Overflow tags from a storage bucket and holds them in memory in the service. This is fine for what is a relatively small number of tags, but as the number of tags increases, the memory requirements will increase to where it is no longer practical to fit in the memory of a single Cloud Run instance. You can use a database to store the tags and retrieve them on demand. This will allow you to scale the service horizontally and add more instances as the number of tags increases, only retrieving the tags when they are needed.

This would be a good case for Cloud Memorystore. Cloud Memorystore is a managed Redis service. Redis is an in-memory data structure store used as a database, cache, and message broker. Redis has built-in replication, transactions, and different levels of on-disk persistence and would be ideal for storing a large amount of simple data. However, the number of tags is unlikely to increase significantly, and in this case, it would be overkill. It is a good principle to only introduce the complexity of a new technology when a limitation of the current technology is likely to be reached.

Google Cloud has many more services than can be covered in this book that only start making sense at scale. Studying for the Google Professional Solutions Architect (discussed in this chapter) is a good way of learning about most of them and, more importantly, their use cases. For now, this chapter will look at how you can scale the fact service with two of Google Cloud's flagship services, GKE Autopilot and Spanner.

Fact Service with GKE Autopilot and Spanner

When building the fact service, I showed how a relatively traditional application built with Java and Spring Boot can make use of Google-specific APIs and services. This is a great way to use Google Cloud if you are fully committed, for example, to a new startup building exclusively on Google Cloud. I also showed how using Spring Cloud GCP libraries that Spring abstracts means that you are not as tied to Google Cloud as you could be. This is the approach Google would encourage because it gives you the best experience on Google Cloud.

However, this is not the only way to use Google Cloud. It is not the only way to use any cloud platform. In some organizations, becoming committed to a cloud in this way can make leaders nervous about lock-in. The question, "What happens if we need to make a forced exit?" can come up. Perhaps Google Cloud suddenly doubles prices or has a major security breach that destroys trust or causes a government or regulator to restrict use. These scenarios are unlikely, but in some industries, they are risks that need to be considered.

You also saw that there are limitations in both Cloud Run and Cloud SQL regarding how they scale. For most applications, these limitations are not a problem. However, if you are building a new application that you expect to scale to millions of users globally, you may need to consider other options. Therefore, let's assume a situation where an organization requires a cloud-agnostic approach and scaling beyond the limitations of Cloud Run and Cloud SQL. Consider how you can take the fact service and deploy it in a way that meets those requirements.

Requirements

Let's look at the specific requirements for this scenario.

User Story

The user story for this requirement is shown in Figure 14-1.

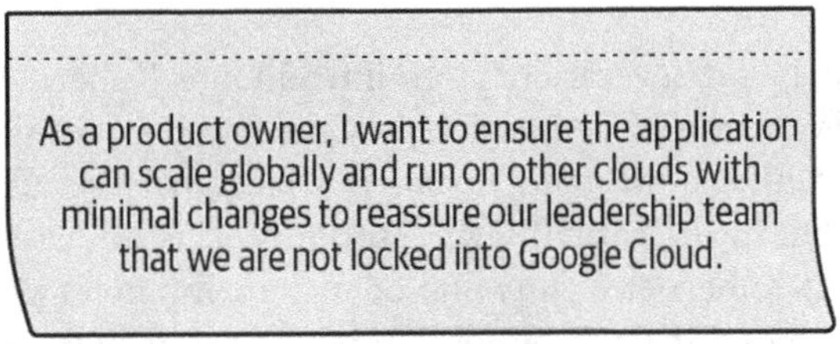

> As a product owner, I want to ensure the application
> can scale globally and run on other clouds with
> minimal changes to reassure our leadership team
> that we are not locked into Google Cloud.

Figure 14-1. Scaling user story

Elaborated Requirements

This example also has the following specific requirements:

- Avoid using any Google-specific APIs or services in code.
- There should be no changes to the code required to host the application on another cloud provider.
- The application should be able to run on any Kubernetes platform.

In this chapter, you will look at how you can take the fact service and host it in a way that is even more agnostic to the underlying cloud provider but still follows cloud native principles. This is a great way to calm nerves by building applications that can be deployed to multiple cloud providers or even on-premises if the emerging topic of "cloud repatriation" takes off.

Solution

This solution calls for some of Google Cloud's more heavyweight services. Here are the details of those services.

GKE Autopilot

In Chapter 13, you used Cloud Run as the runtime for your containers. Although Cloud Run is built upon Knative, which is an open source project, it is still a Google-specific implementation.

In this chapter, you will use Google Kubernetes Engine (GKE) Autopilot as the runtime for your container. GKE Autopilot is a fully managed Kubernetes service that is designed to be easy to use. It is a great way to run containers in the cloud without having to worry about the underlying infrastructure while providing more control than is available with Cloud Run.

I like Kubernetes, but I have never been a fan of the learning curve, the complexity of managing a Kubernetes cluster, or more importantly, the cost. Having a GKE cluster running will cost hundreds of dollars per month even when it is not hosting any applications.

It would be easy to spend several chapters introducing Kubernetes alone, as it is a complex subject. However, GKE Autopilot is a great way to get the power and benefits of Kubernetes without the complexity. It will always be useful to know how Kubernetes works, but in the case of GKE Autopilot, it is not essential. For now, it is enough to know that Kubernetes runs one or more containers in a unit called a *pod* on a cluster of machines. GKE Autopilot is more cost-effective, as you pay on a per-pod basis rather than for several machines or "nodes" in Kubernetes terminology, as you would with a traditional cluster. The cluster supports autoscaling of the machines in it to match what is required at any time. This means that you only pay for the pods that are running, not the entire cluster.

GKE Autopilot is a Google-specific service, but it is built on the open source projects from Kubernetes and Istio service mesh, which are the same building blocks as other public and private clouds. This means that you can use the same container images and very similar configuration to deploy to other Kubernetes platforms, such as Amazon EKS, Azure AKS, or even IBM Cloud IKS, for that matter. This is a great way to build applications that can be deployed to multiple clouds.

Cloud SQL

Previously, you used Cloud SQL for PostgreSQL as the database for your application. This is still a good choice, as every other public cloud provider has a similar managed PostgreSQL offering. There are also many options for running a third-party distribution of PostgreSQL on-premises or on the Kubernetes cluster itself. This means that the database is cloud-agnostic and how it is provided is not a cause for concern. However, there is a limitation to how well it can scale.

Cloud Spanner

If you want to scale the application to millions of users globally, you need to consider how you can scale the database. Cloud SQL for PostgreSQL is a great choice for a relational database, but it can only scale vertically. This means that you can only scale it by increasing the size of the machine it runs on. The other option is to add read replicas, which as their name suggests are read-only. This can help scale reads but not writes.

The alternative is Cloud Spanner, Google's globally distributed relational database. Cloud Spanner is a great choice for a globally distributed application, as it is designed to scale horizontally across multiple regions. It makes full use of all those primitive Google Cloud building blocks described in Chapter 2. Most importantly, it decouples compute from storage, meaning they can be deployed and scaled independently. However, Spanner is also a relational database, which means that you can use it similarly to Cloud SQL for PostgreSQL.

Cloud Spanner challenges the constraints of the CAP theorem, which states that a distributed system cannot simultaneously provide consistency, availability, and partition tolerance. However, it doesn't completely break these boundaries. In the balance between these three pillars, Spanner leans toward consistency and partition tolerance, while making certain concessions in availability.

What sets Spanner apart is its innovative approach to managing availability. Leveraging highly precise clocks, it significantly reduces the availability trade-off. Spanner's reliance on TrueTime API, which uses atomic clocks and GPS receivers, allows for precise synchronization across its global network. This system enables Spanner to make strong consistency and high availability a practical reality, making it a unique offering in the world of distributed databases.

As you will see, however, there are a few limitations that you need to be aware of so that an application can run on both Cloud SQL for PostgreSQL and Cloud Spanner without modification.

Kubernetes Service Accounts

Previously, you created a service account to use from Cloud Run with permissions to access Cloud SQL and the secret stored in Secret Manager. You can refer to this as a Google service account.

In Kubernetes, there is also the concept of service accounts. Similarly, this is a way to grant pods access to other services. However, this is a completely separate concept from the Google service account you created before. You can refer to this as a Kubernetes service account; it is generic to Kubernetes and completely different from a Google service account.

Workload Identity

In this chapter, the goal is for the fact service pod running in a GKE Autopilot Kubernetes cluster to be able to access the database and secret, which are Google Cloud resources. To allow a pod on GKE Autopilot to access Google Cloud resources, you need to bind the Kubernetes service account to the Google service account. This is done through a mechanism called Workload Identity.

Skaffold

Previously, you used Skaffold to automate the building of containers and deployment to local Kubernetes. In this case, you can use it to automate your development process to a GKE Autopilot cluster on Google Cloud.

Preparation

There are some small changes to the fact service needed to prepare it for Kubernetes and Cloud Spanner.

Getting Ready for Kubernetes

For Cloud Run, you are not strictly required to configure health checks for the application. For GKE Autopilot, you will need to use the Kubernetes readiness and liveness probes to check the health of the application. This is a great way to ensure that the application is running correctly and is ready to receive traffic:

Liveness check
> This indicates that a pod is healthy. If it fails, Kubernetes restarts the application.

Readiness check
> This indicates that the application is ready to receive traffic. Kubernetes will not send traffic to the pod until it is successful.

As your Spring Boot application takes several seconds to start, it is helpful to use the readiness probe to ensure the application is ready to receive traffic before Kubernetes sends any.

Fortunately, Spring Boot provides a health endpoint that you can use for this purpose. You can configure the readiness and liveness probes to use this endpoint.

First, you need to add the Spring Boot Actuator dependency to your `pom.xml` in the `dependencies` section:

```
<dependency>
    <groupId>org.springframework.boot</groupId>
    <artifactId>spring-boot-starter-actuator</artifactId>
</dependency>
```

Then in `application.properties` you can add the following to enable the health endpoint and the readiness and liveness probes:

```
management.endpoint.health.probes.enabled=true
management.health.livenessState.enabled=true
management.health.readinessState.enabled=true
```

These expose the two endpoints:

- *Liveness* at *http://localhost:8080/actuator/health/liveness*
- *Readiness* at *http://localhost:8080/actuator/health/readiness*

You use these endpoints in the Kubernetes configuration to configure the readiness and liveness probes.

Getting Ready for Spanner

There are a few things to consider when using Spanner. Although it is PostgreSQL compatible, it is not fully PostgreSQL compliant, and this means there are some limitations.

The first is that it does not support sequences, so it is not possible to automatically generate primary keys, as it was with Cloud SQL. This version of fact service in this chapter uses universally unique identifiers (UUIDs) for primary keys instead of an ID that is auto-incremented by the database.

Hibernate, the ORM library the fact service uses, has a nice feature of automatically updating schemas. This is not supported by Spanner, so you need to manually create the schema. Fortunately, the single table is simple in this case, so it's not a big issue. However, this does add an extra step to the deployment process.

In Google Cloud Spanner, you can use the TIMESTAMP data type to store timestamp values. The precision of the TIMESTAMP data type is up to nanoseconds, but it does not store time zone information as Cloud SQL does. This means there is more information in the LocalDateTime Java type that can be stored in Spanner's TIMESTAMP type.

To solve this issue, the common practice is to use two fields in your entity, one for the timestamp and another for the time zone. You store the timestamp as a String in a standardized format, like ISO 8601, and you store the time zone as another String. When you retrieve the data, you can parse the timestamp and apply the time zone. This is what has been done in this version of the fact service.

These are the type of limitations you need to be aware of when using Spanner; they are small but significant. It is not a drop-in replacement for PostgreSQL. An application written to work with Cloud SQL for PostgreSQL will not necessarily work with Spanner. However, an application written to work within the limitations of Spanner's PostgreSQL will likely work with Cloud SQL for PostgreSQL. If you just target PostgreSQL, you will likely not be able to use Spanner without modification.

 This is the trade-off you make when using a cloud native database. You get scalability and performance, but you lose some features of a traditional database. However, in this case, the benefits are large and the limitation relatively small.

Kubernetes Configuration

The project also contains several generic Kubernetes YAML configurations in the *k8s* directory. These would be the same for any Kubernetes platform and define how to deploy the application:

namespace.yaml

> A namespace is a way to group resources in Kubernetes much like a project does in Google Cloud. This configuration defines a `facts` namespace.

deployment.yaml

> In Kubernetes, the smallest deployable unit is a pod. This is made up of one or more containers. In this configuration, the pod contains two containers: the fact service instance and the Cloud SQL Proxy. A deployment is a way to deploy and scale an identical set of pods. It contains a template section with the actual pod spec.

service.yaml

> A Kubernetes service is a way to provide a stable network endpoint for the pod with an IP address and port. If there are multiple instances of pods, it also distributes traffic between them and stops routing traffic if a readiness or liveness probe fails.

ingress.yaml

> An ingress is a way to expose a Kubernetes services to the internet. Here you are using it to expose the fact service.

serviceaccount.yaml

> A Kubernetes service account is a way to grant a pod access to other services. It is a way to provide a stable identity for the pod.

Implementation

With the preparation done, you are now ready to deploy the application to GKE Autopilot. First, you will deploy the application to connect to Cloud SQL, as you did with the Cloud Run implementation. Then you will configure Cloud Spanner and use that as an alternative.

Create a GKE Autopilot Cluster

Unlike Cloud Run, GKE Autopilot is a Kubernetes cluster, albeit a highly managed one, not a serverless service. You need to provision a cluster to run your application on.

Ensure you are in the citadel project where you have been deploying applications, not the management project:

```
gcloud config set project $PROJECT_ID
```

Enable the Kubernetes API:

```
gcloud services enable container.googleapis.com
```

Then create a GKE Autopilot cluster with the command:

```
gcloud container clusters create-auto $PROJECT_ID-gke \
  --project=$PROJECT_ID \
  --region=$REGION
```

 Services like GKE (and later Spanner) are a lot more expensive than the likes of Cloud Run and Cloud SQL. I recommend keeping a close eye on your billing if using these services. Also, if you are experimenting, don't be afraid to destroy a GKE cluster when you finish with it. You can always recreate a new one later. For example, use the following command to destroy the cluster you just created:

```
gcloud container clusters delete $PROJECT_ID-gke \
  --project=$PROJECT_ID \
  --region=$REGION
```

This will take around 10 minutes to create. On completion, a context for the cluster will be automatically added to the *kubeconfig* file on your machine. This is a file that Kubernetes uses to know how to connect to the cluster. Alternatively, you can use the gcloud command to update the *kubeconfig* file with the following command:

```
gcloud container clusters get-credentials $PROJECT_ID-gke --region $REGION --project $PROJECT_ID
```

If you have the kubectx command installed, you can enter it to list all the contexts in the *kubeconfig* file. This is all the clusters available to you. You should see the context for the cluster you just created and possibly any other Kubernetes clusters you have, for example, a local Minikube.

You will then be able to use the kubectl command to interact with the cluster, and commands will apply to the highlighted cluster. For example, you can use the kubectl get nodes command to list the nodes in the cluster:

```
kubectl get nodes
-----
```

This should return a list of nodes in the cluster like this:

```
[source,text]
-----
NAME                                                  STATUS  ROLES   AGE  VERSION
gk3-skillsmapper-org-gke-nap-1q1d8az0-cdee423f-xdcw   Ready   <none>  13d  v1.24.9-gke.3200
```

As GKE Autopilot is a fully managed Kubernetes cluster, the nodes are managed by Google, and you do not have access to them. For most people, this is a good thing, as managing a Kubernetes cluster yourself can get complicated very quickly.

Service Account Binding with Workload Identity

Kubernetes, like Google Cloud, has the concept of service accounts. These are a way to grant permissions to pods running in the cluster. You will create a Kubernetes service account and bind it to the Google service account you created earlier using Workload Identity. This will allow the pods to access the Cloud SQL instance.

This is not particularly straightforward, but when working, it provides a nice way of integrating workloads on Kubernetes with Google Cloud services without an explicit dependency on Google Cloud.

Define a name for a Kubernetes namespace and a Kubernetes service account in environment variables:

```
export K8S_NAMESPACE=facts
export K8S_SERVICE_ACCOUNT=facts-sa
```

Then create a facts namespace in Kubernetes using this command:

```
kubectl create ns facts
```

This is the Kubernetes configuration to create a service account with the name facts-sa in the facts-sa namespace facts:

```
apiVersion: v1
kind: ServiceAccount
metadata:
    name: $K8S_SERVICE_ACCOUNT
    namespace: $K8S_NAMESPACE
```

You can then create the Kubernetes service account, substituting the environment variables with the envsubst command:

```
envsubst < k8s-template/serviceaccount.yaml > k8s/serviceaccount.yaml
```

Then you can create the service account by applying the configuration:

```
kubectl apply -f k8s/serviceaccount.yaml
```

Executing this command isn't directly creating the service account. Instead, it's sending a declarative configuration to the Kubernetes API server. This configuration describes the desired state for a service account, namely how you intend it to exist within your Kubernetes environment.

The kubectl apply command allows you to assert control over the system configuration. When invoked, Kubernetes compares your input (the desired state) with the current state of the system, making the necessary changes to align the two.

To put it simply, by running kubectl apply -f k8s/serviceaccount.yaml, you're instructing Kubernetes, "This is how I want the service account setup to look. Please make it so."

Then use this command to bind the Kubernetes service account to the Google service account:

```
gcloud iam service-accounts add-iam-policy-binding \
"$FACT_SERVICE_SA@$PROJECT_ID.iam.gserviceaccount.com" \
--role roles/iam.workloadIdentityUser \
--member "serviceAccount:$PROJECT_ID.svc.id.goog[$K8S_NAMESPACE/$K8S_SERVICE_ACCOUNT]"
```

This gives the Kubernetes service account the ability to impersonate the Google service account. You then need to annotate the Kubernetes service account with the Google service account name to impersonate:

```
kubectl annotate serviceaccount $K8S_SERVICE_ACCOUNT \
iam.gke.io/gcp-service-account=$FACT_SERVICE_SA@${PROJECT_ID}.iam.gserviceaccount.com \
-n $K8S_NAMESPACE
```

The pod should now be able to access the Google Cloud resources using the Google service account via a Kubernetes service account.

You can test by deploying a test container. First, take a look at the pod configuration file *k8s-test/workload-identity-test.yaml* with the following content:

```
apiVersion: v1
kind: Pod
metadata:
  name: workload-identity-test
  namespace: $K8S_NAMESPACE
spec:
  containers:
    - image: google/cloud-sdk:slim
      name: workload-identity-test
      command: ["sleep","infinity"]
  serviceAccountName: $K8S_SERVICE_ACCOUNT
  nodeSelector:
    iam.gke.io/gke-metadata-server-enabled: "true"
```

Then deploy, substituting environment variables using the following command:

```
envsubst < k8s-test/workload-identity-test.yaml | kubectl apply -f -
```

Observe the state of the container. This can be done by running the following command, which allows you to monitor changes in the pod's status until it transitions to the *running* state:

```
kubectl get pods -n $K8S_NAMESPACE -w
```

Once the Pod is up and running, you can execute a command inside it. This can be done using `kubectl exec`. The following command opens a Bash shell within the running container:

```
kubectl exec -it workload-identity-test --namespace $K8S_NAMESPACE -- /bin/bash
```

You should now find yourself at the command prompt within the container. From here, execute the following command. This will retrieve the email address associated with the Google service account in use within the container:

```
curl -H "Metadata-Flavor: Google" \
http://169.254.169.254/computeMetadata/v1/instance/service-accounts/default/email
```

The output should reveal the service account currently in use, which should align with the format *fact-service-sa@s$PROJECT_ID.iam.gserviceaccount.com*.

Next, issue the following command to fetch a token. If the service account and its permissions are correctly set up, this command should successfully return a token:

```
curl -H "Metadata-Flavor: Google" \
http://169.254.169.254/computeMetadata/v1/instance/service-accounts/default/token
```

If you received a token, this signifies that the service account is functional and properly configured. You're now ready to deploy the application. Remember to close the shell in your container with the `exit` command. Then clean up by removing the workload-identity-test pod using:

```
kubectl delete pod workload-identity-test -n $K8S_NAMESPACE
```

Deploying the Pod

The pod you're about to deploy contains two containers. The first, Cloud SQL Proxy, establishes a connection to the Cloud SQL instance using permissions granted by the Google service account.

The second container holds the application. Unaware of its presence within Google Cloud or its deployment within a Kubernetes cluster, this application functions solely with the knowledge of its need to connect to a database. The connection details it requires are supplied through environment variables.

These environment variables are stored within a Kubernetes secret, specifically named `facts-db-secret`. Here's how you can create it:

```
kubectl create secret generic facts-db-secret -n ${K8S_NAMESPACE} \
  --from-literal=username=${FACT_SERVICE_DB_USER} \
  --from-literal=password=${FACT_SERVICE_DB_PASSWORD} \
  --from-literal=database=${DATABASE_NAME}
```

You are now ready to apply the deployment. Create the *deployment.yaml* from a template:

```
envsubst < k8s-template/deployment-cloudsql.yaml > k8s/deployment.yaml
```

Then use Skaffold, which is configured in *skaffold.yaml*, to build the container and apply all the configurations in the *k8s* folder:

```
skaffold run
```

When completed, you can check the running pods using:

```
kubectl get pods -n $K8S_NAMESPACE
```

You should see 2/2 in the Ready column. This means both the Cloud SQL Auth Proxy and application containers are running successfully:

```
NAME                          READY   STATUS    RESTARTS   AGE
fact-service-57b9c956b6-ckvdv  2/2     Running   0          2m36s
```

With the application now running in Kubernetes, you can now make it more scalable.

Scaling with a Horizontal Pod Autoscaler

In GKE Autopilot, as with other Kubernetes distributions, the number of instances (pods) for a service is not automatically scaled up and down by default as they are in Cloud Run. Instead, you can scale the number of pods in the cluster using a HorizontalPodAutoscaler. This will scale the number of pods based on the CPU usage of the pods. This is also slightly different to Cloud Run, as new pods are created when a threshold of CPU or memory usage is reached, rather than scaling based on the number of requests.

In the *k8s* directory, *autoscaler.yaml* defines the autoscaler. It is configured to scale the number of pods between 1 and 10 based on the CPU usage of the pods. The CPU usage is measured over 30 seconds, and the target CPU usage is 50%. This means that if the CPU usage of the pods is over 50% for 30 seconds, then a new pod will be created. If the CPU usage is below 50% for 30 seconds, then a pod will be deleted.

This helps ensure that there is sufficient capacity to handle requests, but it does not guarantee that there will be sufficient capacity. If there is a sudden spike in requests, then the pods may not be able to handle the requests.

However, as GKE Autopilot will automatically scale the number of nodes in the cluster, there will likely be sufficient capacity to handle the requests.

Exposing with a Load Balancer

When using Cloud Run, you did not need to expose the application to the internet. It was automatically exposed to the internet via a load balancer. For GKE Autopilot, you need to expose the application to the internet using a Kubernetes load balancer and an ingress controller.

GKE Autopilot does have an ingress controller built in, so you don't need to worry about configuring NGINX or similar. You can use this by creating an ingress resource and then annotating your service to use the ingress controller.

This is a point where you take the generic Kubernetes configuration and annotate it with a specific Google Cloud configuration. In this case, annotate the service configuration for the fact service to use the ingress controller. Annotate the service with the following annotation to use the ingress controller:

```
kubectl annotate service facts-service cloud.google.com/neg: '{"ingress": true}' -n $K8S_NAMESPACE
```

You can then check that the ingress is exposed:

```
kubectl get ingress -n $K8S_NAMESPACE
```

If successful, you will see an internal IP address in the ADDRESS column. This is the IP address of the load balancer:

```
NAME                  CLASS    HOSTS  ADDRESS        PORTS  AGE
fact-service-ingress  <none>   *      34.96.74.235   80     11d
```

You can retrieve this IP address to an environment variable:

```
export SERVICE_IP=$(kubectl get ingress -n $K8S_NAMESPACE \
-o jsonpath='{.items[0].status.loadBalancer.ingress[0].ip}')
```

As with Cloud Run, you can retrieve the ID token for the service account using the following command:

```
export ID_TOKEN=$(curl "https://www.googleapis
.com/identitytoolkit/v3/relyingparty/verifyPassword?key=${API_KEY}" \
-H "Content-Type: application/json" \
--data-binary "{\"email\":\"${TEST_EMAIL}\",\"password\":\"${TEST_PASSWORD}\",
\"returnSecureToken\":true}" | jq -r '.idToken')
```

You can then test the application by running the following command, including the retrieved token:

```
curl -X GET ${SERVICE_IP}/facts \
  -H "Authorization: Bearer ${ID_TOKEN}"
```

Then use Apache Bench to check the response time:

```
ab -n 3 -H "Authorization: Bearer ${ID_TOKEN}" ${SERVICE_IP}/facts
```

For me, this returned sub 100ms response time, which was substantially better than with Cloud Run. It is a useful test to compare how GKE and Cloud Run compare for different workloads.

Switching to Spanner

Google Cloud Spanner is Google's fully managed, scalable, relational database service. Cloud Spanner is designed to offer the transactional consistency of a traditional relational database plus the scalability and performance of a NoSQL database.

Unlike Cloud SQL, Cloud Spanner is cloud native and can scale horizontally and globally. Although it can be very expensive, it is a good fit for large-scale applications. While it is certainly overkill for the fact service at the moment, it is useful to demonstrate how to use it and how switching from Cloud SQL is possible.

The cloud-agnostic version of the fact service used in this chapter knows nothing about Google Cloud. Although it connects to a Cloud SQL database, it connects through a proxy. As far as the Spring application is concerned, there is a PostgreSQL instance running on the local host it can talk to using the PostgreSQL wire protocol. The Cloud SQL Proxy is taking care of all the networking, encryption, and authentication required.

While you can connect to Cloud Spanner natively using client libraries, it is also possible to connect to Cloud Spanner via a proxy, similar to how you have with Cloud SQL. The PGAdapter (*https://oreil.ly/WBCic*) provides a PostgreSQL-compatible interface to Cloud Spanner, as again the client application can treat it as a PostgreSQL database running on the localhost. There are several different options for running the

PGAdapter as a standalone Java process, a Java library, or a Docker container. As the fact service uses Kubernetes, the easiest is to use the Docker image provided by Google as a sidecar container in the same way as the Cloud SQL Proxy.

Create a Spanner Instance

To use Cloud Spanner, first, enable the Cloud Spanner API:

```
gcloud services enable spanner.googleapis.com
```

Create environment variables for the instance and database name for a Spanner instance in the same way you would for Cloud SQL. Note that there is no need to pass credentials, as authentication is via the service account:

```
export SPANNER_INSTANCE='facts-instance'
export SPANNER_DATABASE='facts'
```

Spanner instances are configured to have a specified number of processing units. This computed capacity determines the amount of data throughput, queries per second (QPS), and storage limits of your instance. This was previously the number of nodes in the cluster, with one node being equivalent to 1,000 processing units, and one node being the smallest configuration.

This meant there was no cheap way of using Spanner. Now it is possible to specify a minimum of 100 processing units, which is equivalent to 0.1 nodes. This is a much more cost-effective way of using Spanner for small applications, development, and testing.

Create a Spanner instance using the gcloud command-line tool:

```
gcloud spanner instances create $SPANNER_INSTANCE --config=regional-$REGION \
--description="Fact Instance" --processing-units=100
```

 Even with a minimum instance size, Cloud Spanner can be expensive. As with GKE, it is useful to be able to delete the instance when not in use if you are just experimenting. Spanner is very quick to configure again, if needed. Remove the Spanner instance with:

```
gcloud spanner instances delete $SPANNER_INSTANCE
```

When creating a Google Cloud Spanner instance, you'll often observe a notably quick provisioning time compared to Cloud SQL. This expedited setup stems from Spanner's unique architecture, designed for horizontal scaling across a global and distributed system. Instead of allocating traditional "instance-specific" resources, as many relational databases do, Spanner simply reserves capacity within its preexisting, distributed infrastructure. On the other hand, Cloud SQL requires time-intensive provisioning because it establishes traditional database instances with designated resources (CPU, memory, storage) based on the user's configuration. With

Spanner, you're seamlessly integrating into a vast, already-established system, while with Cloud SQL, you're carving out a more personalized, dedicated space.

Create a Spanner Database

Create a database in the Spanner instance. Spanner supports two SQL dialects, Google Standard SQL and PostgreSQL. The fact service uses PostgreSQL so create the database using the PostgreSQL dialect:

```
gcloud spanner databases create $SPANNER_DATABASE --instance=$SPANNER_INSTANCE \
--database-dialect=POSTGRESQL
```

Again, database creation is near instant.

Authenticate the Service Account

Unlike Cloud SQL, Spanner does not have users, so you do not need to create a Kubernetes secret. However, the service account does require access to Spanner. Earlier, you linked a Kubernetes service account to the service account you created for the fact service. Now you need to give that service account access to Spanner:

```
gcloud projects add-iam-policy-binding $PROJECT_ID \
  --member=serviceAccount:${FACT_SERVICE_SA}@${PROJECT_ID}.iam.gserviceaccount.com \
  --role=roles/spanner.databaseUser
```

The fact service will use the service account to authenticate with Spanner.

Redeploy the Fact Service

In the *k8s-template* folder, there is a second deployment template. This time it has the fact service and a Spanner PGAdapter container. Run the following command to replace the *deployment.yaml* with a new configuration generated from it:

```
envsubst < k8s-template/deployment-spanner.yaml > k8s/deployment.yaml
```

Then run the `skaffold` command, and then apply the new configuration:

```
skaffold run
```

You should now have a fact service running against Spanner rather than Cloud SQL, giving potential for global expansion.

Evaluation

Let's evaluate the solution in terms of scaling and cost.

How Will This Solution Scale?

Here, you have seen a mixture of cloud native and traditional technologies. Although GKE Autopilot is not serverless, it is cloud native. As demand increases, more instances of the fact service will be created by the horizontal autoscaler. As more instances are scheduled, the GKE Autopilot cluster will automatically add additional nodes to deal with the extra pods.

GKE Autopilot also appears considerably faster to service requests than the same container running on Cloud Run. This could be down to the way networking is configured, with requests reaching the service by a more direct route.

This solution will not scale to zero in the same way as Cloud Run, and there will always need to be one pod running to service requests (if individual instances are still running in a single pod). Remember, however, that if demand suddenly increases, it will take a few minutes for both the GKE Autopilot cluster to provision the extra resources required for running the post and then for the pods to start.

While the service can be scaled almost indefinitely, the real bottleneck is the Cloud SQL database, which is not cloud native. There are two related limitations. The first is that the database cannot be dynamically scaled. You have to specify the tier of the machine used for the database, and while this can be changed manually with a database restart, it cannot change automatically in response to load. More importantly, there is a limit to the number of database connections from the instances of the services.

This means that if the instances increase without limit, they will exhaust the number of connections available to the database and fail to connect. For this reason, it is important to limit the number of instances so that the number (instances × connections per instance) is below the maximum number of connections available to the database.

However, you have seen that with some minor adjustments, you can allow the fact service to work with Google Cloud Spanner, a cloud native database with the potential to scale far beyond the limitations of Cloud SQL, creating a full cloud native solution.

How Much Will This Solution Cost?

Unlike Cloud Run, GKE Autopilot does not have a cost per request; you will be billed for the pods running on the cluster and a cluster management fee per hour. At the time of writing, the first 720 hours of cluster management per month are included per account, so you effectively get one cluster free.

The cost of pods is based on the amount of CPU, memory, and ephemeral storage requested by scheduled pods. This is billed per second. The most significant cost is for CPU. Therefore, it is very important to make sure the resources you request for your pod are adequate but not excessive. Remember that a Kubernetes pod can use additional resources up to the limit specified; the requested resources are the ones that are reserved.

As each pod is charged per second, it does not make sense to keep a pod running for a second longer than it needs to. Therefore, using horizontal autoscaling to dynamically increase and decrease the number of running pods to fit demand will help keep costs down.

The cost of Cloud Spanner in this minimal configuration is under $100 per month. That is still ten times the cost of a minimal Cloud SQL instance. However, another advantage of the cloud is that it allows you to experiment with services like advanced databases for short periods, without the massive outlay of money or effort you would have if you were to experiment on-premises. On the cloud, you just switch off the service again and stop paying, so if you wanted to try Spanner for an hour for a few cents, you can.

Summary

This chapter should have given you a glimpse at how you can go further in Google Cloud. However, it is a powerful platform with many services and features. There is a lot more to learn.

For this project, you used the following services directly:

- GKE Autopilot is used as the container runtime to run the container.
- Cloud SQL is used as the database backend for the application.
- Cloud Secrets Manager is used to securely store the database password.
- Cloud Spanner is used as an alternative database backend for the application.

Chapter 15 wraps up your Google Cloud journey and looks at some options for further learning.

Going Further

This book has aimed to lay a solid foundation for you to build upon. If you've come this far, you have covered a lot of ground, but there's still much more to learn.

Fortunately, there's a vast community of people who are eager for you to succeed and willing to lend a hand. Regardless of how good the platform is, the applications that run on it are only as good as the people who build them. The most daunting task any platform faces is not just attracting skilled individuals but also nurturing their success. This is true for Google Cloud as well; a scarcity of necessary skills can make organizations apprehensive about adopting the platform.

In 2021, for instance, Google pledged to equip 40 million people with Google Cloud skills (*https://oreil.ly/RcKgL*). That is a huge number, equivalent to the entire population of California. From my perspective, Google is addressing this by promoting four key areas for Google Cloud learning:

- Professional certification
- Online learning resources
- Community groups
- Conferences and events

Professional Certification

Google, in line with other cloud providers, offers certifications on many facets of Google Cloud. These certifications are structured into general certifications and specialist certifications, which align with the common job roles in the industry.

Each certification requires passing an exam that is normally two hours long. The exam typically consists of 50–60 multiple-choice or multiple-select questions. However, don't be fooled into thinking that the exams are easy. The questions are designed to test your knowledge and understanding of the platform, often requiring you to make a judgment on the best answer from several possible options. The questions are not designed to trick you but to make you think. They are not designed to test your ability to remember facts but to test your ability to apply your knowledge to solve problems.

A third-party provider administers these exams. Professional-level exams are priced at $200 plus tax (as of the time of writing); the Associate Cloud Engineer costs $125 and the Cloud Digital Leader is around $90. All these exams can be undertaken either at a testing center or from the comfort of your home, with a remote proctor overseeing the process via your webcam. Further information about the exams and registration can be found on the certification site (*https://oreil.ly/z0lP4*).

The Cloud Digital Leader certification serves as the entry point. It is a foundational-level exam intended for individuals with no prior Google Cloud experience. It is a good place to start if you are new to Google Cloud; this certification is often pursued by less technical people wishing to grasp the basic understanding of Google Cloud. Nonetheless, it requires a surprisingly broad understanding of the diverse products and services Google Cloud provides.

The Associate Cloud Engineer certification is the next tier, aimed at individuals with 6+ months of Google Cloud experience. It is a good starting point for developers or administrators and covers the basics of Google Cloud, requiring a comprehensive understanding of the various products and services offered by Google Cloud. This exam also includes the most hands-on skills, such as gcloud commands, while remaining multiple choice. Even though it is promoted as an associate rather than a professional-level qualification, there is a substantial amount of material to cover, and the knowledge gap is not as large as it might initially seem.

In this book, you have covered content applicable to the Associate Cloud Engineer exam, Professional Cloud Architect, and Professional Cloud Developer. You also touched on aspects of the Professional Cloud DevOps Engineer in Chapters 12 and 13. The Professional Cloud Architect certification covers the broadest scope of the Google Cloud Platform and is often deemed the most challenging of the exams. All professional-level exams recommend over a year of Google Cloud experience.

If you have diligently worked through this book, I suggest starting with the Associate Cloud Engineer exam, progressing to the Professional Cloud Architect, and thereafter, tailoring your certification journey based on your interests and career aspirations. Although there is no rigid sequence for taking the exams, there is some overlap between them, and the more you undertake, the easier they become. For instance, once you've prepared for the Professional Architect exam, the Professional Developer exam does not require a great deal of additional preparation. Following is the full list of certifications available at the time of writing:

Cloud Digital Leader
Focuses on a foundational understanding of Google Cloud's capabilities and their benefits to organizations

Associate Cloud Engineer
Highlights the hands-on skills needed for managing operations within Google Cloud

Professional Cloud Architect
Concentrates on the design, management, and orchestration of solutions using a comprehensive range of Google Cloud products and services

Professional Cloud Database Engineer
Addresses the design, management, and troubleshooting of Google Cloud databases, with an emphasis on data migrations

Professional Cloud Developer
Emphasizes the design, build, test, and deployment cycle of applications operating on Google Cloud

Professional Data Engineer
Designed for professionals constructing and securing data processing systems

Professional Cloud DevOps Engineer
Covers DevOps, SRE, CI/CD, and observability aspects within Google Cloud

Professional Cloud Security Engineer
Prioritizes the security of Google Cloud, its applications, data, and users

Professional Cloud Network Engineer
Concentrates on the design, planning, and implementation of Google Cloud networks, having significant overlap with security concepts

Professional Google Workspace Administrator
Targets professionals managing and securing Google Workspace, formerly known as G Suite

Professional Machine Learning Engineer
Serves those involved in the design, construction, and operationalization of machine learning models on Google Cloud

The exams are not easy—that is what makes them valuable—but they are not impossible either. Different people will have different preferences for how to prepare. When I have prepared for exams, I prefer to do a little, often: an hour of reading or watching a video in the morning followed by an hour of hands-on experimentation in the evening. I find that this helps me to retain the information and to build up my knowledge over time. As I get closer to the exam, I do more practice exams; Google provides example questions for each in the exam guide, to get used to the style of questions and identify any gaps in knowledge to work on.

I have a ritual of booking my exam for 10 AM and having Starbucks tea and fruit toast followed by a walk before the exam. I arrive or set up in plenty of time, so I am relaxed. When the exam starts, I recommend reading questions very carefully, as there is often a small detail that makes all the difference to the answer.

Sometimes a difficult question can use up time; in this case, I flag it and move on. I also flag any questions I am not completely sure about and come back later. At the end of the exam, I am usually much more confident about my answers.

Often, there will be a piece of information in one question that may unlock a difficult question earlier on. Most importantly, if you are not sure, make a guess. You will not be penalized for a wrong answer, but you will be penalized for not answering a question.

When you finish and submit your exam, you will get a provisional pass or fail. Google does not give you a score or a breakdown to tell you which questions you got wrong (like AWS, for example). You will get an email a few days later with your final result. You may also receive a code to redeem for a gift from Google (at the time of writing and depending on the exam), which is a nice touch. You can also list your certification in the Google Cloud Certified Directory (*https://oreil.ly/S_IgP*). For example, you can see my profile in the Directory site (*https://oreil.ly/jtzNi*).

Resist the temptation to use exam dumps for preparation. These question compilations are often shared in violation of the exam's confidentiality agreement and tend to be outdated and misleading. The optimal way to prepare is to tap into the vast amount of learning material available, get hands-on experience, and take the official practice exams.

I've interviewed candidates who relied on exam dumps, and it's usually clear: they struggle with basic questions. These exams are meant to gauge your understanding and proficiency with the platform, not rote memorization of facts. Encountering a familiar question in the exam is not as gratifying as being able to answer based on a solid understanding and practical experience.

It is a great feeling when you pass, and if you find the experience useful, there are many other specialties. One thing to note is that certification expires after two years, so if you do many exams at once, you will need to do them all again in two years to stay certified. The exception is that the Cloud Digital Leader and Associate Cloud

Engineer certifications are valid for three years. Good luck on your certification journey!

Online Learning Resources and Communities

To help you gain a comprehensive understanding of Google Cloud, a wide array of online resources is available. Your learning journey could continue with the following:

Official Google Cloud documentation (https://oreil.ly/cHM2Y)
    This is a powerful tool offering in-depth coverage of all the services.

Google Cloud blog (https://oreil.ly/pCDwK)
    This provides timely news, helpful tips, and insider tricks.

Google Cloud community (https://oreil.ly/nK7rG)
    This forum is a space for discussions on various Google Cloud topics.

Developer center and community (https://oreil.ly/LzD7f)
    This resource is specifically designed for the Google Cloud Developer community, offering events and articles tailored to their interests.

Remember, these are just the tip of the iceberg; a multitude of other resources are also at your disposal.

YouTube

Google, being the owner of YouTube, ensures the platform is a valuable source of freely available content related to Google Cloud. Here are a few standout channels and playlists:

Google Cloud Tech (https://oreil.ly/kMpYt)
    This is the primary channel for all the latest updates on Google Cloud, including the *This Week in Cloud* series with recent developments.

Serverless Expeditions playlist (https://oreil.ly/V0xPa)
    A comprehensive video series on serverless development on Google Cloud. It aligns well with this book, featuring a significant focus on Cloud Run.

Google Cloud Events (https://oreil.ly/oBUF3)
    This channel hosts recordings from Google Cloud Next conferences and other events. It's a valuable resource since many of these talks come directly from the product developers themselves.

Google for Developers (https://oreil.ly/MWfUd)
> Here, you can find recordings from Google I/O and other developer events. While not exclusively focused on Google Cloud, it provides a wide range of developer-oriented content.

Podcasts

For those who prefer audio content, there are several Google Cloud–related podcasts worth mentioning:

Google Cloud Platform Podcast (https://oreil.ly/0vLtn)
> A weekly podcast that keeps you updated with the latest developments in Google Cloud. It also boasts an extensive back catalogue of episodes, offering insights into various aspects of Google Cloud.

Google Cloud Reader (https://oreil.ly/tfctR)
> A unique podcast that summarizes and presents the best articles from the Google Cloud blog on a weekly basis. It's a great resource to keep up with important Google Cloud discussions without having to read through every article.

Kubernetes Podcast (https://oreil.ly/ojNbj)
> Although it's not exclusively about Google Cloud, this podcast produced by Google offers comprehensive information about Kubernetes, a crucial component in many Google Cloud services. This podcast is informative and handy for anyone wanting to deepen their understanding of Kubernetes and its applications in cloud environments.

Qwiklabs

Google Cloud's Qwiklabs or Google Cloud Skills Boost (*https://oreil.ly/H-AqZ*) offers an online learning environment featuring practical training labs for those seeking to deepen their understanding of Google Cloud. Each lab hones in on a particular topic, and with step-by-step instructions, guides you in interacting with Google Cloud resources directly via your web browser. Labs span from beginner to advanced levels, and topics cover machine learning, security, infrastructure, and application development. Qwiklabs is a great platform for acquiring new skills and reinforcing ones previously learned through other methods, such as Google Cloud's certification programs.

While Qwiklabs usually requires paid access and operates on credits, they often run promotions offering free credits or access to select courses.

As of this writing, Google offers an annual subscription named Google Innovators Plus (*https://oreil.ly/zNe9X*). For $299, you receive a year's unlimited access to Google Skills Boost, cloud expert consultations, and $500 of Google Cloud credit. The package also includes a voucher for a Google Cloud Professional Certification exam (valued at $200), and if you pass, you're granted an additional $500 of Google Cloud credit. The cloud credit from this subscription proved invaluable for funding my Google Cloud projects while writing this book: it was unquestionably a sound investment for me.

A monthly subscription option is also available for $29/month. However, this package doesn't include the cloud credit and exam voucher benefits.

Non-Google Communities

Other non-Google platforms offer valuable content and engaging discussions:

Google Cloud Collective on Stack Overflow (https://oreil.ly/O5QD6)
A community on Stack Overflow where developers can post queries, share knowledge, and help resolve Google Cloud–related issues. It's a reputable place for technical discussions and detailed problem-solving.

Google Cloud on Reddit (https://oreil.ly/IDZC0)
This subreddit is a vibrant community of Google Cloud users. Members can share their experiences, ask questions, discuss the latest trends, or even vent their frustrations about Google Cloud. It offers a mix of technical, business, and general content about Google Cloud.

Google Cloud community on Medium (https://oreil.ly/3jEEJ)
This Medium publication provides a variety of articles about Google Cloud written by the community. Topics range from tutorials and use cases to insights and trends. It's a great place to consume long-form content related to Google Cloud.

Community Support

Google Cloud hosts a vibrant community comprising Google staff, partners, customer groups, and the developer community, all providing substantial in-person support.

Google Staff

Google employs a host of experts, including developer advocates, customer engineers, and professional services personnel, who are all dedicated to supporting various aspects of Google Cloud. While customer engineers and professional services cater predominantly to Google Cloud's customers, developer advocates work to support the broader developer community, producing online content and presenting at conferences.

Partners

Google has partnered with a wide array of businesses, from global system integrators to boutique consultancies, to aid customers in utilizing Google Cloud effectively. They offer help in areas ranging from strategic planning to implementation and often specialize in certain areas. In addition to providing expertise and professional services similar to Google, some partners are authorized to provide training, boasting individuals certified as Google Certified Trainers.

Customer Groups

The Google Cloud Customer Community (C2C) (*https://oreil.ly/xfI8Y*) is a peer-to-peer network that fosters a sharing platform for Google Cloud customers. This community spans across regions, enabling members to share ideas, experiences, and insights to address common challenges and encourage innovation. It welcomes anyone to join and participate in online forums and frequent free events, both online and in person.

Developer Community

Google supports several developer community programs catering to individual developers as opposed to customer organizations:

Google Developer Groups (GDG) (https://oreil.ly/BUSN0)
These are local groups of developers who meet online or in person to share experiences and learn from each other. These groups often utilize platforms like Meetup to advertise their events.

Women Techmakers (https://oreil.ly/PGzMi)
This initiative provides visibility, community, and resources specifically for women in technology.

Google Developer Student Clubs (GDSC) (https://oreil.ly/B6oXK)
Functioning much like Google Developer Groups, these are targeted toward university students, helping them learn about Google technologies across 1,900+ chapters in over 100 countries.

Google Developer Experts (https://oreil.ly/zwopr)
This is a global network of over 1,000 professionals across 30+ countries, recognized for their expertise in Google technologies and their contributions to the community.

The Road to Google Certification (*https://oreil.ly/kBhpT*) is another significant initiative. Sponsored by GDG and held several times a year, this program is designed to help participants prepare for Google Cloud certifications at no cost. It comprises six weekly online sessions and supporting material, with the program being open to anyone interested. Note that it is managed by the GDG independently from Google.

Conferences and Events

Google hosts two significant events annually: Google Cloud Next and Google I/O, each serving distinct audiences and covering unique areas of focus.

Google I/O, typically held in the second quarter, is a developer-oriented conference. It's designed primarily for software engineers and developers utilizing Google's consumer-oriented platforms, such as Android, Chrome, and Firebase, as well as Google Cloud. The event offers detailed technical sessions on creating applications across web, mobile, and enterprise realms using Google technologies. It's also renowned for product announcements related to Google's consumer platforms.

Conversely, Google Cloud Next is aimed at enterprise IT professionals and Google Cloud developers, taking place usually in the third quarter. Its focus revolves around Google Cloud Platform (GCP) and Google Workspace. The event provides insights into the latest developments and innovations in cloud technology. It also presents networking opportunities, a wealth of learning resources, and expert-led sessions dedicated to helping businesses leverage the power of the cloud for transformative operational changes. Its feel is notably more corporate than Google I/O.

Both conferences record the hundreds of talks presented and make them accessible on YouTube. This wealth of knowledge is a fantastic resource for keeping abreast of the latest developments in Google Cloud and gaining an in-depth understanding of technical areas.

In addition to these main events, numerous local events tied to Google Cloud Next and Google I/O are organized by local Google teams or community groups. These include Google I/O Extended and Google Cloud Next Developer Days, which offer a summary of the content from the larger events. The Google Events website (*https://oreil.ly/PMI7A*) is a reliable source to stay updated on upcoming happenings.

Summary

As you turn the last page of this book, my hope is that it has kindled a fire in you—a deep, consuming desire to explore the vast and fascinating world of Google Cloud, but more importantly, to build with it and innovate. If it has, then this book has served its purpose.

Remember, you are not alone on this journey. There's an immense community of like-minded cloud enthusiasts and Google Cloud experts, eager to support and guide you on this path. They're rooting for your success—so embrace their help!

Writing this book has been an enriching experience, filled with growth and discovery. I trust that you've found reading it just as enjoyable. I would be thrilled to hear about your unique experiences and journeys with Google Cloud. Your feedback on this book is not only welcome but greatly appreciated.

To share your thoughts and experiences, or simply reach out, please visit my website at *https://danielvaughan.com*.

As you venture further into the world of cloud computing, remember: every day brings new opportunities for growth and innovation. Embrace them with open arms.

Happy cloud computing, and here's to the incredible journey that lies ahead!

Deploying Skills Mapper

In most of this book, you have been using gcloud commands to deploy everything. If you wanted to ship the product, you could do what I have done in the book and produce a step-by-step guide to the commands. However, it is easy to make a mistake when following instructions. What would be much better is to automate all those commands in a way that could consistently deploy everything for you with a single command.

One option would be to put all the commands in shell scripts. However, when using gcloud commands you are effectively calling the Google Cloud API in the background. What is better is to use a tool that makes the same API calls but is designed for this type of automation. This is the principle of infrastructure as code (IaC).

In this appendix, you have the opportunity to set up everything discussed in this book in one go with automation.

> The code for this chapter is in the terraform folder of the GitHub repository (*https://oreil.ly/2ep0_*).

Reintroducing Terraform

The tool designated for automating the creation of infrastructure in this context is Terraform, an open source offering from HashiCorp. Terraform exemplifies an IaC tool, a concept briefly explored in Chapter 5 when it was utilized to deploy the tag updater.

While Google Cloud offers a similar tool called Deployment Manager (*https://oreil.ly/qi-W2*), it is limited to supporting only Google Cloud. On the other hand, Terraform's applicability extends to all public clouds and various other types of infrastructure. This broader compatibility has made Terraform more widely accepted, even within the Google Cloud ecosystem.

To understand the distinction between using Terraform and manual methods like gcloud commands or shell scripts, consider the difference between imperative and declarative approaches:

Imperative approach

Using gcloud commands or shell scripts is an imperative method. Here, you act as a micromanaging manager, explicitly directing the Google Cloud API on what actions to perform and how to execute them.

Declarative approach

Terraform operates on a declarative principle. Instead of micromanaging each step, you define a specific goal, and Terraform takes the necessary actions to achieve it. This approach is similar to how Kubernetes functions; you declare the desired state, and the tool works to realize that state.

The declarative nature of Terraform allows for a more streamlined and efficient process, aligning the tool with the objectives without requiring detailed command over each step.

What Terraform is effectively doing is taking the destination defined as a YAML configuration and working out the route to get there, provisioning the entire secure environment. This is reproducible and repeatable, so if you wanted to have multiple environments with the same configuration (e.g., dev, QA, and prod) you could build them with the same recipe, ensuring a consistent product.

Terraform also allows you to specify variables and compute values to customize the deployment. It also understands the dependencies between resources and creates them in the right order. Most importantly, it keeps track of everything that is created; if you want to remove everything, it can clean up after itself.

The code used to define the desired state also acts as a way of documenting all the infrastructure. If anyone wants to understand all the infrastructure used in the system, the Terraform configuration is a central source of truth. As it is code, it can be shared in a source code repository and versioned with an audited history. This means developers can issue pull requests for changes, for example, rather than having to raise tickets with an operations team. It is a great example of how a tool enables DevOps or SRE practices.

This appendix is here to help you use Terraform to deploy your own Skills Mapper environment. It is not intended to go into Terraform in depth. For that, I recommend the Terraform documentation (*https://oreil.ly/pBnT1*) or *Terraform: Up and Running* (O'Reilly) by Yevgeniy Brikman.

Installing Terraform

Terraform is a command-line tool that you can install on your local machine. It's compatible with Windows, Mac, and Linux, and you can download it directly from the Terraform website (*https://oreil.ly/QUKq-*). After downloading, you'll need to add it to your system's path to enable command-line execution. You can verify the installation by running `terraform --version`, which should return the installed version.

Terraform makes use of plugins that allow it to communicate with the APIs of service providers like Google Cloud. Not surprisingly, in this setup, you will mainly be using the Google Cloud provider. Terraform is not perfect, though, and it is common to come across small limitations. The Skills Mapper deployment is no exception, so there are a few workarounds required.

Terraform Workflow

Using the Terraform tool has four main steps:

`terraform init`
Initialize the Terraform environment and download any plugins needed.

`terraform plan`
Show what Terraform will do. Terraform will check the current state, compare it to the desired state, and show what it will do to get there.

`terraform apply`
Apply the changes to the infrastructure. Terraform will make the changes to the infrastructure to get to the desired state.

`terraform destroy`
Destroy the infrastructure. Terraform will remove all the infrastructure it created.

Terraform Configuration

Terraform uses configuration files to define the desired state. For Skills Mapper, this is in the *terraform* directory or the GitHub repository. There are many files in this configuration, and they are separated into modules, which is Terraform's way of grouping functionality for reuse.

Preparing for Terraform

Several prerequisites need to be in place before you can deploy using Terraform.

Creating Projects

First, you need to create two projects, an application project and a management project, as you did earlier in the book. Both projects must have a billing project enabled. The instructions for this is are Chapter 4.

Ensure you have the names of these projects available as environment variables (e.g., `skillsmapper-application` and `skillsmapper-management`, respectively):

```
APPLICATION_PROJECT_ID=skillsmapper-application
MANAGEMENT_PROJECT_ID=skillsmapper-management
```

Terraform Backend

Terraform records the state of all the infrastructure it has created so that when the configuration is applied, it only makes the changes needed to get the infrastructure to the desired state. There could be no changes, the configuration could have been changed, or the infrastructure could have been changed outside Terraform, for example by someone issuing gcloud commands. Terraform will work out what needs to be done to get to the desired state.

By default, Terraform keeps this state on the machine that was used to apply the configuration. This means it cannot be shared. Alternatively, Terraform state can store the state of the infrastructure in a backend. In the case of Google Cloud, you can use a Cloud Storage bucket for this purpose.

Create a Cloud Storage bucket to store the Terraform state using gcloud in the management project. As bucket names need to be unique, using the project number as a suffix is a good way to ensure this.

Get the project number using gcloud:

```
PROJECT_NUMBER=$(gcloud projects describe $MANAGEMENT_PROJECT_ID --format='value(projectNumber)')
export BUCKET_NAME='skillsmapper-terraform-state-'${PROJECT_NUMBER}
```

Then use `gsutil` to create the bucket:

```
gsutil mb -p $MANAGEMENT_PROJECT_ID -c regional -l $REGION gs://$BUCKET_NAME
```

Configure Identity Platform

In Chapter 7, you enabled Identity Platform. If you have created a new application project, you will need to enable it again in the project and make a note of the API key, as you will need to pass it to Terraform as a variable.

Setting Terraform Variables

Terraform uses variables to customize the configuration. These are defined in a *terraform.tfvars* file in the *terraform* directory. Many of these have defaults you can override, but you will need to set the following variables before deployment.

Create a *terraform.tfvars* file in the *terraform* directory with the following content:

Key	Example value	Description
domain	skillsmapper.org	The domain name to use for the environment
region	europe-west2	The region to deploy the environment to
billing_account	014...	The ID of the billing account associated with your projects
management_project_id	skillsmapper-management	The ID of the management project
application_project_id	skillsmapper-application	The ID of the application project
api_key	AIzaSyC...	The API key for Identity Platform
app_installation_id	skillsmapper	The ID of the app installation for GitHub used when setting up the factory
github_repo	https://github.com/Skills Mapper/skillsmapper.git	The name of the GitHub repository to use for the factory
github_token	ghp_...	The GitHub token to use for the factory

If you have set all the environment variables for other chapters in this book, you can generate the *terraform.tfvars* from the file *terraform.tfvars.template* in the example code:

```
envsubst < terraform.tfvars.template > terraform.tfvars
```

With this file created, you are ready to deploy using Terraform.

Deploying with Terraform

To deploy the environment, you need to run the Terraform commands in the *terraform* directory.

First, initialize Terraform to download the needed plugins with:

```
terraform init
```

Then check that you have set the required variables in your *terraform.tfvars* with:

```
terraform validate
```

All being well, you should see Success! The configuration is valid.

Although Terraform can enable Google Services, and these scripts do, it can be unreliable as services take time to enable. Use the `enable_service.sh` script to enable services with gcloud:

```
./enable_services.sh
```

As you have created the two projects manually, you will now need to import them into Terraform:

```
terraform import google_project.application_project $APPLICATION_PROJECT_ID
terraform import google_project.management_project $MANAGEMENT_PROJECT_ID
```

You can now run the `plan` command to see what Terraform would do to achieve the required state:

```
terraform plan
```

Terraform will then show how many items would be added, changed, or destroyed. If you have not run Terraform on the projects before, you should see a lot of items to be added.

When you are ready, run the `apply` command:

```
terraform apply
```

Again, Terraform will devise a plan for meeting the desired state. This time, it will prompt you to approve applying the plan. Enter yes and watch while Terraform creates everything from this book for you. This may take 30 minutes, the majority of which will be the creation of the Cloud SQL database used by the fact service.

When completed, you will see several outputs from Terraform that look like this:

```
application-project = "skillsmapper-application"
git-commit = "3ecff393be00e331bb4412f4dc24a3caab2e0ab8"
management-project = "skillsmapper-management"
public-domain = "skillsmapper.org"
public-ip = "34.36.189.201"
tfstate_bucket_name = "d87cf08d1d01901c-bucket-tfstate"
```

The public-ip is the external IP of the global load balancer. Use this to create an A record in your DNS provider for the domain you provided.

Reapplying Terraform

If you make a change to the Terraform configuration, there are a few things you need to do before deploying Terraform again.

First, make sure you are using the application project:

```
gcloud config set project $APPLICATION_PROJECT_ID
```

Terraform is unable to change the API Gateway configuration, so you will need to delete it and allow Terraform to recreate it.

However, first you need to delete the API Gateway that uses the configuration:

```
gcloud api-gateway gateways delete ${API_NAME}-gateway \
--location=${REGION} \
--project=${APPLICATION_PROJECT_ID}
```

Then you can delete the configuration:

```
gcloud api-gateway api-configs delete ${API_NAME}-api-gw-config --api ${API_NAME}-api-gw
```

Also, if Cloud Run has deployed new versions of the services, you will need to remove them and allow Terraform to recreate them, too, as Terraform will have the wrong version.

If Cloud Build has run, delete the services, as it will be a newer version than the Terraform configuration:

```
gcloud run services delete skill-service --region ${REGION}
gcloud run services delete fact-service --region ${REGION}
gcloud run services delete profile-service --region ${REGION}
```

Now you are ready to apply the updated configuration as before with:

```
terraform apply
```

This time you will notice only a few added, changed, or destroyed resources, as Terraform only applies the differences to what is already there.

Deleting Everything

When you have finished with Skills Mapper, you can also use Terraform to clean up completely using:

```
terraform destroy
```

This will remove all the infrastructure that Terraform has created.

At this point, you may also like to unlink the billing accounts from the projects so they can no longer be billed:

```
gcloud beta billing projects unlink $APPLICATION_PROJECT_ID
gcloud beta billing projects unlink $MANAGEMENT_PROJECT_ID
```

Index

(see also factory)

P

pack CLI, 54
performance testing, 41
    (see also Apache Bench)
PGAdapter, 216
podcasts, 226
pods (Kubernetes), 80, 210, 214
populate function of main.go file, 77
port binding (12 factors), 28
PostgreSQL, 97-101
    connecting to, 102-104
    creating a database and user, 99-100
    service account creation, 102
processes (12 factors), 27
professional development, 221-230
    communities and community support,
      227-229
    conferences and events, 229
    online resources, 225-226
    professional certification, 221-225
profile service, 109-121
    costs, 119-120
    implementation, 112-118
    requirements and solution, 109-111
    summary of services, 111-112
    testing, 118-119
progressive decomposition, 93
projects, in Google Cloud Platform, 50
Pub/Sub, 111, 112-119
    configuration, 114-115
    costs, 120
    HTTP endpoint setup, 112-114
    pushing messages, 116
    service account configuration, 115
    subscription creation, 117-118
    testing the profile service with, 118-119
PubsubOutboundGateway interface, 114

Q

Quiklabs, 226

R

Redis, 204
region and zone, 49, 66
regional versus zonal databases, in PostgreSQL,
    98-99

repositories, 174, 177
    Artifact Registry, 66, 148, 174, 183
    choosing, 148
    Container Registry, 148
    GitHub, 174
    one codebase (12 factors), 24
resilience, built-in, 11
REST APIs, 34-35, 57
    (see also fact service)
run stage, 26
    (see also citadel)

S

saturation, 187, 190
scaling up, 203-220
    implementation (see GKE Autopilot)
    preparing the fact service, 208-210
    requirements and solution, 204-207
    skill service, 203-204
    Spanner (see Spanner)
    vendor lock-in, 204
scaling, vertical versus horizontal, 28
secret management services, 25, 101, 176
Secret Manager, 101, 176
securing the software supply chain, 172
security (see citadel)
    and environment variables, 25-26
    as principle, 30, 81
    secret management services, 25, 101, 176
    securing the software supply chain, 172
    service accounts (see service accounts)
    Skills Mapper (see API and user interface)
    zero-trust, 12
security testing, 41
sensitive data, 25-26
separation of concerns, 31
service accounts, 53
    for API and user interface, 128, 132
    Cloud Build P4SA, 176, 182
    Cloud Run, 182
    for fact service, 102
    for skill service, 154
    Kubernetes, 207, 210, 211-214, 216, 218
    for profile service, 115, 117-118
    for skill service, 80-82, 84, 199
    for tag updater, 68-69
service integration testing, 41
@ServiceActivator annotation, 113
Siege, 54

W

Workload Identity, 207, 211-214
Workspaces, in Google Cloud, 187
Workstations, 143
Wyner, Adam, 24

X

XP (extreme programming), 39

Y

YouTube channels and playlists, 225
yq command-line tool, 54

Z

zero-trust security, 12
zonal versus regional databases, in PostgreSQL, 98-99

About the Author

Daniel Vaughan is a Cloud Native Architect, combining his deep technical experience with a background in software development. His work focuses on collaborating with both senior stakeholders and hands-on engineers to optimize the utilization of cloud technologies. While holding many Google certifications, Daniel's particular interest lies in cloud native development and the pursuit of sustainable software practices. His professional experience spans several domains, and he is presently engaged in the financial services sector. Outside of his daily responsibilities, Daniel coorganizes the GDG Cloud Cambridge community group, where he helps fellow developers explore and thrive on Google Cloud. Living in Saffron Walden, UK, with his wife Michelle and son Alex, Daniel attempts to maintain a balanced life that reflects his commitment to both technological innovation and community engagement.

Colophon

The animal on the cover of *Cloud Native Development with Google Cloud* is a great snipe (*Gallinago media*), a wading bird native to northern Europe.

The species name *Gallinago* means "resembling a hen" in Latin. The birds reach a length of about 12 inches, with a 17-inch wingspan. Both males and females are a mottled brown with a barred pattern on their underfeathers. They have a long, thick bill. They eat insects and worms around marshes and wet meadows.

Great snipe migrate to sub-Saharan Africa for the winter. They can fly up to 60 miles per hour and have been known to fly nonstop for up to 84 hours. During nonstop flights, the birds rely on their fat stores so that they do not need to stop to feed.

The great snipe population is dwindling due to habitat loss and hunting. It is listed as Near Threatened by the IUCN. Many of the animals on O'Reilly covers are endangered; all of them are important to the world.

The cover illustration is by Karen Montgomery, based on an antique line engraving from *British Birds*. The cover fonts are Gilroy Semibold and Guardian Sans. The text font is Adobe Minion Pro; the heading font is Adobe Myriad Condensed; and the code font is Dalton Maag's Ubuntu Mono.

Printed in the USA
CPSIA information can be obtained
at www.ICGtesting.com
JSHW051929141123
52069JS00005B/45